51.

international art exhibition

PARTICIPATING COUNTRIES

COLLATERAL EVENTS

la Biennale di Venezia

Contents

Special project

Fabrizio Plessi
Mare verticale

Special project
promoted by
La Biennale di Venezia
and Ministero degli Affari Esteri

Suspicion and not security is the proof of Plessi's mannerist use of video, of his non-monumental insertion. He is aware that reality is not redeemed by art, because art is not frontal to the world. So he does not stop at simple reproduction of the image. He slows down its time, expands the frame and makes a series of strange linguistic dislocations that highlight the neo-mannerist features of the operation. This horizontal use of the television confirms that the artist does not believe in a purely grammatical contemplation of the medium, but one that is vexed and intellectual, emotional and expressive, relative and problematic.

Plessi's 'superficialism' denotes a use of the linguistic tools in a consistent way, but without this damaging the result that always inhabits the places of the complexity of art. Because contemporary art is aware of its operation at the level of the gaze; is aware of the fact that the reproduction always occurs on a surface that allows its duplication. 'Depth must be hidden. Where? On the surface'. Hofmannsthal's declaration is the emblem of Plessi's operation. He keeps to the codes of the medium, introducing substances of the imaginary that filter under the thin patina of the screen and flow into the interior space of the installation. Plessi also introduces the persuasive force of the baroque festival, the enrichment of an elaborated and expensive scene, capable of putting numerous means that indicate a kind of overturning of the rules at the service of his imagination.

Persuasion also comes naturally from the electronic scene, from the function of the automata that are an incentive for contemplation.

Plessi does not respond to the noise of the world with the bewilderment of a still, silent image, but accepts the competition and adorns his works with kinetic and sound elements capable of precipitating the approach. On the other hand, the baroqueness is redeemed by the fact that these machines bring processes of awareness and psychic examination that contest the surface appearance with which the images are presented. They do not carry out but in. In this sense Plessi is an Italian artist; he adopts forms that in their necessary completeness bring breadth and involvement in the direction of the constituent elements of life, but with a tone of vital movement. Such a character necessarily implies a conciliating tension of the natural and the artificial, of the hot and the cold.

Extensive dream fields govern the installations. Everything responds to a design, but is supported by a principle of bewilderment.

Inside, the observer moves her own senses of learning and moving, nourishes her own image brushing the edges of the objects, amplifies her perception, inhabits a time and a space arranged in circular terms, outside every symmetrical frontality with the outside.

Plessi's work moves under the tangent of a sensibility that can assume the structural coldness of the expressive means, bending them to a different temperature, which is that of a fantasy that plays between designing and slipping out of it. Such a result has an elaborative, executive precision that in the perfecting of the mechanism finds the possibility to better realise the imaginary plant.

Plessi's work is armed with the sense of construction of the historic avant-garde and the sense of elaborated separateness that makes it current.

Achille Bonito Oliva

Extract from *Plessi Videocruz*, exh. cat., Madrid, Museo Español de Arte Contemporáneo, 1988

Born in Reggio Emilia, Italy, in 1940. Lives and works in Venice, Italy, and Palma de Mallorca, Spain.
www.Plessi.it

SOLO EXHIBITIONS
- 2004, *Traumwelt*, Martin Gropius Bau, Berlin, Germany
- 2002, *Paradisoinferno*, Stables of the Quirinale, Rome, Italy
- 1998, Guggenheim Museum Soho, New York, USA

GROUP EXHIBITIONS
- 2001, Guggenheim Museum, Bilbao, Spain
- 1987, Documenta 8, Kassel, Germany
- 1986, Biennale di Venezia, Venice, Italy

PUBLICATIONS
- 2001, C. Haenlein, *Plessi Waterfire*, Electa, Milano
- 1999, C. Ahrens and C. Haenlein, *Fabrizio Plessi - Der Hangende Wald*, Kestner Gesellschaft
- 1997, G. Goodrow, *Plessi-Progetti del Mondo*, Dumont, Köln

EXHIBITED WORKS
- *MARE VERTICALE* (Vertical Sea), 2005. Self-supporting steel structure, big screen with bright LED displays, computer programme, sound; 44 × 4 × 4 m

MAIN SPONSOR
GRUPPO "MARE VERTICALE"
CALEARO SPA
DAINESE SPA
DAL LAGO UGO
FASE SPA
GROTTO SPA
STAHLBAU PICHLER SRL
TELWIN SPA
ZAMPERLA SPA

In collaboration with
BMW

1 Fabrizio Plessi, *La Flotta di Berlino* (Berlin's Fleet), 2004. Video installation, self-supporting metal structure, 10 upturned and self-moving boats, 70 monitors, DVD programme, sound; 4 × 40 × 20 m. Martin Gropius Bau, Berlin.
© Photo Gunter Lepkowski

1

2 Fabrizio Plessi, *La Foresta di Fuoco 2* (The Forest of Fire 2) 2000. Video installation, 10 metal structures containing 12 types of trunks, 12 monitors, DVD programme, sound; 300 × 1200 × 60 cm. Stables of the Quirinale, Rome. © Photo Gunter Lepkowski

3 Fabrizio Plessi, *L'Enigma degli Addii* (Farewell Enigma), 1999. Video installation, big worked trunk, 11 monitors, DVD programme; 100 × 1200 × 100 cm. Kestner Gesellschaft, Hannover, 1999. © Photo Gunter Lepkowski

on the following pages
4-5 Fabrizio Plessi, *MARE VERTICALE* (Vertical Sea) 2005. Self-supporting steel structure, big screen with bright LED displays, computer programme, sound; 44 × 4 × 4 m

2

4

5

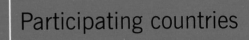
Participating countries

Afghanistan

Given its tragic history over the past two decades, Afghanistan's problems have become synonymous with real or imagined threats to 'civilisation' itself. This is unfortunately what many believe and in so doing they reduce a whole people to a monolithic perception. Drugs, warlords, the subjugation of women, lawlessness: all of these, which are undoubtedly real problems, are the lenses through which Afghanistan is viewed by the popular media of the world. Is it any surprise then that little if anything is known about the art and culture of Afghanistan?

There are many Afghanistans, but unfortunately the one least known is that of its textured, complex history: the vibrant culture of painting and sculpture that was systematically destroyed during the Russian invasion, and the hybrid musical traditions that absorbed and appropriated the numerous influences brought to the country by its conquerors. These can only be appreciated if the simplifications about Afghans that are commonplace in major European and American cities today are transformed.

Afghanistan has never had any representation at the numerous international art festivals, but it is, ironically, in the news almost daily. It is easy to find famous *National Geographic* pictures of Afghan refugees or aerial pictures of the desolate, battle-scarred Afghan countryside. But there is little available of the work of Afghan artists, who have been silently making art for decades both in the country and abroad. Afghanistan is a subject for documentaries and photo-essays, but where are the collective dreams and reveries of the Afghans? One Afghan artist whose work engages both aesthetically and intellectually with Afghanistan is Lida Abdul, who is representing Afghanistan at this Venice Biennial. Born in Kabul a few years before the Soviet invasion of the country, Lida works in many media. Engaging both with the long history of Western art and the less-well known histories of the indigenous cultures of Afghanistan, Lida's work is suffused with the immediacy of ritual and the beauty of meditative forms. I am proud to have her represent Afghanistan at the Venice Biennale and hope that with her the art world will finally begin to recognise artists from Afghanistan as necessary contributors to the global art and culture debate.

Said Ismael Noori

COMMISSIONER
Said Ismael Noori

ARTIST
Lida Abdul

www.lidaabdul.com

1

Rahim Walizada is an artist whose works retain the ancient knowledge of the women of Afghanistan: the weaving and the natural colours of the wool. Woollen works in Afghanistan were once made with sheep's wool and camel hair. Now the wool from a sheep known as a caracol is mainly used. The richness of the updating is mainly expressed in the simple, clear design, though the ancient method of weaving is used. Apart from being a highly talented artist, Rahim helps liberate the women of his country by offering them a chance to express themselves through work. As well as having a workshop employing 20-30 women in the countryside a long way from Kabul, Rahim also allows women who cannot leave their house due to family commitments or other reasons, to take the work directly to their homes. With the support of our committee 'Le Studentesse di Faizabad – Sapere è Libertà' founded in 2001 mainly to help women, it has been possible to bring Afghanistan to an international art exhibition, the 2005 Biennale di Venezia, for the first time, or rather to open Afghanistan up to the world through the representation of women's work.

Chicca Conti Olivetti

M. Rahim Walizada thanks the committee 'Le Studentesse di Faizabad – Sapere è Libertà' for the support given to his own participation and all the women who work with him on the Venice Biennale, 2005

COMMISSIONER
Chicca Conti Olivetti

DEPUTY COMMISSIONER
Sergio Quattrocchi

ARTIST
M. Rahim Walizada

SPONSOR
Banca Intesa Spa
Siemens Communications
Farmindustria

2 M. Rahim Walizada, *Chuk Palu 2*. Wool, cotton, vegetable color (madder root, indigo, tumelic yellow, walnut, onion); 3 × 2 m. Courtesy the Artist. This piece depicts squares that are hybrids of traditional tribal features, squares and color abrash. The piece also relates to aesthetic consumption

2

Albania

The first official participation of Albania at the Biennale began with the critical consideration of its social and artistic role in the international context.

The project was proposed by Andi Tepelena and Cecilia Carmela Tirelli, supported by the National Art Gallery of Albania and developed by various people whose sense of responsibility for cultural representation is reflected in the artistic commitment of Sislej Xhafa.

Sislej Xhafa

As an untiring traveller, in the west and elsewhere, Sislej Xhafa constantly finds himself in contact with social, economic and aesthetic transformations, and merges these into his work. The formulation of complex and, above all light, conceptual strategies becomes the primary operational tool. This allows the artist to approach areas of humour, to upset points of view, to elaborate easy stereotypes, to penetrate to the heart of the problem without setting off mechanisms of rejection. Contact with the political and social dimension is always caught laterally, through marginal processes that are reflected in the conditions of life, or through the exposure of 'forced illegality'. In this direction, not only the condition of abuse but the experience of tourism and the readiness of the community to receive others can become the means for confronting more complex problems. Different emotive registers appear in Xhafa's works: at times intense, direct methods are imposed, at others light, delicate, aesthetic connotations emerge. The operational flexibility actually builds a further force field from which energy may be drawn, so the relationship that is established between the identity of the artist and the constantly developing world can be reshaped. Every formal element in play must in any case give rise to an intense but supervised concentrated aesthetic. In this way the apparent simplicity and immediacy of his works hide a plurality of readings available to the more attentive observer.

Guido Molinari

Ceremonial Crying System or 'The Spectacle of Insurgency'

It appears to our sight and causes confusion. I remember when seeing it for the first time, I thought it must have been some kind of tower, covered in this plastic material, under reconstruction. I was partially right. It is a tower, and it even has to do with reconstruction, albeit not physical, but when you move closer you can notice the two eye-shaped cuts, and the water dripping from them. It is stunning, it strikes you like lightning – a huge Ku-Klux-Klan mask that is crying. Its intended socio/aesthetic function perfectly fits the description of 'insurgent' actions, originally non-political, but cynical and cruel enough to become 'politically most efficient'. This virus-like operation, the confusion and contamination it arouses in

COMMISSIONERS
Andi Tepelena
Cecilia Tirelli

ARTIST
Sislej Xhafa

SUPPORTED BY
Abaz Hado, director
of the National Arts Gallery
of Albania

SPONSOR
Galeria Kombetare e Arteve,
Tiranë
Magazzino d'Arte Moderna,
Rome
Manfredi della Gherardesca,
MDG Fine Arts Ltd, London

www.padiglionealbania.org

the viewer, is precisely the kind of 'guerrilla' method implied by insurgency. 'Insurgent' – the term one is most frequently confronted with on a daily basis in today's headlines. It is something that pops up, attacks/makes a statement and disappears, as if it were not there, just to pop up somewhere else, incessantly, endlessly. Hence perhaps the rise of this new term that embodies a major clash in every corner of the globe: between the corporate world and civil society. In a world where politics, culture and even art is subjugated to corporate rule, insurgency seems to be a new strategy of confrontation, a new way of dealing with that 'system', its tears and its ceremonies.

This is how I think Xhafa's piece and his artistic work functions: it appears somewhere among us, at first unnoticed, but definitely signalling a presence, an important one, almost a reflection of a hidden part of us. Until we come close and see the crying eyes. The spectacle of insurgency unfolds, and art hits back at us...

Edi Muka

Argentina

Jorge Macchi with Edgardo Rudnitzky / *The Assumption*

Duet in the ancient Oratorio di San Filippo Neri,
Jorge Macchi with Edgardo Rudnitzky
The uncertain melody that can be obtained by gluing the titles of a police note onto a pentagram, a newspaper article used as the raw material to construct a pentagram, and nails as notes are some of the works in which Jorge Macchi composes music and images.

One of his latest videos, *Caja de Música 2004*, involves such cohabitation through the rhythm of a traffic light and the occasional arrival and departure of cars, elements that comprise a melody, presenting an everyday event that is normally ignored. These small interventions make us look again in a new way at that which, being familiar, passes unobserved.

The production of works with both image and sound is one of his constants over the years. This aspect exists in parallel with the rest of his photographic texts and the works on paper featuring expert craftsmanship. It would almost seem as if the 'event' could not be produced by the visual register without the sound register. Such is the case, for example in *Buenos Aires Tour*, one of his latest composite creations – in this case in a book – in which music, poetry and objects found walking around the big city are gathered together.

Such meetings or cohabitations are not two disciplines that unite in a certain moment like a changing illustration, but are the essence of the work, which may his own or the result of a collaboration. Could Macchi be defined as a 'visual composer'? Called to represent our country at the 51st Biennale, the artist has produced a new body of work conceived specifically for the space of the Oratorio di San Filippo Neri. The religious architecture, his musical piece and the images of the *Assumption* in the baroque ceiling fresco are the elements of this space that Macchi takes possession of and uses in his work. And in order to obtain this signing of the space he again turns to the musician Egardo Ridnitzky.

From a visual point of view, the exhibition presents a spring board, the only object present in the space. Its shape precisely repeats that of the frame containing the baroque fresco. Even the dimensions are the same. It is positioned under the uppermost element and in the same place. Is it an allegory, a metaphor or simply a raptus of an ancient, ancestral shape? The elastic bed offers the possibility of the game of jumping and falling; and the sequence of this ascending and falling produces a repetitive rhythm of movement and sound. Gestures of exclamation, surprise, joy or fear may appear. Some of the infinite choreographies of this movement are recorded by the musician while at the same time a viola da gamba player interprets the composition.

Macchi and Rudnitzky reject the label of musical piece, installation or performance, because these are concepts that refer directly to music or the visual arts, as if they were two independent disciplines. They prefer the concept of 'intervention' or 'duet'. This musical form underscores the dialogue between the visual and the sonorous. The two voices, the fresco, the bed, the leap, the music, the space, the presence of fiction and the strength of the real are always present. The exhibition becomes an allegorical landscape of new and infinite auditory and sonorous visions. Macchi acts subtly on the space without presuming to modify it or transform it to present his work. On the contrary, he accentuates it, puts it between speech marks, he points to it by playing with the elements in a new combination, the result of which is the experience of a paradoxically changed space.

Adriana Rosenberg

COMMISSIONER
Adriana Rosenberg

ARTIST
Jorge Macchi in collaboration
with Edgardo Rudnitzky

Maria assunta in cielo tra gli angeli che spargono rose
Tommaso Cassani Bugoni da Anton Maria Zanetti (1771)
Fresco. Ceiling of the Antico Oratorio San Filippo Neri, Venecia.

Jorge Macchi in collaboration
with Edgardo Rudnitzky,
La ascensión, 2005.
Installation and performance.
Elastic bed, musical piece
for bass viol and elastic bed

cama elástica

Elastic bed below the fresco
on the floor of Antico Oratorio San Filippo Neri, Venecia

La ascensión, 2005. Proyect for the
Antico Oratorio San Filippo Neri, Venice

Australia

This Time, Another Year

The inevitable passage of time and the life span of things are recurring themes in Ricky Swallow's art. For almost a decade he has made 1:1 translations of objects that are affected by time in various ways: pushed back to the prototype stage, recast as archaeological remains or proposed as future scenarios. Through his intricate sculptures carved in wood, he preserves things at a specific moment, immortalising them so that they might be remembered before obsolescence or natural decay sets in.

Swallow traverses time, referencing historical models and recent popular culture, constantly testing the resilience and adaptability of different genres and iconography. The end result is an expanding repertoire of poetic meditations on the commemorative role of sculpture and the enduring nature of objects.

Swallow is drawn to Dutch still life painting of the seventeenth century, the genre that speaks so eloquently of life, death and the transience of material possessions. His installation for the 2005 Venice Biennale includes a number of works that recall the formal composition and fidelity of the still life tradition. *Killing Time* (2003-2004) is a sculptural inventory of marine animals Swallow caught in his youth, arranged in a banquet style on a replica of his family kitchen table. An accompanying 'air/ground campaign' wall relief features lizards, rats, birds and rabbits, artfully hung and displayed within the medallion format mastered by the British carver Grinling Gibbons. In each three-dimensional still life carving, the artist's collection of memories is condensed into a single scene and the presence of ordinary living things is intensified. The tableaux of creatures he has literally turned from 'real life to still life' are vivid stand-ins for episodes in Swallow's history, put forward to be noted and possibly accounted for in the present.

COMMISSIONER
John Kaldor AM

CURATOR
Charlotte Day

ARTIST
Ricky Swallow

www.ozco.gov.au/venice2005

1

2

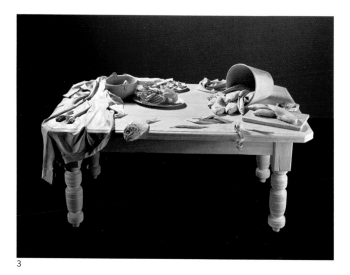

3

4

As well as delving into his past, Swallow proposes new unexpected relationships and extended narrative possibilities for objects in a time after our own. The artist refers to these as 'occupied sculptures', wherein a shifting order is anticipated by objects that are worn out by their original human owner/dwellers and then re-occupied by unlikely inhabitants. The objects still resonate with their previous occupants, but appear adjusted to their new circumstances. This is exemplified in *Come Together* (2002), a curious but strangely reassuring symbiosis of a human skull and beanbag, in which the skull anchors down the bag that in turn provides support and comfort for the toppled skull. In *The Arrangement* (2004) snakes anxiously intertwine through the designated ventilation spaces of a bike courier's helmet, oblivious to its inherent protective function. Along with allegorical associations (for example, to Medusa), this work is an exploration of the complex formal relations between objects – in this instance, between the fluidity of the snakes and the hard-edged architecture of the helmet.

In many of Swallow's sculptures the way objects are marked by time is of particular significance. *Field Recording / Highland Park Hydra* (2003) is a rendering of a prickly pear cactus roughly inscribed by passers-by, treated as a kind of impromptu organic notice-board. Swallow painstakingly reproduces the various names and messages, and the way the inscriptions have been incorporated by the plant as it grows. Although uprooted and transplanted to an ordinary garden pot, Swallow's cactus continues to thrive as a remarkable illustration of endurance and a living thing ennobled by the tests of time. By contrast, in *The Exact Dimensions of Staying Behind* (2004-2005) a solitary skeleton sits fused to a chair, clutching an ornately whittled staff in one hand and a carving knife in the other. With its head tilted back gazing upward to the heavens in a markedly dramatic gesture, the skeleton appears in the final moment before transformation or departure. As in all Swallow's sculptures, the skeleton depleted by time is a *vanitas*; a poignant reminder of our mortality, a weighing up of losses to gains, and an invitation to experience the present moment more profoundly.

Charlotte Day

1 Ricky Swallow, *Come Together*, 2002. Laminated jelutong; 66 × 63.5 × 81 cm. Collection of Peter Norton, Santa Monica, USA © Ricky Swallow. Photo Fredrik Nilsen

2 Ricky Swallow, *Field Recording / Highland Park Hydra*, 2003. Laminated jelutong; 105 × 104 × 40 cm. Image Courtesy Modern Art, London. © Ricky Swallow. Photo Robert Wiedemier

3 Ricky Swallow, *Killing Time*, 2003-2004. Laminated jelutong, maple; 108 × 184 × 118 cm. © Ricky Swallow. Purchased with funds provided by the Rudy Komon Memorial Fund and the Contemporary Collection Benefactors' Program 2004 Art Gallery of New South Wales Collection. Photo Karl Schwerdtfeger

4 Ricky Swallow, *The Arrangement*, 2004. Laminated lime wood; 51 × 46 × 24 cm. © Ricky Swallow. Photo Andy Keate

Austria

The national pavilions at the Venice Biennale are there for the artists, not the curators. The latter should select the artist most able to exploit the opportunity of creating a project in a specific pavilion, at a decisive point in his or her career. The Biennale pavilion should thus be conceived as a unity, as a singular space. It is not simply the site of an exhibition, but an element, an object of artistic intervention.

Hans Schabus is representing Austria at the Biennale this year. He was born in 1970 and studied with the sculptor Bruno Gironcoli, whose works were exhibited in this same pavilion two years ago. Schabus's work combines mental and physical experience in an extraordinary way and with analytical precision. He brings himself and the viewer to a level of experience that is physical, emotional, and intellectual in equal measure – a level that has increasingly been out of the reach of recent art. It is not, however, a collective experience, only a very intimate, personal experience of a situation, expressed in terms of the relation between the artist and the artwork and between the artwork and the viewer. In his understanding of the artist's role as that of a researcher and explorer, Schabus also finds a way out of an art scene that is increasingly based on irony and detachment.

Hans Schabus's sculptures, films and interventions always relate to the site for which they are created. No matter whether it is a video installation in which Schabus glides through Vienna's sewerage system in a boat he built himself and turns up in New York's East River, or in his large solo exhibitions at the Vienna Secession or the Kunsthaus Bregenz in which he associates the place with a network of references.

A meticulous process of drawing closer is the basis of the present work for the Austrian Pavilion. The pavilion is located on the island of Sant'Elena, which was formed in the late nineteenth century with materials excavated from the recently constructed industrial port. At first the new island was left uncultivated and used by the Italian army for exercises. In the 1920s under Benito Mussolini it was zoned for working class housing and a small section was ceded to the Biennale di Venezia, set up in 1895. The Austrian Pavilion was built in 1935 at the rear of the *Giardini* to a plan by Josef Hoffmann. Hans Schabus has constructed his work on these historic parameters and on the nature of the listed building, and gone beyond them. The corpus of the building and the location of the property are translated into a new structure. The architecture is visually weighed down and freed of its function. A new outer skin – a forceful barrier, a mountain, like a part of the Alps that separate Italy from Austria – almost makes the outside of the pavilion disappear. An alpine fortress is reached only through its interior. From darkness into light. From the subsoil to a safe place when the water rises in the lagoon city.

Hans Schabus's works are processes of personal appropriation. He encircles the site of the event; he appropriates the structures and emotional qualities of the site and transforms it. Venice will see the Austrian Pavilion in a new way: barely visible but massive in its presence.

Max Hollein

COMMISSIONER
Max Hollein

ARTIST
Hans Schabus

1

2

3

1 Hans Schabus, Austrian
Pavilion, 2005. Model.
Photo Bruno Klomfar.
Courtesy Hans Schabus

2 Hans Schabus, *Wienfluss,
Wien, 16. Februar 2002*.
Cibachrome. Courtesy Hans
Schabus

3 Hans Schabus, Opening
of the Austrian Pavilion, 1935.
Courtesy Galerie Metropol, Wien

Belgium
The Quest

The creative practice of Belgian artist Honoré δ'O is formally based on the illogical nature of oxymoron and paradox. A great lover of the uncanny magic of matter, stuff and things, δ'O remains notoriously suspicious of the 'materialist', object-based economy of the art establishment. As a prime practitioner of 'process art', he has little time for the persisting cult of the sacramental art object. This penchant towards process (and attendant preference of 'project' over 'object') has led the artist to take up the videocamera in recent years, resulting in a spate of diary videoworks that celebrate the moment – the temporal, the ephemeral – and question the cult of endurance and longevity that continues to inform so much art production. This preoccupation with both dematerialisation and the transitory aspects of image 'production' defines the gestural nature of his practice. Most widely known for his large-scale sculptural installations in the 'scatter art' idiom, he abhors both the monumental and the monolithic: sprawling and unwieldy though these works may be, his heart goes out to the minor gestures that buttress these grand designs, to the transient and the haphazard. Disorientingly chaotic in outlook, these works are in fact extremely well-balanced and meticulously choreographed; the apparent result of some idiosyncratic 'scientific' design, they reflect the tortuous path of the creative thought process; if they impress us because of their immersive, landscape-like quality, it is precisely because they lend such wonderful form to the inner workings of the artist's mind as a landscape of its own. Finally, in these very choreographies and rational-looking designs, the romance of 'science' – systemic thought, procedure, method – is always subverted, however subtly, by the posture of 'poetry', of magic even. There is a deliberate obscuring of logic and thought, as there is as much method in the madness as there is madness in the method.

These observations, however, pertain primarily to the formal aspects of his practice. On a more fundamental level, Honoré δ'O is concerned with the enduring questions that have propelled the development of art since its inception in the early mists of time – and hopefully will continue to do so: what is art and why do I make it?, why am I an artist? – or, phrased in a slightly more confrontational way, what am I doing in this 'art' place?, what does art 'do'? These are all questions that have perhaps been eclipsed too long by the overtly 'political' leanings of a standard contemporary art questionnaire that only inquires, unimaginatively, after the artist's role in contemporary society, and after art's share in bringing about change in this society. While we can or should never aspire to achieve a satisfying answer to the ontological questions of art's quidditas, it is precisely the business of each artist to ask them anew, and this impulse to constantly confront the preconceived notions of 'art' – of artist-hood, art production and the art world in general – is at the very heart of the project Honoré δ'O has developed for the Belgian Pavilion.

COMMISSIONERS
Inge Braeckman
Bart De Baere
Ilse Joliet
Dieter Roelstraete

ARTIST
Honoré δ'O

Honoré δ'O, *The Quest*, 2005.
Mixed media (wood, PVC,
video); 2100 × 1600 × 580 cm

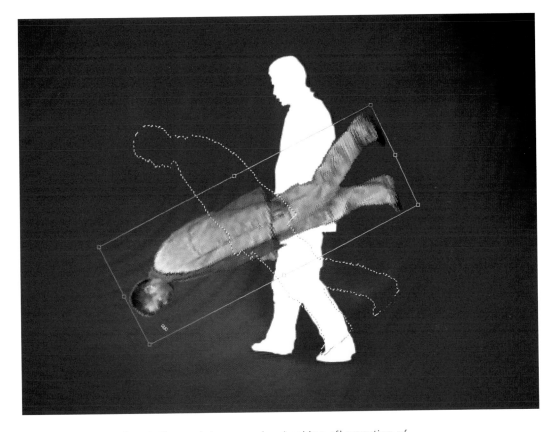

Fittingly titled *The Quest*, the work is as much a 'making-of' narration of δ'O's own odyssey-like struggle with the many aspects of contemporary art (with the artist casting himself in the role of the art world's generic Everyman), as it is a stage set on which this quest can be re-enacted. A meandering trail of video works, lumbered together in a seemingly random fashion, reminding us of the quandaries that litter the path towards Art, leads up to a 'chroma key' room, the shrine-like centrepiece in δ'O's installation: a non-site devoted to asking the questions that really matter in our common 'quest' toward the Riddle of Art – more so than ever before.
Dieter Roelstraete

Brazil

A Library in the Tropics

According to Umberto Eco there are two kinds of libraries: Don Quixote's earthly one, from which we go forth to take up the challenges of life, and the one imagined by Jorge Luis Borges, which we do not want to leave because it is the universe and exists *ab aeterno*.

Rio de Janeiro's Real Gabinete Português de Leitura, perhaps the most beautiful library in the tropics, belongs to the first variety. The Lusophone world in the Atlantic triangle between Lisbon, Rio and Luanda lies at the feet of all those who step out of this architectural jewel inaugurated in 1888.

Caio Reisewitz's Real Gabinete photographs belong to the second category described by Borges in his Library of Babel – that enormous hexagonal gallery that has no end: 'Each wall has five shelves, each shelf holds thirty-two books of the same size, each book consists of four hundred and ten pages, each page of forty lines, and each line of eighty letters in black ink' (Borges). No two books are the same in this library. When it was announced to the people that the library was complete and comprised all the books that had ever been written, they considered themselves fortunate, for there was no problem whose solution was not to be found in one of the hexagons. It is also worth remembering that Goethe's Faust experienced the infinite in a library, only to lose it again later in real life.

Like all good works of art, Reisewitz's pictures create a space that expands parallel to the real world. If you spend long enough inside it, you no longer need any excursions into so-called real life. In Rio's Real Gabinete you can quote individual titles, because it is a finite space. In Caio Reisewitz's newly invented library, you don't want to name a specific book, because the shape and aura of the library interest us more than the topics of the books. In art, books cease being the prose of the world.

The Oldest Musical Instrument in the World

Chelpa Ferro (Barrão, Sérgio Mekler and Luiz Zerbini) is a performance group from Rio de Janeiro resembling the adventurer in Alejo Carpentier's novel *Los pasos perdidos*, who searches for an archaic musical instrument in the jungles of the Orinoco.

Art has always been a time machine that is equally at home in the dim and distant past as in the present. Therefore, its points of reference can be the first days of creation or banal objects from present-day city life. The members of Chelpa Ferro, a phrase that used to mean 'money' in old, colloquial Portuguese, love the aura of everyday articles they find, particularly if a sound can be wrung out of them. A rusty drill from a dental clinic sounds like an electronic techno sample; a mysterious rustling penetrates the forest from branches vibrated by miniature motors. Or is it perhaps an experimental music concert? No-one except Chelpa Ferro knows how the flute made of swan bone that was recently discovered by archaeologists in southern Germany sounded; it is the oldest musical instrument in the world – 35,000 years old.

COMMISSIONER
Manoel Francisco Pires da Costa

CURATOR
Alfons Hug

ARTISTS
Chelpa Ferro
Caio Reisewitz

COORDINATION
Fundação Bienal de São Paulo

http://bienalsaopaulo.globo.com/
noticias/51bienalveneza.asp

As curators of an organographic museum, whose location in the tropics is no coincidence, Chelpa Ferro rummage through the treasure troves of both past and contemporary art and music. They unearth a gramophone, and finally a flute made of fired clay which the Amazon Indians use while hunting to imitate a bird's song. Then again they produce the noise of an aircraft turbine or an alarm siren or the sound of a techno rave. The sounds abruptly alternate between dark, rural sound colours and the hectic noise of a big city. It goes without saying that percussion rhythms taken from Brazilian popular music crop up repeatedly. Chelpa Ferro cheerfully unite the extremes of nature in the tropics and the inventiveness of art. There are often seemingly absurd situations that initially make us feel helpless; in the end, however, thanks to their fine irony, they send us back into our everyday lives with a quiet smile on our lips.
Alfons Hug

1

2

Canada

Belmore's art, whether it is installation, video or photograph, has its basis in performance, which she in turn sees as a medium shared by old traditions and modern expression – a medium both indigenous and international.

As a vehicle for polemics, Belmore's performance art almost always features her body, and her presence in the work calls forth a sense of loss for something absent. That sense of loss is for the great losses suffered by North America's First People since European colonisation.

In an early performance at the Havana Biennial (1991), *Creation or Death, We Will Win*, Belmore moved a pile of dirt up a long staircase, stair by stair, in a state of desperate frenzy. Dirt is lost at every stage and it is not at all certain that any of it will make it to the landing at the top of the stairs. The title of the piece reveals its intention to have the viewer experience the piece as the struggle of First Nations people to reclaim their territories and culture.

The sense of loss in Belmore's work has been explicit and specific. In addition to lost battles and the scourge of racism, there is a loss of cosmology and nature, a remapping and reimagination of the inhabited world that imposes itself and erases culture, language and ways of apprehending.

In working with the transitions between performance, video and installation, Belmore pays special attention to the screen. The surface receiving the projection was punctured by light bulbs in her 2002 work, *The Named and the Unnamed*. The light bulbs solidify the screen, making it a wall as well as a window. One's attention is always split between the palpability of the surface of the screen and the transparency of the moving image projected upon it. This cleavage she creates in the perception of the viewer, who is both invited into and rebuffed from entering the depth of the projected image, produces a disturbance many viewers will find distressing but compelling.

Rebecca Belmore's new work, *Fountain*, was conceived for the Canada Pavilion at the Giardini in Venice. An image is projected onto a water screen. The projected image is an edited DVD of a video shot cinema-style on an industrial zone beach near Vancouver, Canada. It is a cold, grey winter day, typical of the North American Pacific Northwest in January. The action is in five parts. The artist flails in the water near the shore struggling with a bucket. Next, in a calm state, she kneels and holds the vessel beneath the surface of the water. Then she rises and walks onto the shore. After that, she stops and tosses the contents of the pail toward the lens, covering the screen with a sheet of blood. And, lastly, she is seen through the film of blood that fragments and distorts the image. The action has an ambiguous meaning that is associated with awakening and emerging. There is a sense of a task to be done; one of ritual and portent.

Fountain deals with elementals or essences: fire + water = blood. The time is both now, in the industrialised landscape of North America, and in another zone, a time of creation, myth and prophecy. The element of water is represented both as a body of water in the projection and literally as a wall of falling water. Water turns to blood. As befits our times, we don't know whether this is a metaphor for creation and connectedness or an apocalyptic vision.

Jann L.M. Bailey, Scott Watson

COMMISSIONERS
Jann L.M. Bailey
Scott Watson

ARTIST
Rebecca Belmore

www.belkingallery.ubc.ca/belmore

1

2

3

4

5

6

Croatia

The exhibition by Goran Trbuljak, Tomo Savić Gecan, Pasko Burdelez, Alen Floričić, Zlatan Dumanić and Boris Šincek at this year's Biennale opens a possible window onto Croatian art. My view is driven by emotion, intuition, recognition and self-identification; slippery categories, all of them, that resist definition.

In one of his former works Goran Trbuljak states that 'I don't want to show anything new or original', and the same is true of this presentation, which proposes something similar. The characteristic defensiveness of all six artists is one of the key points for recognising that in this context it becomes a strategy. These artists offer no solutions. They are not the conscience of the world. They take no pains to be right. The are linked by contradiction. Although they are passive, motionless, absent, closed, detached and self-referential, they deal directly with relations and contrasts of power, in their own roles as artists, creators and people in the contexts of art and society. Their speech is immediate and without redundancy, which is read as a sign of deficiency and uncommunicativeness.

In a time dominated by form, they remain loyal to substance.

Everything at this exhibition has either already happened or is happening somewhere else.

Slaven Tolj

COMMISSIONER
Slaven Tolj

ARTISTS
Pasko Burdelez
Zlatan Dumanić
Alen Floričić
Tomo Savić Gecan
Boris Šincek
Goran Trbuljak

ASSISTANTS
Antun Maračić
Srdjana Cvijetić

COORDINATOR IN VENICE
Živa Kraus

ORGANIZATION
Museum of Modern Art,
Dubrovnik, Art workshop
Lazareti, Dubrovnik

www.ugdubrovnik.hr

1

1 Pasko Burdelez, *Untitled*, 2004. Video and photo documentation of the performance. Photo Ana Opalic

2 Goran Trbuljak*, *The need to add a footnote to a text is more important than whatever might be in the footnote 30 years later*, 1976-2005. Episcope text projection

3 Zlatan Dumanić, *The Play*, 2003. Weld-painted tin-zinc; rice; 25 × 119 × 16 cm. Photo Luka Bezic

4 Tomo Savić Gecan, *Untitled*, 2003-2005. Interactive installation. Courtesy Isabella Bortolozzi Gallery, Berlin

5 Boris Šincek, *Shooting*, 2002. Video still from the video documentation of the performance. Photo Miha Fras

6 Alen Floričić, *Untitled N° 03/04*, 2004. Video still from the three channel video installation. Photo Alen Floričić

Goran Trbuljak*, 1976.

*
———
Potreba da se tekstu doda fusnota važnija je od onoga što bi se u njoj moglo naći 30 godina kasnije.

2   3

The passing of visitors during the Portal 2 exhibition in Kunsthalle Fridericianum, Kassel (XII 2003 - II 2004) causes small changes in the architecture in Isabella Bortolozzi Gallery, Berlin (XI 2004 - I 2005).

4

5   6

Denmark

The most important task of the Danish Arts Council's Committee for International Visual Art is to communicate and situate Danish visual art within an international context. The Committee aims to enhance the dissemination of Danish contemporary art abroad and of foreign art in Denmark. The Committee seeks to establish and secure the best possible conditions for Danish visual art on the international art scene and thus contribute to a professional art dialogue on equal terms. The Committee aspires to an organic set of principles where integration, dialogue and openness are fundamental values.

The Committee for International Visual Art is responsible for the Danish Arts Agency's Visual Art Centre's international activities in Denmark and abroad. These include appointing Danish participating artists for the two major international biennials in Venice and Sao Paulo as well as responsibility for the selection of artists for studio visits to New York, Los Angeles, Berlin and Paris, respectively. In addition to these activities, the main task of the Committee is to give grants to Danish visual art abroad and to foreign visual art in Denmark.

The Committee for International Visual Art is appointed for a four year period from July 2003 to July 2007 by the Danish Arts Council's representatives and the Minister for Culture.

Curators of the exhibition are Sanne Kofod Olsen and Jacob Fabricius.

Sanne Kofod Olsen is a curator employed at the Danish Art Agency's Visual Art Centre, Copenhagen. She has been working as a curator and writer since the mid-90s.

Jacob Fabricius is freelance curator who lives and works in Copenhagen. He has been working as a curator and critic since the mid-90s and is the founder of the publishing company Pork Salad Press.

COMMISSIONERS
Danish Arts Council, Committee of International Visual Art
The committee counts following members:
Anders Kold (chairman), curator at Louisiana Museum of Modern Art, Denmark, Kirsten Ortwed, artist, Köln, Germany, Olafur Eliasson, artist, Berlin, Germany, Åsa Sonjasdotter, artist, Copenhagen, Denmark, Peter Weinberger, gallerist

CURATOR
Sanne Kofod Olsen

ASSISTANT CURATOR
Jacob Fabricius

ARTISTS
Eva Koch
Joachim Koester
Peter Land
Ann Lislegaard
Gitte Villesen

COORDINATOR IN VENICE
Daniela Murgia

ORGANIZATION AND CARE OF
Troels Bruun

www.biennalen.dk
www.danish-arts.dk

1

2

3

4

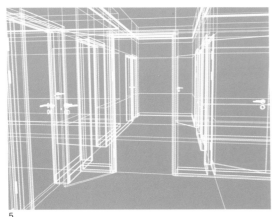

5

6

Egypt

Every two years the Venice Biennale, like a sacred amulet surrounded by artists from all over the world, launches a few magic words, such as the *Arts in the Mirror* theme, which I witnessed as one of the artists exhibited in the Egyptian Pavilion at the 41st Biennale in 1984 *Art Alespuico - Art Traditions*.

Today, this great 51st Biennale, with its giant mirrors, observes man floating with his imagination, mind and spirit, going beyond the boundaries of time and place, surpassing all art schools and trends incorporating the remote past and the endless future. The Biennale always calls upon artists, intellectuals, philosophers, critics and lovers of art and knowledge to look at everything in life with a human eye; to interact with the feelings and emotions that have reflected man's features on his journey since the dawn of history, through human awareness, experience and the mind; to contemplate man's world, which he creates everyday, and to contemplate his genius, madness, mania, weakness, aggressiveness, gentleness, superiority, deterioration and worries. One day, Dante Alighieri's *Divine Comedy* will be an appropriate theme for examining man on his journey through hell, purification and paradise, by all media and the languages of fine arts and literature in close cooperation with the arts of place and time.

The Italian city of Venice is a curious eye that re-examines man's existence. Throughout Venice's history, art and creativity have created a powerful atmosphere and a dynamism in which art, science and philosophy balance in a new continuity and a new awareness of man's reality in interacting with his world and his existence. It is backed up much contemplation and interaction in all the fine arts presented here by artists from all over the world. We came here with our faith in art, its role and mission, the value of the free expression of our thoughts, our vision and our dreams.

The young artist Nagy Farid presents his sculptures floating within the three dimensions of time, reflecting his worries about the contradictions of our contemporary world, expecting the arrival of a new age. His materials are granite, leaping into vast horizons and searching for new existence. The heritage of our forefathers is the aesthetic gauge; the symbols clear sentences and words in the language of form.

The young artist Salah Hamad presents his boats, which renew the journey in the labyrinth of departure toward the sun boats – the source of myths of Death and Life. These boats awaken contemplation of the secrets of earth and heaven. The elements of theatrical construction in his works seek to introduce a dialectic by using different media, including music.

Abdel Salam Eid

COMMISSIONER
Abdel Salam Eid

ARTISTS
Nagui Farid Tadros
Salah Hammad

1

2

1 Nagui Farid Tadros, *Another Time*, 2005. 14 pieces in one composition

2 Salah Hammad, *Migration*, 2005. Construction wood, granite, marble, metal, sand, bowling, sound effect (music); 4 × 5 m

Estonia
Isolator

'In my opinion such Estonian "men and women" are enemies of the Estonian state and should be isolated: let them operate within closed walls' (M. Sults, 'A Duty to Preserve the Country', *Postimees*, 28 July 2004).

'The first thing the Germans did was to forbid Jews access to swimming pools; it seemed to them that if the body of an Israelite were to plunge into that confined body of water, the water would be completely befouled' (J.-P. Sartre, 'Anti-Semite and Jew', *Temps Modernes*, 1946).

The intimate exhibition rooms in the Palazzo Malipiero where the Estonian display is located act as a conceptual apartment. Mark Raidpere's solo exhibition examining his personal identity contradictions marks the co-ordinates of privacy in social space. The viewer, who for the first time encounters the abundant grotesque of the homo-erotic motives of Raidpere's earlier pictures of himself, is taken by surprise. Whence this pain, strained to its limits, discreetly brought to attention by the cigarette-burned stigmas on the hands in the black-and-white photographs? This was the time Raidpere photographed himself at home, recovering from the crisis that led to self-burning – working with his father's Zenit E that was probably just as old as he was. Later this became an exhibition titled *Io* (1997) where personal material became public evidence. A theme of personal fragility was taken up in another key in the video *Father* (2001). It is a trip through the environment of a small flat in a district of grim dormitory-type houses, belonging to the artist's father who had recently suffered a psychotic condition. The interview-based works of today return to earlier traumas mapping emotional breaking points between himself and his closest people. They are psychoanalytical strolls in the father-mother-home-and-myself quadrate of interpersonal relations, characterised by the high-tension between the private and the public, natural and staged, conditional and comprehensive. Everything eccentric hidden in the limelight – for example the condemned men at the prison photo session in the video *16 Men* (2003), who show him their tattoos – has fascinated him personally. Paradoxically the video has an effect of the artist's self-portrait. Here a parallel emerges between home as man's personal defence zone and prison as a social rejection zone. Raidpere's heightened awareness of the performative nature of his identity reveals an agonising sign of danger, a symptom of something worrying, a state of a pariah. We get the impression that his presence always makes the others point their finger at him, thus increasing his need for solitude and privacy, romanticising even the forced isolation. According to Habermas, the isolation and privacy of a small-family sphere used to be the historical birthplace of content and free inner life, and part of the artist still believes in that. In contemporary reality, colonised by the camera lens, this romantic notion naturally remains in the field of unsatisfied Ego-Ideal, which escalates tension between the values of an artist and society. The ideological determination of the private sphere leads to insoluble tensions between relatives and friends, something Raidpere tries to open with new means. Tension between the public and the private is stronger in transitional societies than in Western Europe with its longer experience of democracy and tolerance. In the motto of the current writing, taken from a homophobic article of a Tallinn school director and published last summer in a major local daily, we find a reference to the social background of Raidpere's enforced dramatics. For a foreign observer, as a rule, this remains concealed behind the grand scenes of the PR-conscious New Europe, but is firmly evident in the private sphere. Joining the discussion, the editor in chief of the same daily later added that if the private life of homosexuals becomes a public affair, 'there is no knowing when the majority's thin coating of tolerance regarding

COMMISSIONER
Sirje Helme

CURATOR
Hanno Soans

ARTIST
Mark Raidpere

ORGANIZATION
Museum of Contemporary Arts, Estonia

CO-ORGANIZER
Arte Communications, Venice

www.cca.ee
www.cca.ee/en/tegemised/
naitused/venice/estonian_
exhibition_
www.artecommunications.com

1

2

minorities suddenly rips, and the streets are full of quite different parades' than the gay-pride. From Raidpere's point of view this no doubt sounds threatening. We should perhaps try to regard the slogan introducing Estonia internationally – the land of improvement – without any irony. It might actually come in useful.
Hanno Soans

Translated from Estonian by Tiina Randviür

FYROM (Former Yugoslav Republic of Macedonia)
Mozart's Boat

Mozart's Boat: Sailing on Silence

Over the last fifteen years, young artists in the Republic of Macedonia have been maturing in complex social conditions as a result of global world movements and of turbulence in the country and the immediate region. Their reaction is reduced to quiet resistance or aggressive resistance.

As a member of the current fine arts scene, Antoni Maznevski chooses quiet resistance, although he shares the universal desire to overcome the restlessness, conflict and uncertainty of the time. His project, *Mozart's Boat*, with its sophisticated feeling for the common dilemmas of today's world, reflects alienation and withdrawal into one's own 'psychic depths', into the inner sanctum of art. His space for meditation, contemplation and survival is the boat of wishes with its trajectory. With it, Maznevski's silent resistance sails toward metaphysical spaces: from the height of the individual to that of the trans-individual, where he can rediscover the sense of reality in this world, which forces him to feel unreal and false.

The *Mozart's Boat* project is visually very simple. It is made of two basic structures: a wooden boat (100 × 650 × 200 cm) placed in a clean white space, and a line of bows fixed on the surrounding walls. The body of an old, worn-out yacht has been restored and its upper horizontal surface been shaped as a stringed instrument. The ambiguity of this invented object arose in the imagination, which still requires dialectic. The dynamic lines of the bows are contrasted with the imagined energy enclosed in the physical stillness of the musical instrument-boat, as a specific visual support for an imaginary itinerary 'engraved' on the watery horizontal.

The initial germ of this work came from the wish to understand infinity, the risks of adventure, and opens up opportunities for extended associations. The musical instrument-boat awakens myths and personal fantasies of sea voyages and adventures, it reopens symbolism and relations between fear and curiosity, risk and caution, music and water, male and female, real and imaginary, the ontological and non-ontological. The meaning of the voyage also denotes the uniting of extreme distances and different times. In this narration about boats, Maznevski does not approach the closed structure of Jules Verne's Nautilus (boat-house), but prefers the free, open sailing of Rimbaud's *Drunken Boat*, which 'conveys man from cave psychoanalysis to the genuine poetics of the need to explore', on the other side of truth, in the regions of the transcendental. These reminiscences are also related to Maznevski's affinity with oriental philosophy and Zen aesthetics. In order to identify 'that which cannot be named' the author forgets his own 'I' and concentrates on appearances and things to find out their essence, their real self-nature.

The *Mozart's Boat* project merges with the simplicity of silence. Parsimony of

COMMISSIONER
Sonja Abadzieva

DEPUTY COMMISSIONER
Zoran Petrovski

ARTIST
Antoni Maznevski

ORGANIZATION
Museum of Contemporary Art, Skopje

www.msuskopje.org.mk

Antoni Maznevski, *Mozart's Boat*, 2004. Installation, ready-made wooden boat; 100 × 650 × 200 cm, and 10-15 wooden bows of variable dimensions. Photo Courtesy Rumen Kamilov

discourse is the need to be free of the scream of images, letters and texts that cause the fatigue in contemporary society. Maznevski considers that silence, beauty and perfection are those forces that can free us from the tyranny of rhetoric and return us to the freshness and spontaneity of the source.

Mozart's Boat, ideally smoothed and adjusted, together with the technical refinement of the linear strings and the elegant bows, does not hide the artist's irresistible desire to also include the general notion of beauty as perfection existing in itself, and the concrete beauty of shape and form, in order to give them back the lost glow of active beauty.

Sonja Abadzieva

Translated into English by Irena Apostolova

France

The artist has conceived a specific project for the French Pavilion at the Venice Biennale that uses all the available space. Drawing inspiration from a legendary work of Italian literature featuring a now universal 'hero', she has designed a pathway that conjures up a story, our story, in an allusive and poetic manner. It also deals with the creative process and artistic parentage in a game where, in tragic alternation, the immortality of a puppet would stands for innocence without rule and regained humanity would condemn it to a lethal norm.

The project is arranged in three rooms, each with its own rhythm, referring to a stage in the development of the 'hero'.

Having crossed a forest of bolsters – between sleep and death – supported on human organs, the visitor coming into the second room is seized by a fantastic, organic vortex whose colour evokes the violence of birth and the passage into life.

In the third room, the mechanical movement of a hellish machine forces the 'hero' to make strange contortions. Is it a game or an ordeal ?

The world of childhood hides a dangerous mechanism whereby the person who thinks she is playing is being played with. Suffering is there, ever present, for the manipulator and the manipulated.

Annette Messager has from the start turned her condition as a woman and an artist, which she felt was devalued, into works of art, accentuating their tensions. She uses everyday elements – press cuttings, strands of wool, nets, pencils, cushions, cuddly toys, etc. – sometimes combining them with drawings and photographs and, more recently, with apparently shoddy technological equipment, to create a universe that is both fascinating and repulsive, obvious and ambiguous. The ordinary nature of life with its banality, triviality, commonplaces, things unsaid, fears and fantasies are her basic materials. The overtly intrepid nature of the approach does not mask any secretly maintained vulnerability.

Over the years her work has developed considerably in space, while taking on a more solemn dimension, with the artist reacting to the often violent disruptions that perturb contemporary society – like the spectacular installation, *Articulé-Désarticulé*, presented at Documenta 11 in 2002.

More recently, this solemnity has been displaced by a more introspective tone, where mysterious allusions are mingled with more public elements, where personal history meets History. This is exemplified in the work entitled *Pudique, Publique*, produced at the Palazzo delle Papesse in Siena in 2002 and in *Sous vent*, presented by the Musée d'Art moderne de la Ville de Paris at the Couvent des Cordeliers in the summer of 2004.

Annette Messager's constantly questioning work demands the absolute freedom to be part of the present, to renew itself, to be serious and playful, and sends us back the echo of society taking root in a sophisticated and popular imagination and subconsciousness, allowing a complex interpretation that reverberates in each of us.

Suzanne Pagé, Béatrice Parent

COMMISSIONERS
Suzanne Pagé
Béatrice Parent

ARTIST
Annette Messager

Germany

Thomas Scheibitz and Tino Sehgal

What links them is their fundamental engagement with what contemporary visual art could be. Against a backdrop of vast diversity and a constant intermingling of modernity and postmodernity, both artists explore the specific aspect of art which cannot be replaced by other experiences and means of representation. In their own different ways they thus explore the emergence of form and meaning. But neither in Thomas Scheibitz's painting and sculpture nor in Tino Sehgal's site, space and body-related works are these questions solved or treated in an abstract way. Instead, both artists are fundamentally interested in complex kinds of content, form and association.

In a very peculiar way, Thomas Scheibitz's (born in 1968) paintings and sculptures combine a high level dynamism with what might be seen as a rather cool attitude towards the world and its interpretation. They exist in a zone between recognisable signs and painterly autonomy. The motifs he uses derive from many very different sources. They extend from the built environment via landscape to the figure, from older works of art via popular pictorial media to everyday design. But these fragments of reality are subjected to formal processes that are both calculated and intuitive. Without a doubt, Scheibitz's works produce an image of the present. But this is the result not of reproduction, but of pictorial construction, a process of knowledge produced using visual means.

Tino Sehgal (born in 1976) has developed a specific form of art that takes shape only at the moment of one's encounter with it. His works are performed by interpreters (such as museum attendants) and consist of movements, spoken words, song or communication with the visitor. Sehgal replaces the production of objects with works related to the body, space and time, which act as though they are objects in exhibitions, museum collections and the art market, but which are actually not. They exist only as a situation, conversation, in transformation, in memory and in the past. Consequently there are no filmic or photographic records of the works. Sehgal is less concerned with a critique of the institutional space than with making works of visual art in which production is formulated in essentially new and different ways.

What is so fascinating about Thomas Scheibitz and Tino Sehgal is their treatment of basic issues in art under the conditions of contemporary culture. Using very different means both artists explore the emergence of form and meaning. In doing so they refer to universal phenomena of the present day, but do not illustrate them. In an age with a strong tendency to 'cross-over', they are interested in that which still remains specific in visual art, that which is not replaceable.

Julian Heynen

COMMISSIONER
Julian Heynen

ARTISTS
Thomas Scheibitz
Tino Sehgal

COORDINATION
Katia Reich

IN CO-OPERATION WITH
Auswärtiges Amt
in collaboration with Institut
für Auslandsbeziehungen

SPONSOR
DekaBank Deutsche
Girozentrale, Partner
of the German Pavilion

www.biennale2005.de

Thomas Scheibitz, work
in progress for the German
Pavilion

Japan
mother's 2000-2005 --- traces of the future

Miyako Ishiuchi's *Mother's* provides a portrait of a woman who was a forerunner of the independent women of today's Japan. The heroine of this story was a woman born in a rural village in the Northern Kanto region in 1916. She obtained her driver's license at age 18 and went to Manchuria to work. She was married there, but her husband was quickly drafted and sent to the front.

She returned to her hometown in Japan during the war and drove a truck hauling military materials. During that period, she met a young student who had been mobilized and sent to work at a nearby air field. When the war ended, she encouraged him to return to college and after he graduated they began living together in the village. Her husband had been reported dead but returned after the war. She was pregnant at the time, so she paid severance money to her husband and obtained a divorce by mutual agreement.

Ishiuchi's *Mother's* series begins with an old photograph of the woman who lived this turbulent life. It shows a large truck, probably of American make, with the door open on the driver's side. A small young woman wearing a long skirt and blouse, a belt cinched tight around her waist, stands next to it with a dazzling smile. The rest of the works in the exhibition show objects she once owned.

These photographs, including 'portraits' of chemises and girdles, seem to embody the will of the person who wore them. There are also images of several partially-used tubes of lipstick in different colours, a comb with hair still stuck in it, false teeth and wigs, and close-ups of plants and skin. Ishiuchi carefully selected a variety of 'things' left by her mother as a way of quietly observing their relationship, which she reports as discordant, and contemplating a 'sadness beyond imagination'.

She is performing the task of resuscitating the existence of her mother as a woman. She links her name as an artist with the name of her mother in this series. As Miyako Ishiuchi, an independent contemporary woman, she pays homage to Miyako Ishiuchi, another independent contemporary woman who has continued to live vigorously for 84 years. Her work gives a realistic picture

COMMISSIONER
Michiko Kasahara

DEPUTY COMMISSIONERS
Jun Takeshita
Hiroshi Omori

ARTIST
Miyako Ishiuchi

ORGANIZATION
The Japan Foundation

1 Miyako Ishiuchi, *Mother's # 8*, 2002. Gelatin silver print; 108 × 74 cm. Collection of the artist

2 Miyako Ishiuchi, *Mother's # 15*, 2002. Gelatin silver print; 108 × 74 cm. Collection of the artist

3 Miyako Ishiuchi, *Mother's # 49*, 2002. Gelatin silver print; 108 × 74 cm. Collection of the artist

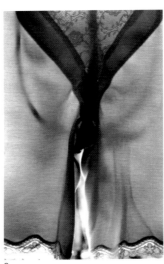

1
2
3

4

6

7

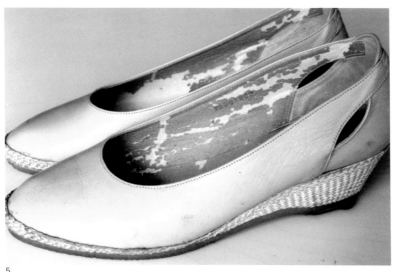

5

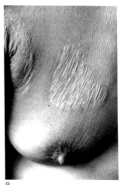

8

of the great changes that have occurred in the consciousness of contemporary women.

Contemporary art reflects contemporary society and looks ahead to the near future, and the photographs of Miyako Ishiuchi, who represent Japan at the Venice Biennale, are refined works of art that deal with the dramatic transformation in women's attitudes taking place today.

Michiko Kasahara

4 Miyako Ishiuchi, *Mother's # 37*, 2002. Direct print; 19 × 28.5 cm. Collection of the artist

5 Miyako Ishiuchi, *Mother's # 52*, 2003. Type-C-print; 100 × 150 cm. Collection of the artist

6 Miyako Ishiuchi, *Mother's # 39*, 2002. Direct print; 150 × 100 cm. Collection of the artist

7 Miyako Ishiuchi, *Mother's # 54*, 2002. Direct print; 150 × 100 cm. Collection of the artist

8 Miyako Ishiuchi, *Mother's # 53*, 2000. Gelatin silver print; 108 × 74 cm. Collection of the artist

Great Britain

For their exhibition in the British Pavilion for the 51st Venice Biennale, Gilbert & George present a new group of pictures.

Gilbert & George began working together shortly after meeting on the Advanced Sculpture Course at St. Martin's School of Art, London, in 1967. Their first solo exhibition took place in May 1968, and in January the following year they presented their first 'Living Sculpture' as Our New Sculpture (later re-titled Underneath the Arches and finally The Singing Sculpture). Using themselves as their primary subject, the artists and their artwork became one and the same, and Gilbert & George have continued to develop their singular visual language ever since: 'the content of mankind is our subject and our inspiration'. They began making their first photo-pieces in the early 1970s. Initially incorporating groups of individually framed black and white images, they later utilised a grid format to enable them to work on a more ambitious scale for large series such as Cherry Blossom, 1974, Dead Boards, 1976, and in particular The Dirty Words Pictures, 1977. Here images of East End London street life are juxtaposed with close-up shots of aggressive graffiti, and where the early photo-pieces had seen Gilbert & George alone in their own private world, in The Dirty Words Pictures they are cast as witnesses to the harsh realities of human struggle. This was the inner-city reality of their London and these pictures speak to the viewer in the most direct and uncompromising way, encouraging them to question their own place in the world, their own hopes and fears.

During the following decade, Gilbert & George introduced a saturated field of colour and increased the scale even further for their monumental multi-part pictures such as Death, Hope, Life, Fear, 1984, and Class War, Militant, Gateway, 1986, where they continued to explore such universal themes as religion, class, race, identity, sex and death. The rich allegorical nature and cinematic scale of these pictures in turn led to the groups of pictures of the 1990s, The Naked Shit Pictures, 1994, and The Fundamental Pictures, 1996, which saw them at their most vulnerable and exposed, stripped of any vestige of clothing and appearing naked before the world.

Throughout their career, the streets of London have been a constant source of inspiration for Gilbert & George as they have charted their own journey through life and stood witness to the changes in the cultural fabric of their own neighbourhood. This sense of time and place has become increasingly apparent in the new groups of pictures made in the present decade. The graffiti strewn landscape and sombre tone of Nine Dark Pictures of 2001, seemed to both reprise the pictures of the 1970s and yet anticipate the de-stabilising world events about to take place later that same year. These pictures also looked forward to the direction of the unsettling imagery of their most recent pictures, Thirteen Hooligan Pictures, 2004, and Perversive Pictures, 2004. In certain of these highly charged symbolic pictures the artists' features have been manipulated so that they appear stretched and distorted, halved and doubled, while in others they appear as mere apparitions, ghost-like sentinels watching over the streets of London they have inhabited for almost forty years.

Richard Riley

COMMISSIONER
Andrea Rose

CURATOR
Richard Riley

DEPUTY COMMISSIONER
Brendan Griggs

ARTISTS
Gilbert & George

www.britishcouncil.org/
venicebiennale

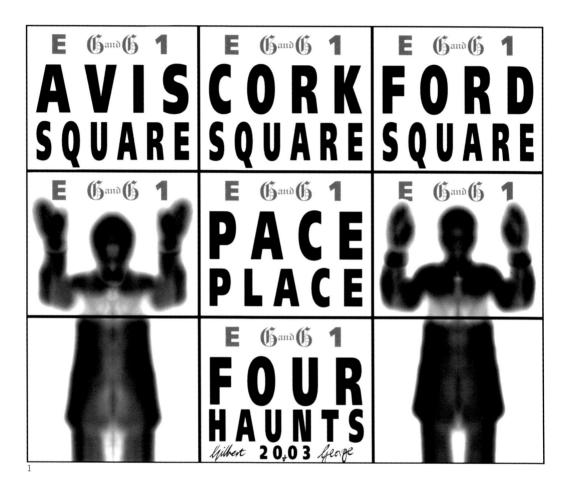

1

2

3

Greece

George Hadjimichalis' *Hospital*

George Hadjimichalis has never stopped wondering about the meaning and the value of painting and, by extension, its viability through the new media of artistic expression. Through his work, he demonstrates that painting is a geographic, philosophical and historical *topos* that has unlimited possibilities of renewal and adaptation to the requirements of contemporary art. He feels as comfortable in a classical painter's studio as in the space where a conceptual work of art could be realised. This is perhaps because he naturally demystifies the meaning of the composite Greek word for painting: ζω-γραφική (depiction from life). It is obvious that George Hadjimichalis understands art as both a conceptual and real space, a microcosm in which man has always been living. His entire work is thus a timeless commentary of the relation between life and art. The artist's world comes complete with its own physical / technical infrastructure, set of historical-mythological references, memories and visual experiences. Overall, an exhibition is for him a display of images. His installation *Hospital* for the 51st Biennale of Venice, is the culmination of both his artistic and existential quests and fears.

This mixed media installation has been conceived as a non-space, devoid of life's trivialities, alluding to art, the triumph of life over death. Hospitals and the art world have this in common: although they are a part of everyday life, they are at the same time apart from it. Their contained worlds are in a permanent critical state because of their insecurity and unpredictability. Tragedies and miracles occur in equal proportions. Art and health both have to be protected and treated. This is the reason why the term 'therapy' ('θεραπεία' in Greek, 'cura' in Latin) was used in both contexts. Today only the word 'curator' betrays the existence of this immediate link. An artist is maybe the only being that still feels the essential connection between those two worlds.

'Crisis' loses its almost exclusively negative connotation and takes on its original meaning of a decisive moment. The concrete and the fleeting, the existing and the predicted, the sacred and the profane, the obvious and the ineffable, the fatal and the suspended coexist in the artist's *Hospital*, which aims to remind of a place where art is survival.

Katerina Koskina

COMMISSIONER/CURATOR
Katerina Koskina

DEPUTY CURATOR
Nadia Argyropoulou

ARTIST
George Hadjimichalis

1-2 George Hadjimichalis, *Hospital, The Building, the Plan, the View from the Windows, the Ward*, 2004-2005 (detail). Installation; mixed media; dimension variable. Photos of the artist

1

2

Indonesia

Actualising Insight Virtuality

Have you ever tried to sense what you feel when you are in the middle of a noisy and crowded market where so many people and businesses represent their various interests? Everyone is occupied with their own thoughts and needs. People are physically close, but emotionally far apart. Other people seem to be competitors or barriers. The market itself is full of diverse, sensually persuasive commercial images: billboards, product brands and leaflets. Such 'noise' has intensified in Indonesia in recent years because of a pronounced socio-political awareness and an excess of media commodification. This situation has been complicated by a series of natural disasters, in particular the tsunami that hit one of Indonesia's provinces, Nangro Aceh Darussalam, at the end of 2004 (26 December), causing unspeakable destruction and killing so many people.

In such situations it seems natural if people start complaining, blaming each other and shouting. People are easily tempted to express feelings and represent such situations with direct emotional and critical language, adopting an overriding pessimism about life. Verbal, visual and gestural language becomes coloured by vulgar, banal or absurd expressions. These kinds of feelings and this atmosphere are increasingly reflected in contemporary art in Indonesia. As a result, many artists in Indonesia who are directly and indirectly influenced by such situations reflect symptoms of necrophilia in their work. Therefore, representing violence, death and pathos seems natural and attractive to many.

In such a gloomy situation, however, one has to be thoughtful and astute when reading the phenomena. One ought to be courageous enough to challenge this sense of claustrophobia and brave enough to imagine the light behind the darkness. One might choose to approach such a predicament differently from the grim ways mentioned above. To take a long deep breath, be with one's self for a moment and extricate one's self from patterns of daily problems and then focus attention on the very moment of 'the now' is an act of imagination that can lead to a new reality. In this way, one has more chance to listen to internal insight and *rasa* (the senses) when responding to a given situation. In other words, one can recognise the microcosm with its virtual potential within oneself, behind which is the potential of the non-local or universal (*brahman*), the well of hope and dynamism.

Indonesia is celebrating its sixtieth anniversary at this 2005 Venice Biennale with four artists whose work generates and vibrates feelings of paradox and expresses the non-linearity of life. They are Entang Wiharso (1967), Noor Ibrahim (1966), Yani Mariani Sastranegara (1955) and Krisna Murti (1957), each creating work which strives to find original answers for their own lives. They don't merely 'grab' the experiences of others as sensationalised by the media, but generate work that directly reflects their

COMMISSIONER
Sumarti Sarwono

CURATOR
Dwi Marianto

DEPUTY COMMISSIONER
Grace Anna Marie

ARTISTS
Noor Ibrahim
Krisna Murti
Yani Mariani Sastranegara
Entang Wiharso

CO-ORGANIZATION
Arte Communications, Venice

SPECIAL THANKS
Telecom Italian Future Centre

www.artecommunications.com

1

2

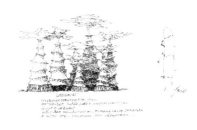

3

4

own experiences. Entang's work for this event is about his reflections on virtual materials (news, opinions and images from the media) that are continuously presented, absorbed and by and large crystallised into dispositions that influence society's point of view. Ibrahim mainly represents his insights about Indonesian cultural diversity in various traditional dresses. Krisna Murti shows video art about a therapeutic journey between pleasure and happiness. Yani Mariani reflects on soil and new plant shoots as metaphors for the endless potential of life.

While conscious of the devastation that natural and man-made violence has on individual lives as well as socio-political systems, these artists choose to articulate and map images and ideas that sustain renewal and vitality.

Dwi Marianto

1 Noor Ibrahim, *Angel from Gampingan*

2 Krisna Murti, *Video Spa*, 2004. Video still

3 Yani Mariani Sastranegara, *Lazuardi*, 2005. Sketch of the installation

4 Entang Wiharso, *FORBIDDEN EXOTIC COUNTRY: VIRTUAL STILL LIFE*, 2004. Mixed media installation; dimension variable

Iran

Participation of Iranian artists in the Venice Biennale dates as far back as the 1960's, when works by a number of distinguished Iranian artists taking part in the Tehran Biennale would be selected to be dispatched to Italy.

The post-revolutionary era brought an end to this participation and, after years of reclusion, three Iranian artists – Behrooz Daresh, Hossein Khosrowjerdi, and Ahmad Nadalian – participated in the 50th Venice Biennale in 2003.

Two Iranian artists will be delegated to the Biennale this year for the second time since the Islamic revolution. Conceptual art and modern visual expression by a few eminent academicians, who were closely following on the heels of modern trends and phenomena in the world of art, were presented in classes and a young generation of artists gradually became familiar with this mode of expression. Through various media, this new generation of artists created works of art that revolutionised the conventional and academic modes of expression in Iran's art arena. Nevertheless, the most effective steps in introducing and defining conceptual art and new approaches in artistic expression was taken by the Tehran Museum of Contemporary Art through exhibitions including 'Conceptual Art' (2000) and 'New Art' (2001). These events, together with support provided by the MoCA, promoted modern approaches in art among a new generation of Iranian artists, which produced the two young women who are representing Iran in this year's Biennale.

Bita Fayyazi Azad and Mandana Moghaddam are two distinguished artists whose success in their artistic career impressed the selection committee and who participate in the Venice Biennale as Iran's ambassadors. Today, the emergence of eminent female artists in cultural, art and social arenas is the harbinger of a bright future for the presence of this 'other half' of Iranian citizens in the domain of creativity and contemplation.

Mandana Moghaddam has prepared an installation entitled *Chelgis* (Forty braids of hair). *Chelgis* is taken from an old Iranian myth and tells the story of a beautiful girl, who is incarcerated by a ghoul in a blissful garden. She never sees the ghoul, but it is said that the ghoul has blocked the river so as not to let human beings use water. The ghoul is a brazen-bodied creature and to kill him one must break his spell. The work comprises a block of cement hung from the ceiling by four braids of hair. A red ribbon is stuck into each braid and comes out the other end. The block of cement is on the one hand a symbol of absolute, traditional masculinity, and on the other monotony and coldness. The braid of woman's hair with its red ribbon is a symbol of feminine liveliness, glimmer and sensitivity, and this is what tolerates the heavy block of cement and keeps it in a suspended position. Duality in the work of the artist has turned into a single, inseparable identity and the reality of each side of the equation has merged with the other side. This artist is a woman who, crossing the threshold of modern visual experiments, has created a work of art that not only touches on Iranian national mythology, but also has unfurled hidden realities that rule the relations between modern human beings.

Fayyazi's proposal is titled *Kismet* (Destiny). The term was first used by Edward Fitzgerald in his translation of the Rubaiyat-e Khayyam and entered the English vocabulary.

'The moving finger writes; and having writ / Moves on; nor all thy piety nor wit Shall lure it back to cancel half a line / Nor all thy tears wash out a word of it'. This installation consists of a cubic space of $200 \times 200 \times 400$ centimetres. A

COMMISSIONER
Ali Reza Sami-Azar

ARTISTS
Bita Fayyazi Azad
Mandana Moghaddam

ORGANIZATION
Teheran Museum
of Contemporary Art

CO-ORGANIZER
Arte Communications, Venice

COORDINATOR
Kambiz Sabri

www.artecommunications.com

1 Bita Fayyazi Azad, *Kismet*, 2005. 50 sculptures of aluminium casted life-size new-born babies positioned within a purpose built structure made from aluminium plate sheets; 200 × 200 × 400 cm. Courtesy the Artist

2 Mandana Moghaddam, *Chelgis II*, 2005. Sketch for the installation at the 50. International Art Exhibition La Biennale di Venezia, 2005

metal sheet is inserted into one of the walls acting like a diving board. Fifty life size sculptural infants made of aluminium are placed on the board. They are arranged into an archipelago that is suspended in space. A female figure, whose stomach is emitting a yellow light, is lying on the floor. This work, without doubt, possesses certain features that have their roots in the sense of femininity, motherly productivity, immortality and birth. Similar to primitive seas, where life was blown into small particles, water symbolises light and life. Dominant cold, metallic grey in the installation is a symbol of coldness and water that is especially glittering inside the golden womb of the figure and is akin to the beating of life in the work. Cold metallic grey is a symbol of home, while yellow colour suggests warmth and life.

Mandana Moghaddam and Bita Fayyazi are female artists who are in conflict with the existing traditions of society. The central theme of their works is confrontation and a proper reaction to mythological phenomena. Their works reflect the sensitivities of mankind willing to live in and react to a tumultuous world.

Ali Reza Sami-Azar
Director of the Teheran Museum of Contemporary Art

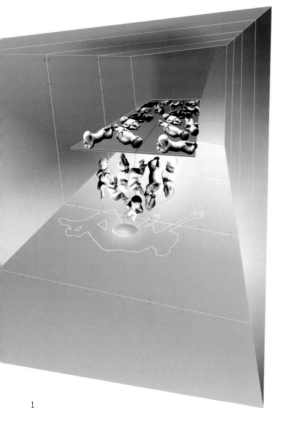

The Image of the sketch for the installation that will be created in Venice biennial
Name: Mandana
Surname: Moghaddam
Title: Chelgis II
Technique: Installation

Detail

1

2

Ireland

Seven artists represent Ireland at the 51st Biennale; Stephen Brandes, Mark Garry, Ronan McCrea, Isabel Nolan, Sarah Pierce and the collaborative partnership Walker and Walker. Housed for the third time in the Scuola di San Pasquale, Campo della Confraternita in the Castello district, Ireland's participation brings together six independent practices into a collaboration with the distinct context of the Scuola and its surrounding area.

Stephen Brandes' large drawings stem from a visual diary he made during a recreation of his grandmother's flight through Europe to escape the pogroms in Romania. In the resulting work his relationship with this history is interwoven with his own experience and invention resulting in fantastical, dysfunctional landscapes that suggest the imagined places of history and fairytales, yet from a distinctly suburban viewpoint.

Mark Garry uses a range of natural and craft materials such as thread, beads, coloured paper, origami and plants, and a range of methodologies (colour, line, objects and space) to create refined part installations and part drawings that delicately intersect the space and leave the viewer open to an imaginative response to the visual, spatial and associative interactions created by the materials.

Ronan McCrea is developing for Venice a new expanded version of his photographic slide installation *Sequences, Scenarios & Locations (after* Hänsel and Gretel*)*. Several photographic sequences follow a teenage girl acting out elements based on a scene from the Grimm fairytale when Hänsel unsuccessfully uses a trail of bread to find his way home through the forest. Here 'host-like' paper fragments cut from a *post mortem* drawing of the artist's father stand in for the bread dropped by Hänsel and the narrative is set in city locations associated with the father's biography.

Isabel Nolan uses various means – drawing, painting, text, video and photo-graphy – in an eclectic body of work that tentatively describes her uncertain and shifting relationship to her real and imagined surroundings. The work offers glimpses of the world that are given temporary significance by our desire to define our situation and relationships with others.

Based in Dublin, Sarah Pierce organises The Metropolitan Complex, a practice embedded in contemporary arts meta-discourses: talks, archives, publications, exhibitions etc. Fundamental to this project is the local as a discourse articulated through one-to-one and group exchanges. For Venice, a collaborative pavilion in the garden of the Scuola di San Pasquale is an experiment in finding one's place.

Walker and Walker have continued their exploration of representations of the sublime with their first film project *Nightfall*. The 16mm film follows a central protagonist through a Lakeland landscape that is reminiscent of the ideals of

COMMISSIONER
Sarah Glennie

ARTISTS
Stephen Brandes
Mark Garry
Ronan McCrea
Isabel Nolan
Sarah Pierce
Walker and Walker

SPONSOR
An initiative of Culture Ireland, the Department of Arts, Sport and Tourism, supported by the Arts Council/An Chomhairle Ealaíon. Collaborating partner the Lewis Glucksman Gallery, Cork

www.irelandvenice.ie

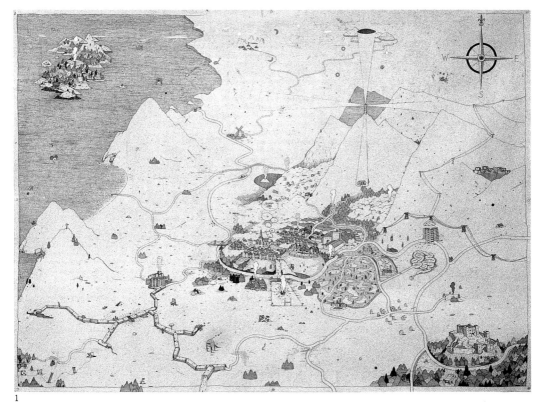

1

Romanticism. The film uses three formal devices to address the sublime in nature; the echo, repetition as the protagonist is shadowed by a *Doppelgänger*, and the passing of day into night, which evokes the allegorical opposites of darkness and light and the Romantic interpretation of the sublime as a passion best aroused by uncertainty.

Additionally, *Printed Project*, a journal published by the Sculptors' Society of Ireland, launches its fifth issue, curated/edited by artist Alan Phelan, as part of Ireland's participation at Venice. The themes from various world biennales serve as titles for contributions examining various participatory, collaborative and discursive practices.
Sarah Glennie

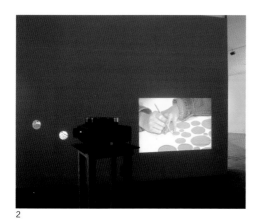

2

2 Ronan McCrea, *Sequences, Scenarios & Locations (after Hänsel and Gretel) version 2*, 2004 (installation view). Slide installation, continuous loop. Courtesy the Artist. Photo Ronan McCrea

3 Mark Garry, *One Thought*, 2004. Mixed media and plant; dimension variable. Courtesy the Artist

4 Isabel Nolan, *Beseiged with Sadness*, 2004. Acrylic on canvas; 108 × 78 cm. Courtesy the Artist

3

4

5

6

5 Sarah Pierce, *Scuola di San Pasquale*, February 2005. Photo Sarah Glennie

6 Walker and Walker, *Nightfall*, 2004. 16 mm film; 7'. Courtesy the Artists

Iceland
Versations/Tetralogia

While the history of Icelandic art is a short one, a remarkable narrative tradition, whose roots lie in the Middle Ages and which has had a profound influence on most Icelandic artists, has evolved there.

The work that Gabríela Friðriksdóttir is showing at the Venice Bienniale 2005, *Versations Tetralogia*, makes oblique reference to this narrative tradition, which appears in the present day in the most unlikely forms and often in a highly paradoxical fashion. Icelanders are said to read more books than any other nation, yet when they come together they either say nothing, or won't let each other get a word in edgeways. Nobel-prize-winning author Halldór Laxness maintained that the Icelanders remain unconvinced by logic, and that when they talk to each other it is generally on a very personal level, often ending with an argument. 'Icelanders' thinking is in accord with the windy climate: they swing from one opinion to another and detest a dead calm. A draught blows through the Icelandic mind. Like the young rock on which the Icelanders live, their thinking is similar: young, raw and insubstantial – unlike the solid marble of the Continent', says Gabríela.

Gabríela addresses this illogical Icelandic tradition of discourse in her work, and underlines this with the title *Versations*, where she has omitted the prefix con- from conversations, implying that this is not a true conversation but an attempt at conversation. Perhaps it is the most powerful who seize the right to be heard; but words are vital, although their virtual reality traps us ever more securely in its net. Gabríela delves beneath the surface of the words, strives to find the reality beneath, gives herself over to a fantastical imagination which she unleashes, seeking inspiration equally in literature, mysticism, music and visual arts. She has taken a piano melody that she improvised and has been composing since she was a teenager, and asked four musicians – Daníel Ágúst Haraldsson, Björk Guðmundsdóttir, Borgar Thor Magnússon and Jónas Sen – to compose a piece based on the melody. The video and musical works are then edited together to form the *Tetralogia*, which as a whole forms a quartet, although each video is autonomous.

In Ancient Greece the term tetralogy meant a series of four plays by the same playwright, in which the first three were tragedies, the fourth a satire or comedy. The aim was to win a contest held among playwrights at a feast held in honour of the god Dionysus. Gabríela's *Tetralogia* could thus be an ode to Dionysus. An ode in which the artist is the catalyst which unleashes the ions and permits them to rearrange themselves, inviting a select team to join her and contribute to creating a splendid outcome.

But *Tetralogia* is just part of this multivoiced installation, which is an attempt at bringing together different media. The facade of the pavilion has been altered in accord with the content, the music of the videos is heard through loudspeakers, and the visitor has a vague premonition of what waits within. The visitor is gradually drawn into the spiritual and mental world of the artist, becoming an explorer in this wonderland of symbols, images and sounds, encountering on his/her journey through the pavilion all sorts of bizarre beings, which drift between dream and reality, truth and illusion, heaven and hell.

In *Versations* Gabríela also addresses the chaos – the disintegration and disorder – of today. She explores our perceptions, emotions, longings, the boundaries of emotion and the unification or tension between different art forms. 'Where is the line?' asks Björk on her latest album, *Medúlla*, in which the human voice is the basis of expression, and its palette of colour is explored

COMMISSIONER
Laufey Helgadóttir

ARTIST
Gabríela Friðriksdóttir

www.gabriela.is

to the utmost. Gabríela and Björk joined forces, together with dancer Erna Ómarsdóttir, and created the idea for a video for Björk's song; Gabríela uses the same material in one of the videos of *Tetralogia*, in which she addresses the imbalance of emotions and their expulsion from the body, or catharsis, as she did in the video *Catharsis* of 2004. Björk becomes an upholstered host, a sort of Venus of Willendorf, who gives birth to a demon coated in a white stickiness – dancer Erna Ómarsdóttir – who, after a wild dance, withdraws back inside the host. In the final scene everything explodes, and hay-wraiths emerge from the background, as if a mutation has occurred in the electrifying atmosphere, and plunge down on the host, who vanishes and is absorbed into the whole.

The primal energy of the narrative, the desperation and claustrophobic atmosphere, are intensified by the rough, raw texture, strong visual contrasts and the bizarre hay-scape of the barn.

Gabríela focuses, like the surrealists, on the spontaneous, but with the proviso that the spontaneity grows from the seed of the forefathers. She takes arms against rationalism and bends the rules to her will. She seeks answers in what happens between waking and sleeping, the objective and subjective, or in the tension between the mind and the material world. She entangles the observer in her web of symbols, as she did in her first show, *The Nameless One*, in 1997, thus activating the web.

Laufey Helgadóttir

Gabríela Friðriksdottir,
Versations/Tetralogia, 2005.
Pen drawing: Gabríela
Friðriksdóttir; design: M/Mparis,
Photographs: each D100/
6Mpxls. Photo Lode Saidane

Translated into English by Anna Yates

Israel

Guy Ben-Ner: *Treehouse Kit*

After his trajectory into making videos centered on his own performative presence, directly addressing his relationship with his immediate family, Guy Ben-Ner now creates a piece for the Israeli Pavilion in Venice that takes us back to his early adventure films. These included *Berkely's Island* (1999), in which the artist enacted an over-philosophical Robinson Crusoe; *Moby Dick* (2000), where he featured the famous hunt for the white whale in his domestic kitchen; and *House Hold* (2001), where he concocted an escape scheme from under his son's crib. This time, however, Ben-Ner's piece is not a mere video, but rather an 'interactive' work, between a sculptural object and a film. In this respect, while differing in appearance from Ben-Ner's videos of recent years, *Treehouse Kit* (2005) is their extension in terms of subject matter, drawing on the cinematic and artistic referents of previous works. The object is not a disposable prop as in his earlier films: it is a tree; a tree made of dismantled furniture. It is an 'artistic object' manifesting the artist's creativity. The film is an 'instruction tape' intended to teach the viewer how to make the furniture necessary for a cosy living from the 'tree.' Neither the object nor the film would have any significance without the other. In the film, Ben-Ner resumes the role of Robinson Crusoe, the protagonist of his first video, *Berkeley's Island* (1999). Back on his island, possibly already trained in survival techniques, this time he is less inclined to self-pity and philosophical lucubration, and sets straight to work, dismantling parts of the tree and building the furniture he needs, in much the same way that Daniel Defoe's protagonist built his household from the ship's wreckage. First a ladder – a utilitarian piece that enables him to sleep on top of the tree, far from the reach of animals. Then a rocking chair and an umbrella, followed by a table, chairs and, finally, a proper bed. *Treehouse Kit* also goes back to the early films that influenced Ben-Ner's oeuvre, such as Buster Keaton's *One Week* (1920), which, similar to *Treehouse Kit*, is a slapstick story of objects rather than a human being, and a successful attempt to ridicule the modern DIY myth. A mishap in Keaton's comedy makes the newlywed build his proto-IKEA house the wrong way, with no door, nor a proper roof. Keaton makes a point by using objects in a creative rather than normative way, just as Ben-Ner's creative role-house appliances function in his works – whether using the fridge for lighting or as a book, the kitchen as a ship, a crib as a cage, etc. The combination of the film and the object clearly indicates that a process has taken place before we entered the scene. We can imagine a slapstick situation whereby the artist appropriated the household contents, 'snatching' the furniture – the chairs, tables and beds – from under his wife and children, and assimilating them into his work. Like his video *Elia* (2003), which followed the migration of the Ben-Ner family walking in reverse dressed as ostriches, *Treehouse Kit* goes backwards, restoring the 'tree' into the 'natural' shape of the furniture. The work also relates to the modernist myth of the ready-made. It re-creates and acts out the principle enunciated by Picasso when referring to his *Head of a Bull* sculpture made of a bicycle's handlebar and seat (1942, Picasso Museum, Paris) – that someone could find this 'head of a bull' and make a bicycle from it – thus opening the linear process of the artification of common objects to a circular process of the commonisation of artifacts.
Sergio Edelsztein

COMMISSIONER
Sergio Edelsztein

DEPUTY COMMISSIONERS
Diana Shoef
Arad Turgeman

ARTIST
Guy Ben-Ner

1

2

1 Guy Ben-Ner, *Berkeley's Island*, 1999. Still from video

2 Guy Ben-Ner, *Wild Boy*, 2004. Still from video

Italy

Ministero per i Beni Culturali e le Attività Culturali
Dipartimento per i Beni Culturali e Paesaggistici
DARC - Direzione Generale per l'Architettura e l'Arte Contemporanee
"Un'opera per il Museo Nazionale delle Arti del XXI secolo - MAXXI.
Premio per la giovane arte italiana 2004-2005"

The Ministero per i Beni Culturali e le Attività Culturali, through DARC - Direzione Generale per l'Architettura e l'Arte Contemporanee – is organising the third Premio per la giovane arte italiana (Italian youth art prize) at the 51st Biennale di Venezia. The award was established to promote artistic research in Italy and bring together the most significant examples.

The competition is open to Italian and foreign artists (resident in Italy for at least one year) under 30. The selection jury, chaired by Maria Vittoria Marini Clarelli, superintendent of the Galleria Nazionale d'Arte Moderna in Rome, consisted of Paolo Colombo (curator of MAXXI - Museo Nazionale delle Arti del XXI secolo, Rome), Anna Mattirolo (director of the contemporary art section of DARC), Angela Vettese (independent curator and art critic), Vicente Todoli (director of the Tate Modern, London), Ludovico Pratesi (director of the Centro Arti Visive Peschiera, Pesaro) and Beatrice Buscaroli (university teacher). The jury selected the following four winners from 377 participants:

Carolina Raquel Antich, born in 1970 in Rosario, Argentina, who lives and

COMMISSIONER
Pio Baldi

CURATORS
Paolo Colombo
Monica Pignatti Morano

ARTISTS
Carolina Raquel Antich
Manfredi Beninati
Loris Cecchini
Lara Favaretto

1

works in Venice. A painter, she has exhibited several times in collective exhibitions both in Italy and abroad.

Manfredi Beninati, born in Palermo in 1970. He studied jurisprudence, then attended film courses at the Centro Sperimentale in Rome. In 1994 he started working as a painter in London, where he lived briefly. He has lived in Campagnano Romano, near Rome, since 2001.

Loris Cecchini, born in Milan in 1969, lives and works between Milan and Prato. He attended the Florence Accademia di Belle Arti and the Brera, Milan. He has exhibited numerous times in collective and personal exhibitions both in Italy and abroad.

Lara Favaretto born in Treviso in 1973, attended the Brera Accademia di Belle Arti in Milan and has won important prizes in Italy and abroad, exhibiting numerous times in collective and personal exhibitions. She lives and works in Turin.

The artists will present a work at the Padiglione Venezia inspired by the theme of the competition *Un'opera per il MAXXI*. The works will eventually go into the collections of the National Museum of 21st-century Arts in Rome (formerly the Centro Nazionale per le Arti Contemporanee), which are expanded not only by purchases and donations, but also, precisely, by competitions.
Pio Baldi

1 Carolina Raquel Antich, *La prova*, 2003. Video projection on a wall, animated painting; 10' loop

2 Manfredi Beninati, *Palermo*, 2004. Oil on canvas; 149 × 200 cm. Courtesy Galleria Lorcan O'Neill, Roma

2

3

4

3 Loris Cecchini, *Monologue Patterns (reading books in the park)*, 2004. Metal, transparent polycarbonate, 3M film. 'Zone Artistiche Temporanee', Gallarate, Milano, 2004. Photo Ela Bialkowska

4 Lara Favaretto, *È uno spettacolo*, 2004. Wood table (200 × 100 × 73 cm), nautical engine, resin paddle, iron weight, tank. Six black & white photographic prints on barite paper: Performance 11 am 24 × 43 cm, Performance 9 am 65 × 84 cm, Performance 2 pm 100 × 100 cm, Performance 8 am 90 × 115 cm, Performance 7 am 80 × 150 cm, Performance 10 am 120 × 154 cm. Installation view. © Galleria Franco Noero, Torino. Photo Ela Bialkowska

Latvia
Dark-Bulb

It all ends with an accidentally spotted story: 'In the days when electric light bulbs were being used more and more, Aristotle Operandi discovered and manufactured the first dark bulb. When it is switched on it turns any light into pitch-black darkness. Unfortunately, Operandi died during the first completely successful experiment with his dark bulb. He had not been able to find the way out of his laboratory. Operandi died of starvation and his body was only discovered a month later when the landlord cut off the electricity for non-payment'.

A story about the dark of the mind or the light of the mind. What exactly is the source of a discovery and when does the light of the mind turn into darkness of the mind? Does an invention, the result of a discovery sparked off by a brainwave, necessarily lead to catastrophe in the end?

The earth is a dark planet and it becomes light during those hours when it is lit by the sun. That is why the human mind mainly circles in the dark, only occasionally displaying flashes of light thoughts.

An immense number of things have been discovered and invented that enable accidents to occur. But the cool mind of man the inventor is concentrated only on the object of research itself. Everything outside it is irrelevant.

Everything begins with an accidentally found piece of news: 'While working on his project "Eternal Daylight" using soothsayer Zinta's method of stretching the fabric of time, Kavala, the third level sorcerer-sociologist from Kurzeme, has transformed the Moon into the star 'Light'. A short circuit created by an unknown orbiting object caused an explosion sending an impenetrable layer of dust into the atmosphere plunging the entire Earth into darkness. Why not?'.
F5

COMMISSIONER
Līga Marcinkeviča

CURATOR
Līga Marcinkeviča / F5

DEPUTY COMMISSIONERS
Signe Pucena
Paivi Tirkkonen

ARTISTS
Group F5
(Līga Marcinkeviča, Ieva Rubeze, Martiņš Ratniks, Ervins Broks)

CO-ORGANIZATION
Arte Communications, Venice

SUPPORTED BY
Ministry of Culture
of the Republic of Latvia Culture Capital Foundation of Latvia

SPONSOR
Culture Capital Foundation of Latvia, Ministy of Culture of the Republic of Latvia, Rietumu Banka, Kolonna, Ventspils Nafta

www.artecommunications.com

1-4 Group F5, Sketch design for the installation *Dark Bulb*, 2005

1

2

3

4

Lithuania
Jonas Mekas. Celebrations Of The Small And Personal In The Times Of Bigness

Jonas Mekas was born in 1922 in Semeniskiai, Lithuania. Since his arrival in New York in 1949 he has established himself as one of the leading figures of American avant-garde filmmaking. Mekas's extensive personal film collection includes celebrated films like *Guns of the Free* (1961), *The Brig* (1963), *Walden* (1969), *Lost, Lost, Lost* (1975), *Reminiscences of a Voyage to Lithuania* (1972), *Zefiro Torna* (1992) and *As I was Moving Ahead, Occasionally I Saw Brief Glimpses of Beauty* (2001), and stretches in time from the early fifties up to this very day. Apart from filming, he has also been an important force in the development of American independent cinema. In 1954 Jonas Mekas became editor-in-chief of *Film Culture*; in 1958 began writing his *Movie Journal* column for the *Village Voice*; in 1962 he co-founded the Film-Makers' Cooperative and in 1964 the Filmmakers' Cinematheque. The latter grew into Anthology Film Archives, one of the world's largest and most important repositories of avant-garde films.

For the *Celebration Of Small And Personal In The Time Of Bigness* project at the Lithuanian Pavilion of the Venice Biennale 2005, Jonas Mekas focuses on his diary films as well as on the visuals related to his view of Lithuania, which comes across powerfully in a large part of his work. His presentation includes extensive film screenings, his most recent video work, still images and selected extracts from his writing projects.

Liutauras Pšibilskis

COMMISSIONERS
Liutauras Pšibilskis
Lolita Jablonskienė

ARTIST
Jonas Mekas

COORDINATION
Troels Bruun

Celebration Of Small And Personal In The Time Of Bigness

In this exhibition, as in my work in general, I am concerned with the discovery and celebration of small, insignificant, personal, moments in our life – in my life, the life of my family, my close friends; joys, celebrations, being together, small daily events, feelings, emotions and friendships. I consider that too much attention is given today in the arts to big, dramatic events, themes, actions, exceptional situations, dramatisations and to psychological and other perversions – all at the expense of what I consider is really important: the deeper, subtle, invisible events of our existence that make us what we are.

Jonas Mekas

1 Jonas Mekas, from *As I was Moving Ahead, Occasionally I Saw Brief Glimpses of Beauty*, 2001. 285'

2 Jonas Mekas, from *Walden*, 1969. 16 mm film; 180'

1

I remember the morning I passed Avignon. The Nice Express was speeding across France. I woke up,

I remember the morning I passed

2

Luxembourg

Mondo Veneziano. High Noon in the Sinking City

'In art there are no schools, only hospitals'[1]
This line by Jean Cocteau, quoted by the Belgian 'pastiche' artist Jacques Charlier, who is in turn quoted by one of the protagonists in *Mondo Veneziano*, is particularly fit to illustrate both the content and form of the quite literal deconstruction of current art discourse – and its flawed transposition into reality – this film undertakes.

A medium-length feature by artist and film-maker Antoine Prum, it portrays a group of four professionals from the art world who meet in Venice to debate on the current state of affairs. In a range of blatantly solipsistic ponderings, the fictional characters – a curator, a theorist, a painter and a 'convivial' artist – announce their respective aesthetic positions, obviously at odds with each other. But it soon appears that their grandiloquent declarations are 'borrowed' or, better still, 'sampled', as all the dialogues are in fact excerpts from recent specialist literature. Quite shamelessly, the film employs the much vaunted technique of sampling – a post-modern variation of collage – said to reflect the 'democratic' use of modern-day technologies by today's artists to produce work and, in a wider sense, express the multiplication, if not equal validity, of standpoints in a global world. Yet, insidiously snatched from their original context and carefully recomposed into deadpan dialogues, the high-flown intellectual efforts fuelling these texts make for a biting parody of today's art circus.

But in *Mondo Veneziano* the artifice is pushed further, as even the setting is a 'sample' of sorts: the somewhat sketchy Venice in which the protagonists progress is clearly a film set, 'quoting' the actual City of Doges. As luck would have it, Prum did not have to scout for a location, because Venice literally showed up on his doorstep: Luxembourg, Prum's home country, boasts a large-scale Venice replica, built on industrial wasteland in the southern town of Esch/Alzette. Designed in 2001 for the purpose of a feature film (*Secret Passage*, dir. Ademir Kenovic), Venice has meanwhile served in various popular and other, notably less exposed productions, thereby contributing to boost the tiny country's fledgling cinematographic industry.

In Prum's film for this year's Biennale, the now rather derelict film decor casts a ghost-town Venice with empty canals as the backdrop to a verbal joust that, come dusk, turns into a physical one. For, besides the diurnal theoretical part, in which the actors confront their irreconcilable positions, a nightly chapter sees them settle their differences in a gory and lusty showdown. The slightly camp 'Venetian Round' then tilts into a *Mondo Cane*-inspired debauchery of bullets, blood and guts, as we witness reality catching up with discourse. Or, to speak in the words of the 'convivial' artist, quoting 'cyberarts' theoretician George Fifield, cited in an interview with artist Angelika Middendorf: 'The shift from theoretical reality towards applied reality'[2].
Boris Patrick Kremer

COMMISSIONER
Ministry of Culture, Executive Director of Education and Research, Grand Ducy of Luxembourg

CURATOR
Boris Patrick Kremer

ARTIST
Antoine Prum

[1] J. Charlier, 'One nor the Other', in *The New Art Report*, November 2004.
[2] G. Fifield, [Angelika Middendorf], 'ID_TRANSiT Interview #02. An interview with George Fifield', in *Men In Black. Handbook of Curatorial Practice*, Berlin: Künstlerhaus Bethanien, 2004 (first published in *ID_TRANSiT Reader*, [ed. Angelika Middendorf], 2000).

Antoine Prum, *Mondo Veneziano*, 2005. High definition video/35 mm; 30'.
Set photo: Christian Mosar

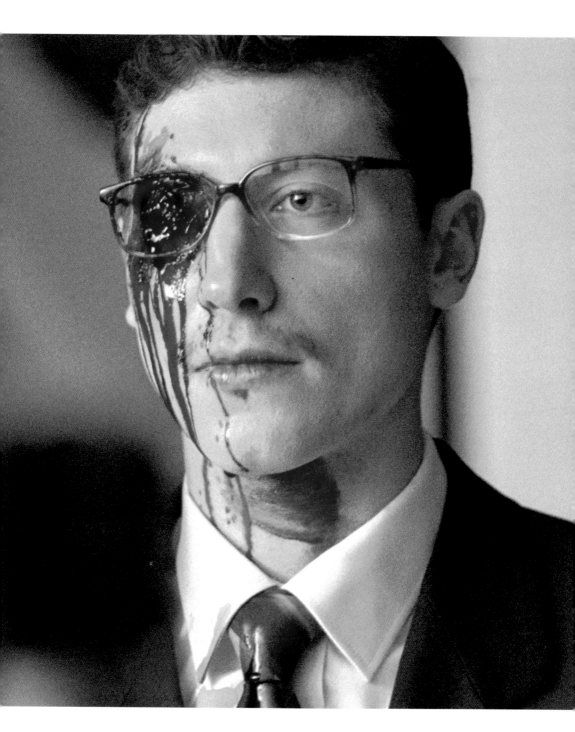

Morocco

The Current Art Trend in Morocco

The Biennale di Venezia is for the first time hosting a selection of plastic art works by artists representing Morocco, a country of great tradition and culture. The changing diversity of its landscapes, the singularity of its light and the richness of its folk art much inspired painters like Eugène Delacroix, Henri Matisse and others who revolutionised universal aesthetics.

Three talented artists, Mohamed Bennani, Fouad Belamine and Fathiya Tahiri, will help, each in their own way, to give some idea of the prodigious diversity and multiple facets of Moroccan artistic expression.

Participation in the 51st International Art Exhibition offers my country a valuable opportunity to promote its image and to show off the singular vibrancy of plastic creation and the contribution of its artists in search of new forms of expression and enrichment of the universal aesthetic.

Furthermore, in these dark times, comparison of artists from the southern banks of the Mediterranean, particularly those representing a country known and recognised for its adherence to the universal values of dialogue and tolerance, with the works of western artists is of undeniable didactic benefit.

My country cannot but be happy to bring its modest contribution to this extraordinary exhibition of contemporary art, which is a genuine opportunity for promoting reciprocal understanding and creativity, certainties of common enrichment.

Furthermore, the Chiesa Santa Maria della Pietà with its marvellous frescoes by Tiepolo, a precious treasure chest for the works of three artists closely engaged in the most original contemporary work, gives their creations an appropriate space for dialogue under the gaze of great masters of the past. In this place of great spirituality, these works will transmit a powerful symbolic message, beyond their meaning and their aesthetic value.

S.E. Tajeddine Baddou
Ambassador of the Kingdom of Morocco

COMMISSIONER
Tajeddine Baddou

CURATOR
Paolo De Grandis

ARTISTS
Fouad Bellamine
Mohamed Bennani Moha
Fathiya Tahiri

ORGANIZATION
Arte Communications, Venice

UNDER THE HIGH PATRONAGE OF
His Majesty Mohammed VI,
King of Morocco

SPONSOR
Pour le Maroc Avenir et Groupe
Caisse De Depot et De Gestion

www.artecommunications.com

In its mix of contributions, correspondences and influences, the Biennale di Venezia becomes a stimulus and catalyst for a fertile and increasingly urgent dialogue between peoples. Thus the first participation of Morocco in a process of confrontation with its own past and re-invention, seems to be of considerable importance.

Morocco is a country in which strongly local traditions and a strong thrust towards change co-exist, so the recovery of styles, models and themes that are part of the acquired cultural baggage must be seen as a natural opportunity for reflection, and a starting point for renewed growth in expressiveness. Today, new forms of elaborating images are gaining ground and new creative itineraries are appearing aimed at overcoming ethnic determinism and testing the significant developments in the expressive forms of contemporary art. The multiplicity of visual art in this country provides important stimuli in the forming of a new vision of cultural contacts exploring historical and territorial specificities, not as inviolable data but as a product of a constant re-evaluation of the concept of identity.

The art of Fouad Bellamine, Mohamed Bennani MOA and Fathiya Tahiri should be seen as a fundamental moment in the instinct to create. The accumulation of memories, and hence a sort of intellectual nomadism, permits the creation of

1

an artistic action that is not, however, lacking in the free influence of imagination and instinct. This recovery can express itself in different ways, whether it takes the form of a simple evocation or textual quotations from traditional imagery.

The painting of Fouad Bellamine is proudly expressive, elegiac and full of memories and moods. The style is independent, characterised by a process of geometric abstraction starting from frequent and symbolic forms, such as the architecture of the Islamic world. Where the strokes emerge, they are serious and violent, but the backgrounds of colour unite or isolate themselves in plastic forms that are immediately legible.

The work of Mohamed Bennani MOA contains nature, the sky, the sea, all constantly changing colour and form, oxidising and corroding, the blinding light vibrating and silent; there is a suspension of silence and of atmosphere, and the dust of the desert can be felt in the air and the objects. The canvases are large painted backgrounds marked with broad strokes of red, blue and ochre. The gesture of making art manifests itself with energetic brushstrokes, with material colour, accrochages and scratches, to graze the conventional signs of superficial aesthetics and reveal the purer, more hidden values.

Fathiya Tahiri is an artist who for years has been experimenting with the potential of different expressive forms in many directions, from architecture to sculpture, forging the most precious materials, until arriving at the classicism of painting. Her vital, generous art reformulates an abstract iconography, a vocabulary of signs which form in accordance with strange syntactic rules: an iconography animated by the painterly medium laid down with vigour and marked by sudden changes.

The work of these artists is the result of a mediation effected between the culture and events of a contemporary civilisation considered through the lens of a profound sensibility of history.

Paolo De Grandis

1 Fathiya Tahiri, *Naissance*, 2003. Oil on canvas; 200 × 140 cm

2 Fouad Bellamine, *Untitled*, 2004. Mixed technique on canvas; 140 × 160 cm. Photo Hafid Jender

3 Mohamed Bennani Moha, *Acrylique et matiére sur toile*, 2004; 180 × 140 cm

2

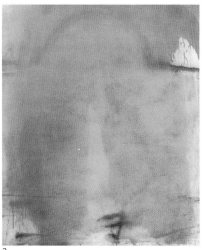

3

New Zealand
the fundamental practice

Tariq Ali has suggested that the religions of Christianity, Judaism, and Islam began as versions of what we would today call political movements[1]. By extension, in order to generate a religious movement one needs a blend of political values, members and ideologues. What we experience in et al.'s *the fundamental practice* is not yet religion, but rather a machine and programme for generating group allegiance to a belief system.

Central to et al.'s work is an exploration of the human tendency to establish truths and orthodoxies in response to the 'unknown'. It is a concern that is reflected in et al.'s long-standing choice not to reveal their identities. The artists involved have a 20-year history of exhibiting under a variety of titles that include personal and group histories, androgynous names and gender switching; identities who in turn have been associated with discrete practices involving objects, paintings, films, sound-works, books and installations. Their work draws on fragments of images, ideas, texts and objects by authors both living and dead, and involves collaboration with musicians, writers, scientists among others in its production. The group is currently steered by one artist who remains anonymous outside the moniker et al., thereby protecting her own mutability, and the homogeny of the group.

Et al.'s focus in recent computerised installations has turned to the practice of mind control and behaviour modification – practices for engineering human enhancement within diverse fundamentalist ideologies. Both the work and the identities deployed together form part of an examination of the role of personality within cultural belief systems, including those of religion, politics, science, and art. Exploiting the potential of their group identity, et al. have begun to investigate cult dynamics. Within the group priority continues to be given to 'et al.' over the individual, with the suggestion that there is an acknowledged but invisible leader.

the fundamental practice itself employs five Autonomous Purification Units (APUs) to pursue a particular line of fundamentalist dogma. Each metal unit is automated by a central control station and progresses haltingly along its track while emitting phrasing from existing texts and sound files pertinent to their

COMMISSIONER
Gregory Burke

CURATOR
Natasha Conland

ARTISTS
et al.

SPONSOR
An initiative of Creative New Zealand, the Arts Council of New Zealand Toi Aotearoa In association with The Museum of New Zealand Te Papa Tongarewa and the Govett-Brewster Art Gallery Supported by The Patrons of New Zealand at the Venice Biennale 2005 and the Supporters of *the fundamental practice*
Principal sponsor 42 BELOW vodka.
Supporting sponsors Montana Reserve and Lindauer Special Reserve wines

1

2

3

1-3 p.mule (dr) et al., *APU /
public projects Venice. Original
research output*, 2004. Photo
Patrick Reynolds

4 et al., *the fundamental
practice* (under construction),
2005. Site specific installation;
various media including audio,
video, computers, and
constructed objects; dimension
variable. Photo of the artists

5 et al., *the fundamental
practice* (site plan), 2005

6 et al., *APU fig. 3, 6.10.04,
public projects Aotearoa*, 2004.
Pencil on postcard

subject. Bodily in scale and industrial in appearance, their job is to recite, translate, and modulate scripture, texts and ideas, cut and shuffled by an absent leader – the programmer. The work brings into close proximity the conflicting forms of fundamentalism associated with art, religion, philosophy, nuclear research, cosmological theory and belief in the paranormal.

The machines are not programmed to find answers; rather their effect is active disorientation. The sources for objects, phrases and sounds are only occasionally recognisable. However, through this disorientation what is presented is a mechanism of significant controls. The APUs are pulled by winches, their movement bound by a pulley system and contained by wire fencing that forms a cage marking their designated area of movement. These allusions to containment and restriction, combined with the autonomous recital of fundamentalist and computer modulated texts, ensure that the viewer is engaged on both a physical and metaphysical level.

4

Confronted in the installation space, with little guide, the viewer is placed in the position of 'explorer', in the poetic sense of that word. They must feel comfortable with a condition of not knowing, while finding a route through belief systems and their mechanised representatives. Despite this uncertainty, the experience is one of privilege for the viewer – the liberty of the unknown – of taking something original from this found matter.

What we are unprepared for as viewers are moments in which the combination of movement, sound and speech are orchestrated into a crescendo as the APUs lapse into a state of seeming bliss. Such harmony envelops the space, thereby increasing the sense that the objects are attempting to 'engineer the viewer's consciousness'. We experience the rapture of fundamentalism, while enclosed in its totalising mind set.

Gregory Burke, Natasha Conland

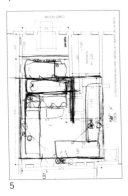

5

[1] Tariq Ali, *The Clash of Fundamentalism: Crusades, Tihads and Modernity*, London: Verso, 2002, p. 24.

Rotoehu Lake.

6

The Netherlands

'Art pays no attention to our definitions'

Since commencing their collaboration in 1994, Jeroen de Rijke and Willem de Rooij's select corpus of 16 and 35 mm films, slide- and photo-works, objects, writings and printed matter has opened up an arena in which images are characterised by a curious kind of detachment. De Rijke and de Rooij's images are polyvalent, often appropriated, but disengaged from their prevailing aesthetic, social, economic and political definitions. For de Rijke and De Rooij, art is a locus from which to reflect upon the artistic image itself and to engage in a dialogue with other arenas where images are produced and acquire meaning, ranging from the reserved approach to imagery in some Islamic cultures to the West's obsession with the image and the resulting image overload generated by its media industry. As artists, de Rijke and de Rooij are intent on elucidating the difference between various genres of imagery and the way these can be 'read'. Tellingly, they maintain several extensive visual archives that include press photos from newspapers and magazines, pictures of artworks, film stills and visual records of their travels. Their artistic programme entails a detached and critical investigation of the context, rules and conventions governing the presentation and interpretation of images derived mainly from reality. In the way they approach their subject and turn it to their artistic purposes there is a clearly perceptible tension between various forms of realism, aestheticising artifice and conceptual definition.

In their filmmaking de Rijke and de Rooij initially focused on the conventions and mechanisms of narrative cinema, as in the 16 mm coloured films *Chun Tian* (1994) and *Forever and Ever* (1995). In three more recent, 35 mm films, they reduced the narrative cinematographic structures to a single shot containing a wealth of visual information that is gradually revealed to the viewer. De Rijke and de Rooij present their filmworks in carefully controlled spatial situations. The exhibition space is decked out with the trappings of a cinema: a projector encased in a soundproof box, a few benches and the wall as projection screen. The spatial relationships between projector and seats, the size of the projected image and the way the viewer and the projection relate to one another are all precisely adjusted to the situation. The films are so constructed that they have a beginning and an end and are consequently shown at specified times so as to enable the viewer to watch the film in its entirety. Between shows there is no screen image and the gaze is directed instead towards the physical attributes of the exhibition space.

For their presentation in the Dutch Pavilion at the 51st Venice Biennale the artists make a new work in which they return to a cinematographic form that focuses on narrative, even theatrical artificiality and in which the imagery, rather than being borrowed from reality, has a highly contrived and fictional character. This work is shot in a studio rather than on location. Within the context of their own body of work, the film for Venice represents a new chapter in their ongoing project to examine representation in a wide variety of contexts, to test the elasticity of images and transpose them to the realm of art. Thereby under-scoring the dictum 'Art pays no attention to our definitions'.[1]
Martijn van Nieuwenhuyzen

Translated from the Dutch by Robyn de Jong-Dalziel

[1] J. Burckhardt, quoted by P. Hecht, *There's no Problem Enjoying it, but the Meaning is Tricky*, in *Senses and Sins – Dutch Painters of Daily Life in the Seventeenth Century*, exh. cat. (Rotterdam, Museum Boijmans Van Beuningen; Frankfurt am Main, Städelsches Kunstinstitut und Städtische Galerie), 2004-2005, pp. 20-29: p. 26.

COMMISSIONER
Martijn van Nieuwenhuyzen
on behalf of the Mondriaan
Foundation, Amsterdam
in collaboration with the
Stedelijk Museum Amsterdam

ARTISTS
Jeroen de Rijke and Willem
de Rooij

ORGANIZATION IN VENICE
Venice Planner,
Ankie Schellekens

www.dutchpavilion.info

Photo Marcel van den Bergh, 1993

Nordic Countries - Norway - Sweden
Sharing Space Dividing Time

Sharing Space Dividing Time:
Matias Faldbakken, Miriam Bäckström & Carsten Höller

Sharing Space Dividing Time, the 2005 exhibition for the Nordic Pavilion at the Venice Biennale, is neither a group show nor a thematic exhibition; rather, it is two separate exhibitions shown on alternate days. The artists participating are Matias Faldbakken and Miriam Bäckström & Carsten Höller in a joint project. One of the decisive factors defining the concept for the Nordic Pavilion in 2005 was the building itself. Architecturally the building is exceptional, not just because of its striking beauty, but because more than any other building in the Giardini, it has the character of a 'pavilion' as we understand the term today. Half of the wall structure consists of glass or glass doors. And the transition between inside and outside is further reinforced by the trees that grow within the building. The transparency of the building affects visitors in a special way as they gain a general impression of the visual form of the exhibition inside before they have even entered the building. This is the quality that has underlain work on designing the physical character of the exhibition.

The artists were invited both to produce new works and to take part in the curatorial process by considering the overall presentation of the exhibition. The idea was to build on the spatial characteristics of the pavilion, i.e. its transparency. Since the works produced by the artists were expected to be of a relatively immaterial nature, an important idea behind the exhibition was that it would be possible to show the works within a common physical framework, which would in itself constitute one of the works of art.

The artists' response took the form of an exhibition design that forms part of a

COMMISSIONER
Ann-Sofi Noring

CURATOR
Åsa Nacking

ARTISTS

NORWAY
Matias Faldbakken

SWEDEN
Miriam Bäckström
& Carsten Höller

1

1 Matias Faldbakken, *Black Screen*, 2005. DVD video, color, no sound; approx. 1'

2 Miriam Bäckström & Carsten Höller, *Utopia Station Group V, Venice*, 2003

3 Miriam Bäckström & Carsten Höller, *Utopia Station Group I, Venice*, 2003

2

3

work in itself. It involves removing all the glass walls, thereby opening up the building to its surroundings and making the transparency even more apparent. Thus the framework represents a reduction of the existing architecture rather than an addition to it. For visitors who are not familiar with the building the changes will be invisible and will merely seem like a natural aspect of the pavilion. The aim of the reduced architecture is to emphasise the intervention between outside and inside, while at the same time promoting a more direct encounter between the works of art and the viewer.

The artists were neither given a theme to work on nor an issue to reflect on. Instead they have had a fixed venue with specific architecture and the joint task of making the presentation as attractive as possible. The works are to be understood independently of each other and the artists are presented separately rather than as in a traditional group exhibition.

The solo presentations are organised so that, throughout the Biennale, the artists will have the entire pavilion at their disposal on alternate days. The aim of this alternating presentation is to share the space between the artists in an alternative but still democratic manner in a way that the normal division of a room showing works of art cannot offer. This is particularly true of the Nordic Pavilion in that the artists, as representatives of different nations, have to be placed equally attractively yet also to the best advantage of the works shown. Solving this delicate equation does not necessarily result in the most interesting use of the space; which is a good reason for trying this new variant. The way in which the spatial and temporal division has been ordered should be seen as an alternative to a situation that really predicates a group show and this is the most radical aspect of the concept for Nordic contribution to the Venice Biennale.

Åsa Nacking

Poland
Repetition

Artur Żmijewski's Experiment

In the project *Repetition* he has prepared for the Polish Pavilion at the 51st Biennale in Venice, Artur Żmijewski intends repeating the famous prison experiment carried out by Prof. Zimbardo at the University of Stanford, USA, in 1971. In this event, which has become a historic threshold in the development of contemporary psychology, a group of volunteers chosen from amongst the students was arbitrarily divided into prisoners and guards. The experiment demonstrated how rapidly abhorrent mechanisms of aggression and the need to dominate and humiliate the prisoners arose in the group cast as guards, while typical defence mechanisms emerged in the prisoners. Just a few days, or to be more precise, a number of hours, were enough for quite normal young people to be transformed into torturers or into oppressed, frustrated prisoners burdened by the trauma of prison. Despite the fact that the carefully stipulated rules of the experiment prohibited the use of physical violence, the intensity of the reactions, the tension and the psychic torment of the experiment were such that those in charge were forced to abandon it after just five days. The results were deeply shocking: the experiment demonstrated nothing less than the predictable nature of human behaviour in particular situations. People who had never had anything to do with prison, transgressions against the law or violence started behaving precisely according to the model known from such situations. In contemporary psychology, the experiment became classic proof that we are all capable of more or less any act dependent on the situation we find ourselves in, and that the most appalling crimes are not so much inhuman, as an intimate part of our human nature. In deciding to repeat Prof. Zimbardo's experiment, Żmijewski wants to repeat all the essential elements of the initial experiment. However, the questions he intends to pose will go well beyond the bounds of the field of contemporary psychology.

Artur Żmijewski was born in 1966 and from 1990-1995 studied in the atelier of Prof. Grzegorz Kowalski at the Warsaw Academy of Fine Arts. His works have been presented at many exhibitions, both at home and internationally, such as at the Centrum Sztuki Współczesnej Zamek Ujazdowski in Warsaw, (1998), Galeria Foksal, (2000), the Peter Kilchmann Gallery, Zurich (2002), Fundacja Galeria Foksal (2003), and most recently at a large scale retrospective presentation at the MIT List Visual Arts Center in Boston (2004). The medium most frequently used by the artist is film of a para-documentary nature. He most often works by arranging certain situations according to a scenario that he has invented, while the action itself, and the behaviour caused by the action's environment, remains open to chance. Żmijewski edits his films from the documentary material recorded in these conditions. In his works, Artur Żmijewski tracks infirmity and all other forms of exclusion as a metaphor for different forms of social relations. He is fascinated by the tension caused by stepping out of one's usual role or the breaking of the regulations imposed by good form and social convention, which on an everyday basis enable the physical interaction of people without collision. An infirm consciousness is seen as potentially just as creative as a person behaving properly, posing the question of how to live with the consciousness of evil and the grotesque inside oneself.
Joanna Mytkowska

COMMISSIONER
Agnieszka Morawińska

CURATOR
Joanna Mytkowska

DEPUTY COMMISSIONER
Ewa Wojciechowska

ARTIST
Artur Żmijewski

www.labiennale.art.pl
www.zacheta.art.pl

1

2

1-3 Artur Żmijewski, *Repetition*, 2005. Video film. Courtesy the Artist

3

Portugal
Intus

Intus or The Experience of the Body in the Place

Since the seventies Helena Almeida's work has been manifesting a confluence of different artistic disciplines and approaches since the seventies. Photography, painting, drawing, video and performance come together in an artistic practice consolidated by self-representation. The artist's body – and its inherent images – is presented as a work in progress, never as a self-portrait, a mise en scène or a fictional representation of other people, but rather as a reiterated presence of itself. It is never presented as a description or an existent representation – we never learn anything about the artist's nature (her personality, tastes, thoughts, the way she conceives the world) by looking at her photographs. In not creating characters or self-portraits, Helena Almeida tells us nothing about her physical being.

Her use of photography reveals this as a *medium* that allows for (and motivates) the use of series, or of meta-narratives, of small movements, some almost fictional, marking the different moments of a movement.

The artist's body becomes an instrument of mediation and communication in the creation of a space – a plastic, architectural space in a phenomenological sense.

This is what also happens in the *Eu estou aqui* (I am here, 2005) series being shown for the first time at the Venice Biennale, at the Scoletta dei Tiraoro e Battioro in San Stae, in which the body is simultaneously hidden and exposed, is bent and straightened, through a minimalist choreography of gesture and posture.

This series reminds us of the gesture of an actor at the final curtain call, and of another dimension: a public offering, like an immolated body-lamb surrendering itself to the gaze of the public.

As is perhaps not the case in previous works, Helena Almeida's recent works have an almost religious and sacrificial dimension. This is evident in the video (a medium the artist explored at the end of the seventies and to which she now returns) *A Experiência do Lugar II* (The Experience of the Place II, 2004) in which Almeida covers the entire space of her studio on her knees, in an act that is both liturgical (i.e. when she kisses the floor) and one of atonement. The objects that were always part of its minimalist and domestic décor – the lamp, the stool – appear in this video, like a cross that can be carried on the shoulders, but also as an offering, in recognition, presented to the camera (that is, to us, the spectators).

The fact that these are the pieces the artist created to show at the Venice Biennale is significant of the corrosive subtlety with which she addresses the great altar of artistic consecration.

In Helena Almeida's work the space is never a measurable abstract space, but rather an inhabited space, taking its shape from the body. One could even speak of bodily architecture – the body as a house and a home. The image is inhabited inside its own walls and shows itself to the outside: *Intus*.

Rather than creating works for specific sites and places, the artist states that her space is her studio and that her studio is her world. In this sense, Helena Almeida works as a classical painter. The artist creates specific works in her own space and refers the works she makes to the space in which they are

COMMISSIONER
Isabel Carlos

ARTIST
Helena Almeida

ORGANIZATION
Instituto das Artes / Ministério da Cultura

www.iartes.pt/bienalveneza2005

Helena Almeida, *Eu estou aqui*
(I am here), 2005.
Black & white photograph;
125 × 125 cm

made, thus dislocating her own domesticity, arousing an element of surprise in
the familiar, everyday space.
The constant search for self-knowledge (an attitude the artist claims in some
interviews) runs parallel to research into the limits and borders of artistic genres
using her own body – a process as contemporaneously daring as her works.
Isabel Carlos

Czech Republic and Slovak Republic
Model of the World / Quadrofonia

We do not conceive of the model as an 'image of the world' which can be read in different directions without falling apart as a whole. Nor do we conceive of it as a 'scheme' which can only be apprehended statically or through linear reading, and if so, only within clearly defined propositions. The model has a holistic nature. The positions of its different elements cannot be changed arbitrarily. As such, the model is more complex than the scheme (not being reductive), yet it lacks the polyvalence intrinsic to a picture where it is the viewer who has the final say. The model sets down a point of view, a position or an approach to be adopted by the viewer, even though the viewer's involvement is not restricted or over defined as far as the functional aspect is concerned. The model conveys the world as a whole, not just separate pieces of information as in the case of a scheme or a formula. The model is non-transferrable. It is determined by the time of its creation and the place of its execution. At another time and another place, it would have to be created anew and would assume a different form, even though its meaning would remain unchanged. The model is not reality, the model is not the whole world, but rather a condensed and controlled analogy of both.

The world forms a continuum in spite of being continuously decomposed and recomposed. The process of composition and the process of decomposition form a unity without which the world would not be apprehensible and habitable. If every thing can be a fascinating starting point for philosophical thought, a theme for an image, a useful object, a source of meditation, a representation of the cosmos, a memory trigger, a musical instrument, a future archaeological discovery, a cipher of destiny, an intersection of functional relationships in post-industrial society, or even a refusal or obstacle, then we are, at any time, in the centre of reality as a whole. Anything in it takes us 'back' to material and physical prerequisites for the existence of the world, and even 'further' towards the 'mystical' interconnection between diverse time-space layers, as well as, introspectively, 'inside', towards the uniqueness of every man.

The perspectives from which we view and in which we 'handle' objects, meanings and the world as an assumed whole of wholes are mutually permeated, interconnected and inapprehensible at the same time. Rather than emerging one after another, the layers of reality appear, in fact, simultaneously and are in permanent motion, preventing us from discerning and – often out of necessity – even defining the borders between them. Definable layers of reality are a mere aid to our perceptive and social system: they are treacherous and yet indispensable mental mirrors of the world.

We tend to take on a safety net of meanings and purposes. The purpose of art is to either break the net, set it up anew for each particular case or project it into infinity while it is being woven. Meanings represent a convention shaken by every single use of analytical and critical tools. The world is being composed

COMMISSIONER
Alexandra Kusa

CURATOR
Marek Pokorný

ARTISTS
Stano Filko
Jan Mančuška
Boris Ondreička
Marek Pokorný

1-2 Sketch of *Model sveta -*
Quadrophonia / Model
of the World - Quadrophonia

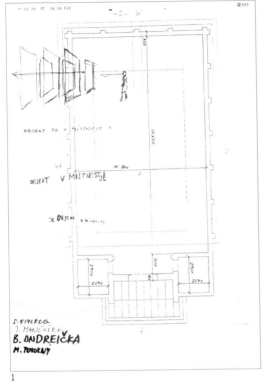
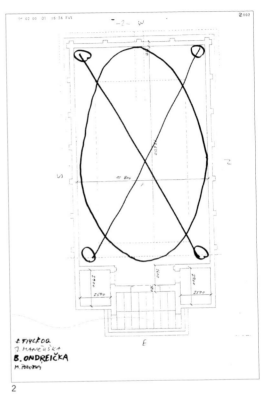

1   2

and decomposed at the same time. Our model of the world is this kind of permanent manifestation of the world in continuous composition and decomposition. It is a utopian/inconceivable attempt at putting an infinite quantity of actions, meanings and possibilities into apprehensible relations.

The members of the project team temporarily relinquished their identities without being deprived – as they believe – of their personal creative search and experience. Individual systems are interconnected in our model of the world to show the common elements which permeate the thought of different generations. Each of the team members has thus had an equal share in the process of creating an up-to-date model of the world valid in the framework of the project, which only comes into being as a result of interaction – of mutual agreement and disagreement.

January 2005 - Berlin, Bratislava, Brno, Prague, Vilnius

Republic of Armenia
Resistance Through Art

Since the mid-nineties, the enthusiasm for revolution in post-Soviet Armenia has turned into an overall state of crisis. This is dominated by apathy, a subjectivist attitude towards social life and mounting nostalgia for the bipolar world, where poverty and deprivation were compensated by the illusive pride of being a citizen of a nuclear superpower. This social phenomenon, which has accompanied the process of globalisation, is one of the basic obstacles to democracy in post-Soviet republics. Globalisation forces the artist to select between making a conscious choice or conforming. However, this is not a simple choice between the past and the future, east and west, war and peace, or 'mine' and 'yours'. This choice is an act of resistance.

According to Theodor W. Adorno, 'Affirmativeness resists the worst, the development of barbarism. ... Life asserts itself by means of culture, including the hope for a better, dignified, true and worthy human life.'

Building on this idea, the artists of the project *Resistance through Art*, using psychological and aesthetic contradictions, display the 'clash of the bodily with the spiritual', and ask whether it is possible to live without violence. What is man's natural environment? Why is culture, which is supposed to be the mechanism of sublimation, unable to determine the boundaries of our natural environment? Why do humans try to escape from the world they create?

In her video *The Logic of Power*, Diana Hagopian is directly asking whether it is possible to reconcile with violence, by displaying the roles assigned to women together with statistics from opinion polls. Is it possible to create a society where self-admiration and authority do not appear as 'attractive games'?

Images follow one another in a fast 'rock and roll' pace to create a dynamic chain, which by its imagery reminds us of the positive effects of the 1960s and 70s emancipation movements.

Diana Hagopian tries to take the viewer on a journey of emancipation, but it continuously collides with various expressions of the neo-patriarchal justification of 'the logic of power', its senseless exploitation and consumption.

Sona Abgarian's video-installation *Tomorrow at the Same Time* is another example of a woman's inability to articulate her identity. By manipulating a monster's mask, the girl simultaneously discovers her own: a mask she had worn in the past at an unknown party. Lonely and abandoned by the guests, she tries to show her present face to her past mask. The theatricality of movement and gesture demonstrates the total bankruptcy of mass culture stereotypes, where the artificial veils its artificiality. The same act is repeated on a second monitor with a time-lapse, as if observing that the only origins of fear and emptiness are the signs of lust and untamed pleasure. The photographs mounted on the backdrop of the monitors carry the same images, scratched and frayed, in a desperate attempt to escape falling into the trap of mass-consumption show business models.

Tigran Khachatrian's video *Thodicy*, according to the artist himself, belongs to his *Corner of the Room or Garage Film Production* series, which he began in 2000. In this series the artist adopts a unique method of re-mixing, where the famous films of internationally acclaimed and commonly 'leftist' film directors are revisited. The artist insists that this re-enactment returns the original attributes of humanity and simplicity to the idolised films. Tigran Khachatrian believes that periodic retrospection of art is didactically effective for the self-consciousness of society. This, in his opinion, is a unique traditionalism.

COMMISSIONER
Edward Balassanian

HONORARY COMMISSIONER
Jean Boghossian

CURATOR
David Kareyan

ARTISTS
Sona Abgarian
Vahram Aghasyan
Diana Hakobian
Tigran Khachatrian

www.accea.info/venice/
2005biennale.htm

Vahram Aghasian in his double screen video-installation *Factories in the Sky* presents an abandoned, dilapidated factory from the era of 'the glorious industrial achievement' of one-time Soviet Armenia. He tries to break free from the prejudiced stare of the viewer who in post-Soviet artists' works searches for documentary description of financial cataclysms. In the passage between very closely placed projection screens, the artist blows artificial 'stage smoke', which is the only tangible reality. If history was written first and attempts were then made to enact it, the world has been turned into smoke.

These four representatives of 'The Art of Resistance' believe that art has an influence on life, hence on how the world should be. From the exhibition *Crisis* (1999) on, the basic feature of exhibitions presented at the Armenian Centre for Contemporary Experimental Art (organiser of the Armenian Pavilion) is the fact that artists reflect upon their real human and social experiences.
David Kareyan

1 Sona Abgarian, *Tomorrow At the Same Time*, 2005. H8 video, DVD; stills from video

2 Vahram Aghasyan, *The Factories in Heaven*, 2005. H8 video, DVD; stills from video

1

2

3 Diana Hakobian, *The Logic
of Power*, 2005. H8 video,
DVD; stills from video

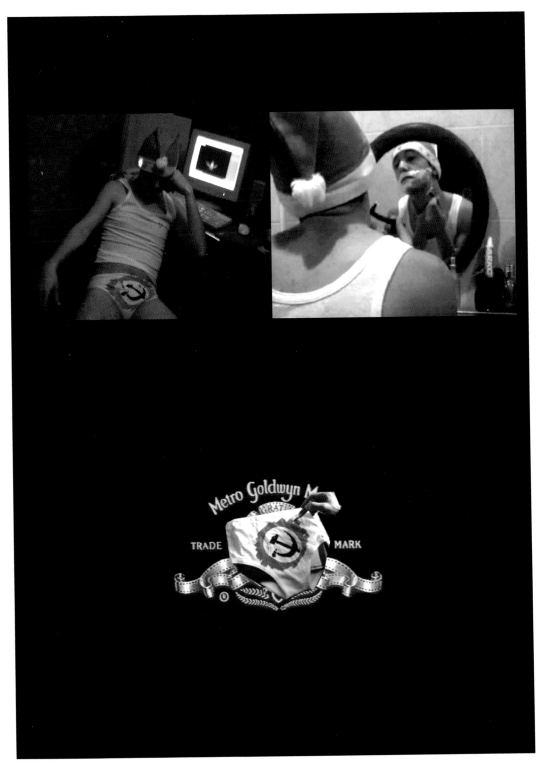

4 Tigran Khachatrian, *Theodicy*,
2005. H8 video, DVD; stills
from video

Republic of Belarus

Belarus is taking part in the Biennale di Venezia for the first time, and for the first time Belarus artists will be present with their work. Nine artists, who differ in terms of methodology, theme and tendency, document the development of contemporary art in Belarus. The artistic world in this country is in constant ferment, is highly productive and develops numerous themes. Almost all the artists have an academic professionalism acquired from their studies in Belarus. On that solid base, at times so heavy as to lead some to an indifferent immobility, many other artists have also been able to create a new direction, find new horizons and different themes and styles for communicating a new originality with their works.

The Belarus artists of the end of the twentieth century and the present have certainly not been forgotten. Nor can we ignore Belarus's important artistic past, including the beginnings of Marc Chagall's art in Vitebsk, the foundation of the art academy in Vitebsk in the 1920s, where artists of the calibre of Kasimir Malevich and El Lissitsky worked, and the first steps of the 'Russian avant-garde' movement with the Unovis group in 1921.

Like Marc Chagall, some artists chose to follow new directions and went to other European cities. They were able to directly acquire an international breadth, as was the case with Igor Tishin, Natalya Zaloznaya and Andrei Zadorine. The other participants in the Belarus Pavilion, Leonid Khobotov, Valerij Shkarubo, Ruslan Vashkevich, Vladimir Tsesler & Sergey Voichenko, have investigated themes peculiar to their culture, further enriching their experience through cultural and professional exchanges with artists from other cultural backgrounds. All have taken part in important exhibitions in Europe and other countries around the world.

The name of Izrail Basov, an artist who died in 1994, is also among those presented at the 51st Biennale di Venezia. He can be considered something of a precursor of a new cultural and artistic orientation in Belarus.

The slow, gradual opening that prevented the Republic of Belarus being reached and subject to sudden change led some artists to create a new and very personal mode of expression on the basis of the most absolute classicism. This

CURATOR/COMMISSIONER
Enzo Fornaro

CURATORS
Larissa Michnevic
Natalia Sarangovic

DEPUTY COMMISSIONER
Adriano Berengo

ARTISTS
Izrail Basov (1918-1994)
Leonid Khobotov
Valery Shkarubo
Igor Tishin
Vladimir Tsesler and Sergey Voichenko (1955-2004)
Ruslan Vashkevich
Andrei Zadorine
Natalya Zaloznaya

1

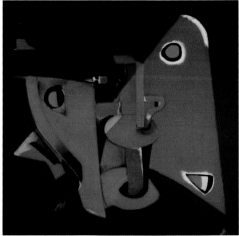

2

1 Izrail Basov, *At Dawn*, 1993.
Oil on canvas; 65 × 74 cm.
Courtesy the Estate

2 Leonid Khobotov, *Refractions*,
1999. Oil on canvas;
140 × 145 cm. Courtesy
the Artist

3 Valery Shkarubo, *Invasion*,
2002. Oil on canvas;
110 × 150 cm. Courtesy
the Artist

4 Igor Tishin, *The Nanny's
Wish*, 2000. Oil on canvas;
174 × 125 cm. Courtesy
the Artist

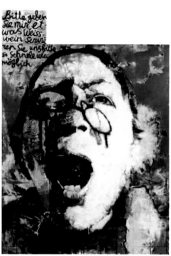

3   4

is the case with Valerij Shkarubo, who is noted for a hyper-realism that borders on abstraction in his landscapes. Ruslan Vashkevich creates his works from tradition, with irony, using different techniques that range from painting to installation, from the object to the verbal text. His creative activity is never at rest, and not without reason is he considered an experimenter.

Vladimir Tsesler & Sergey Voichenko are two artists who transform images into plastic, communicative signs; theirs are representations of post-modern and ironic objects. They interpret classical art with an ascetic radicalism using the traditional technique of oil on canvas, with technological photography and the use of computerised processes.

Leonid Khobotov paints imaginary worlds on the canvas with a lively, pregnant sense of colour, and his poetics seem to have their roots in distant Chagall origins.

Natalya Zaloznaya is noted for her extraordinary, light, ironic lyricism. Although she looks to contemporary German art, she is able to give her works an impalpable and refined lightness.

The work of Igor Tishin is distinguished by eclecticism and varied techniques ranging from photography to collage and from painting, with strong colour tones, to graphics and writing on the surfaces of his works.

Andrei Zadorine immerses the subjects of his paintings in an aura and a singular light; some of them seem to contain references to Balthusian poetics and the light of seventeenth-century Fleming painting.

Enzo Fornaro

5 Vladimir Tsesler and Sergey Voichenko, *Spiral*, 1995. Acrylic paste in relief and oil on canvas; 103 × 130 cm. Courtesy the Artists

6 Ruslan Vashkevich, *Colorblind Triptych*, 2002. Oil on canvas; 90 × 120 cm, 100 × 120 cm, 55 × 120 cm. Courtesy the Artist

7 Andrei Zadorine, *Untitled*, 2004. Oil on canvas; 115 × 145 cm. Courtesy the Artist

8 Natalya Zaloznaya, *Usual Thought 1*, 2004. Oil on canvas; 140 × 200 cm. Courtesy the Artist

5

6

7

8

Republic of Cyprus

GRAVY PLANET
A World Drawing by Konstantia Sofokleous and Panayiotis Michael

The German philosopher Niklas Luhmann claimed that each person is always 'partially displaced', because each one of us plays a multitude of roles and does so in an infinite number of settings. And that we constantly feel 'partially excluded', because of the multitude of voices and projects competing against each other, and the demands urging us to make use of them at all times and in all places. We always feel the here and now as an ephemeral situation. We are a chance permanent transitory 'I', and our whole life could be thought of as a storehouse of identities that have not managed to reach completion.

The Cyprus Pavilion for this year's Venice Biennale is headed by Konstantia Sofokleous (1974) and Panayiotis Michael (1966), two artists whose work to fill the pavilion space comprises drawings on paper, wall interventions and animations. Although their work is based on two individual presentations, the full project must be seen from the viewpoint of a shared aim: to investigate mechanisms that allow us to locate our universe of private worries within the public sphere. By working in a very personal manner and based on the study of how each of us perceives and acts in socio-political and geographical situations, making up our context and defining the references that determine our lives daily, both artists have striven to find meaningful resources in order to create a space where new values acquire form.

Alice's Adventures in Wonderland and a *Popular Children's Poem* are the two animated pieces on which Konstantia Sofokleous' installation is based, while Panayiotis Michael – under the general title of *I promise, you will love me forever* – has chosen to combine different works on paper and wall murals that represent a reinvention of concerns expressed in his previous work, but this time from a totally new perspective. Konstantia Sofokleous' work is based on the episodic, extravagant and even neurotic stories inhabiting and making up the world of children, but that also determine the life of every individual. The artist has created a new world based on universal material and has invented new ways of interpreting it, in order to emphasise the constant game that each story creates in terms of control, success and failure.

The work of Panayiotis Michael is based on an investigation into political imagination and how a relationship can be established between life actions and artistic practice within the socio-historic coordinates of which we are all an integral part. In developed countries, this is based on the idea that individual freedom can only result from collective work, but it can also be claimed that the group colonises our private space. Panayiotis Michael focuses his drawings on that strange border where a complete process that could be defined as the 'privatisation of utopia' takes place.

Beyond therapy and beyond etymological redundancy when tackling the present, both artists present works capable of conspiring against the apathy of the imagination; of creating a planet without a centre. As opposed to looking for collective remedies in our society based on the search for groups with which to close ranks, GRAVY PLANET could be thought of as an endless accumulation of possible answers, of shared worlds and personal visions that are born and circulate in an autonomous society.

Chus Martinez

COMMISSIONER
Loulli Michaelidou

CURATOR
Chus Martinez

DEPUTY COMMISSIONER
Stavroula Andreou

ARTISTS
Panayiotis Michael
Konstantia Sofokleous

1 Panayiotis Michael, *Untitled*, 2004. Pencil, ball pen, photocopy collage on paper; 140 × 160 cm. Courtesy the Artist

2 Konstantia Sofokleous, *Children's Poem*, 2004. Pencil drawing on plain paper; 21 × 29 cm

1

2

Republic of Korea

Chakyoung

In the 1990s Korea faced a lot of cultural changes, and various movements also emerged in the field of art. After the 1990's, diverse art activities by individual artists and groups replaced the previous tendency to follow one massive trend dominating the field. After the 1988 Olympic Games, which ignited international cultural exchanges in Korea, various forms of small-scale interdisciplinary events were staged combining visual art and other forms of art, particularly the performing arts and cinema. These events laid the foundation for various types of exhibition venue, alternative spaces and a number of large-scale biennales. Broad, profound changes that had never occurred in Korea were brought into the culture as a whole in the 1990's and many changes occurred.

This exhibition deals with the period from early 1990 to the present, 2005. Since the time dealt with here is a moment in the past, the exhibition will unfold its story by selecting artists of the times as inscribed in our memory and experience, and weaving a plot out of them.

The exhibition is intended to show the movements of young Korean artists who led contemporary Korean art struggling with those changes. It takes two artists, Choi Jeong-Hwa and Yiso Bahc, as a starting point for Korean contemporary art after the 90s. Choi is well known for his spectacular and colourful objects, whereas Bahc created works with almost no sense of physical existence. Nevertheless, a kind of affinity is found in their artworks. They both use modernist forms to deal with what happened in Korea, particularly the social problems that were hidden below the rapid economic development, thus capturing the ironies of society. Taking these two crucial artists as the basic pillars of the exhibition, it will also include artists who were aligned with them in the midst of the changes as well as younger artists who reflected contrary positions and attempted to fuse them into something new. The exhibition seeks to create a scene that presents various problems and issues from both inside and outside the art field. There are many different kinds of scene: scenes from our reality, from our lives, those in our minds and spirits, void scenes, full scenes, etc. The scenes, in this context, include not only natural scenes, but also virtual scenery. This is represented and processed reality, or an in-between

COMMISSIONER
Sunjung Kim

ARTISTS
Young-Whan Bae
Yiso Bahc (1957-2004)
Choi Jeong-Hwa
Gimhongsok
Ham Jin
Yeondoo Jung
Beom Kim
Sora Kim
NAKION
Kiwon Park
Park Sejin
Hein-Kuhn Oh
Sungshic Moon
Jewyo Rhii
Nakhee Sung

1

2

3

4

5

6

7

1 Yiso Bahc, *Wide World Wide*, 2003. Acrylic and oil on canvas, paper labds; 242 × 415 cm. Courtesy Mr Daeyeol Ku and friends of Yiso Bahc

2 Choi Jeong-Hwa, *Dragon Flower*, 2003. Installation (waterproof cloth, motor, ventilator, timer); 45 × 300 cm

3 Gimhongsok, *Love*, 2004. Steel; 150 × 145 cm

4 Young-Whan Bae, *Pop song*, 2002. Installation, projection, sound; dimension variable

5 Beom Kim, *An Iron in the form of a Radio, a Kettle in the form of an Iron, ads a Radio in the form of a Kettle*, 2002. Mixed media. Collection of the National Museum of Contemporary Art, Kuachon, Korea

6 Ham Jin, *Aewan Love # 2*, 2004. C-print photograph of a sculpture made of polymen clay, fly and mixed media; 155 × 125.5 cm. Courtesy the Artist

7 Yeondoo Jung, *Evergreen Tower*, 2001 (detail). Multi-side projection, 32 images; dimension variable. Courtesy Artsonje Center, Seoul / JGS Foundation, NY / Fukuoka Asia Museum, Fukuoka, Japan

field hanging on the verge of reality and virtuality.

This exhibition provided me and the artists with an awareness of the notion of 'time', our recognition and experience of time, a series of ideas on thinking, memorising, their mode of change and, overall, a whole change in our way of recognising reality. The present lies in the continuum of the past, and connotes what the future holds. Amid the flow of changes, what cultural transformations did the artists of the time accept, how do we at present communicate the changes and how will they be viewed in the future? Ironically, this idea about time and change, a commissioner's intention to take this idea as a subject, are part of the incessant flow from past to future. It was illuminating to see that a well-planned scheme and set of ideas could not but undergo a series of changes, and in the course of these changes, unexpected experiences and numerous revisions, new memories were brought about and became a major part of the plan.

The plan and idea for the exhibition itself, turning into a virtual reality, went through organic mutation and unfolded in the current of diverse situations and ideas.

The exhibition talks about methods and attitudes (referring to attitudes toward objects and also the attitudes taken by those objects). As mentioned above, the Korean contemporary artists who had been through the 1990s learnt many different ways of accepting the diverse cultures and genres, as important international cultural exchanges were made. External factors were introduced and ultimately formed a new culture inside. The exhibition in the Korean Pavilion and the pavilion itself, as a conduit between outside and inside, will embody the method and attitude of such cultural transformation and exchange as happened in Korea: an open channel between Korea and the outside world. This exhibition will attempt to express the relationship between Venice and Korea and, moreover, between the pavilions of other countries and the Korean Pavilion, along with all their harmonies within those frameworks, by borrowing

8 Sora Kim, *CapitalPlus Credit Union*, 2002

9 NAKION, *Omnivision*, 2003. Ink on paper; 155 × 250 cm. Courtesy the Artist

10 Kiwon Park, *Hot Space*, 2004. Vinyl sheet installed on the wall; dimension variable

11 Park Sejin, *Labor*, 2004. Rose and mixed media on paper; 164 × 150 cm

8

9

10

11

the concept '*chagyeong*' from the Korean tradition (*chagyeong* is architectural jargon. A window is a significant architectural factor in building a house or building, and when a window is designed to see the scenery outside the term '*chagyeong*' is used, meaning 'to borrow scenery').

This exhibition will be recognised as a single structural work from outside. However, on coming closer you will find it contains many various scenes revealed spontaneously in the long flow of time, though standing as separate pieces. We would like to show that broken fragments of scenes taken from the site in those times are connected to each other, creating one complete new scene. Each of them is a particular piece, but it is not difficult to notice that important contexts and flows are running through the time they are talking about.

Sunjung Kim

12

12 Jewyo Rhii, *The Half of Basement - Homage to Yiso Bahc*, 2004. Installation; dimension variable

13 Sungshic Moon, *Talking Trees*, 2004. Watercolor on paper; dimension variable

14 Hein-Kuhn Oh, *Twist Kim, Singer, Actor*, 1993. Gelatin silver print; 110 × 85 cm

15 Nakhee Sung, *# 6 (Shangai)*, 2003. Wall drawing with vinyl sheet, marker, paint, and spray paint; dimension variable

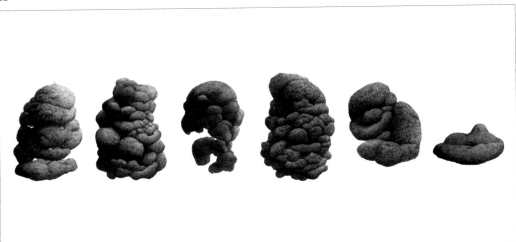

13

14

15

Republic of Slovenia
Another Day

As mounted in the gallery, Vadim Fiškin's project *Another Speedy Day* might be prima facie reminiscent of stage equipment. But what is staged on this set is just the fluctuation of light, increasing and fading at a steady pace. All the physical equipment is merely the support of something that seems to hover – though it is not immaterial – on the verge of material presence. Moreover, light is a precondition for the possibility of seeing and, at the same time, something that is in itself on the edge of visibility. Fiškin has here used the possibilities afforded by the contemporary media and theatre technology to stage something intangible and, as it were, barely visible. The fluctuation of light also determines the duration: the cycle of the light growing brighter and dimming lasts twelve minutes, thus demanding prolonged attention from the viewer and, consequently, producing an increased awareness of time. But although the emphasis laid on the duration seems great, the work's temporal nature also makes the work ephemeral, or even momentary, as it incessantly escapes and disappears into nothingness.

The cycle of light is actually the enactment of a day, 24 hours compressed into 12 minutes. We could also say it is the enactment of one of the most fundamental human fantasies, that of controlling the course of time.

Overcoming gravity and overcoming the restrictions that prevent man from moving at will in any direction of four-dimensional space-time are closely connected. Overcoming gravity also means breaking free of the human body, of being physically bound by the parameters of space and time. The artist has described his project thus: 'The light in the room changes according to a "fast clock". On an electronic display, the hours tick by at an accelerated pace. Daylight and night light follow one another to the rhythm of the electronic clock. For example: 24 hours pass in 12 minutes. If we were on a hypothetical rocket travelling away from Earth at a speed of 299,782 km/s (a mere 10 km/s slower than the speed of light), these 12 minutes would become one Earth day. Several different possibilities can be calculated on the basis of different velocities. The speed of the timepiece is calculated by applying the formula $t = t_0/\sqrt{(1 - v^2/c^2)}$'. The rhythm of light pulsating in Fiškin's installation would thus be experienced by someone a mere 10 km/s from reaching the speed of light, i.e. from overcoming one of the most fundamental and absolute limitations of our universe.

Inke Arns has described Fiškin's works as 'machines (media) that produce the metaphysical'. Indeed, they are machines, technological aggregates, but machines that work in a 'poetic' manner since they are not subject only to production pragmatics but underscore in their work the complexity and contradictoriness of their own fundamental premises. Generally speaking, Fiškin's art could be said to be closely related to the world of modern science

COMMISSIONER
Zdenka Badovinac

DEPUTY COMMISSIONER
Igor Zabel

ARTIST
Vadim Fiškin

www.aplusa.it

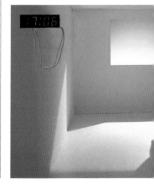

Vadim Fiškin, *Another Speedy Day*, 2003-2005. Electronic clock, light, room construction. Light design: A.J. Weissbard. Photo Vadim Fiškin, Tilde De Tullio.

The light in the room changes according to a 'fast clock'. On an electronic display, the hours tick by at an accelerated pace. Daylight and nighttime light follow one another to the rhythm of the electronic clock. For example: 24 hours pass in 12 minutes. If we were on a hypothetical rocket traveling away from Earth at a speed of 299,782 km/s (a mere 10 km/s slower than the speed of light), these 12 minutes would become one Earth day. Several different possibilities can be calculated on the basis of different velocities. The speed of the timepiece is calculated by applying the formula

$$t = t_0/\sqrt{(1 - v^2/c^2)}$$

and technology. But this does not make it rationalistic or naively technicist. On the contrary, it emphasises that crucial line in the development of modern sciences and technology in which strict scientific positivism has intertwined or literally fused with metaphysical reflections, and technological innovations have acquired poetic or even esoteric aspects.
Igor Zabel

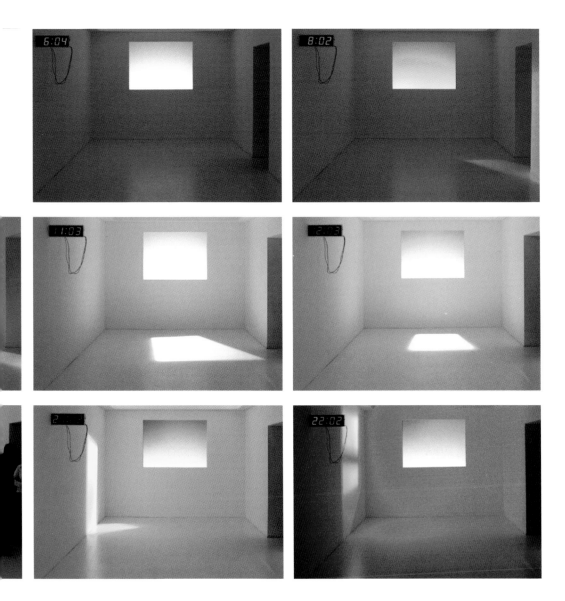

People's Republic of China
Virgin Garden: Emersion

The title of the China Pavilion's first exhibition, *Virgin Garden: Emersion*, taken from the name of the site, represents the romantic symbolism of China's induction into the Venice Biennale, and curatorial themes. *Emersion* reflects the various spirits of the time arising out of the rapid change and development in Chinese society. The idea speaks of the displacement or re-location of China's distinct political, economic and cultural influences onto an international arena, and depicts the astute face of Chinese contemporary artistic practice in an effort to cast off prevailing stereotypes.

The inaugural China Pavilion occupies two adjacent spaces. In the interior there is a video installation by Xu Zhen and a light installation by Liu Wei. The two works embody the human psychological response to fleeting, chance stimulation, while articulating the point of collision between the internal domain of the human psyche and the external world of society. The adjacent outdoor space features three works marrying traditional Chinese culture and contemporary conceptual wisdom. The architect Yung Ho Chang has created a new nomadic landscape in the *Virgin Garden*. The artist team of Sun Yuan and Peng Yu presents a flying saucer that was handcrafted by Chinese farmers and represents their projected ideals for the new century. The *fengshui* specialist and Chinese architecture and town planning scholar Wang Qiheng will conduct a *fengshui* analysis for the national pavilions and Venice at large, revealing dynamics between the China Pavilion and the Biennale enterprise. In short, *Virgin Garden: Emersion* will probe both the conceptual and artistic language of contemporary Chinese artists and the shifting landscape of a nation in the midst of a metamorphosis.

Fan Di'An

There is a hundred-year gap between the induction of the China Pavilion and the establishment of the first national pavilion at the Venice Biennale. So this selection of artists is essentially an investigation into the nature of national pavilions and how to represent the arrival and attitude of the inaugural China Pavilion.

The architect Yung Ho Chang uses bamboo to build an open pavilion in the *Virgin Garden*, which represents an incomplete 'vessel' in progress. Wang Qiheng, an architectural historian and the most renowned *fengshui* specialist in China, uses *fengshui* principles to examine and assess the state of energy of the existing national pavilions, the Biennale and the city of Venice. His investigation into the issues associated with fate and destiny will also take on an unusual perspective in deciding the orientation of the China Pavilion. Artists Sun Yuan and Peng Yu have invited Du Wenda, a Chinese farmer, and his team to Venice to test launch a flying saucer that they spent the past few years earnestly building. The farmers made Chinese headline news for their courage in opening up a way of connecting a rural village to the larger universe. The project is a metaphor for the current developments in Chinese society and the inauguration

COMMISSIONER
Fan Di'An

CURATOR
Cai Guo-Qiang

ASSISTANT CURATOR
Pi Li

ARTISTS
Yung Ho Chang
Liu Wei
Sun Yuan & Peng Yu
Wang Qiheng
Xu Zhen

1 Yung Ho Chang, *Bamboo Shoots*, 2005. Bamboo, galvanized iron wire, hemp cord, iron tube, etc. 52.5 × 29 × 8 m

of the China Pavilion at the Venice Biennale this year. In addition, the indoor presentations, *Shout* by Xu Zhen and *Star* by Liu Wei, emphasise the China Pavilion's sense of arrival.

The collection of the artists' works evolves around the central theme of expressing spirituality and soulfulness. This creative methodology not only relates to Chinese traditional culture but also investigates the contemporary artistic manifestation of the non-material world. The building of an official national pavilion raises the questions of what a national pavilion is, and, in the twenty-first century, what kind of national pavilion we should build.

Cai Guo-Qiang

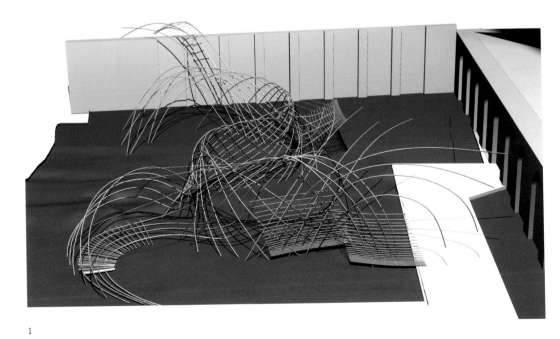

1

2 Liu Wei, *Star*, 2005.
Monolights, digital cameras,
motion detectors; dimension
variable

2

3 Xu Zhen, *Shout*, 2005.
DVD, DVD player, projector;
dimension variable

4 Sun Yuan & Peng Yu,
Unidentified Flying Objects,
2005. UFO. 6 × 2.5 × 6 m

3

4

Romania

The admission of Romania and Bulgaria is planned for 2007 in the European Union (EU); membership negotiations have been taken up with Turkey. Western and eastern Europe are growing together into a transitory space, which is being politically and culturally recast and remapped. This process of growing, which has accelerated since the fall of the Berlin wall, is founded historically on a phantasm and politically on the idea of a common European foreign and security policy independent of the United States. The phantasm of 'Europe' is a noun of bourgeois universalism created in the second half of the eighteenth century, when travelling English authors in particular discovered ancient Greece as the cradle of civilisation and founded an abstraction of civilisation, to give cultural legitimacy to the values and economic interests of a rising bourgeoisie. In the following period the European nation states laid exclusive claim to this core ideal and excluded whole swathes of Europe as 'Asiatic', 'barbarian' and 'oriental.' The process of the appropriation and expropriation of European identity went hand in hand with the colonial forays of the European nation states, whose aggressive national economic competition vented itself in two world wars.

To sum up, the EU project rests on two pillars: the euro and the European army. Further defining features that drive and shape the European superpower internally are the centralisation of political power ('speaking with one voice'), control over advanced technologies and cultural hegemony. It is currently proving difficult to centralise political power because smaller states are not willing to unquestioningly follow the EU core states Germany and France. But once we recognise that Europe is an emerging superpower, what does this mean for the development of democracy in general and for the status of culture in particular? The contours of the 'new Europe' can be seen especially clearly in the cuts in welfare and social services, and also in migration policy, because that is where principles of social construction such as inclusion and exclusion of (cultural) identity and (ethnic) difference can be cemented in place. After the fall of the Berlin wall, mass emigration terrified the western European industrial states; after 9/11 and the Madrid bombings, there is discussion of a series of new security laws and deployment of the army to maintain public security. Europe, which gave birth to public space and the free city, is in the process of raising the state of emergency to the ruling paradigm of urban life.

While the political sphere formalises the EU integration process as a geopolitical vision of a greater Europe and forces norms on society (the new member states had to democratise their political systems on the Western model, accept international rules of competition and integrate thousands of European Union laws to their national legislation), the field of culture – wherever it connects with political and social resistance movements – has the potential to bring forth a perspective that treats the process of European unification as an opportunity for creating a critical Europe. The mixing process of culture and political resistance tends to generate three formats for activity, which interact and reinforce one another: activism as art form; cooperation between artists and activists; art as activist manifestation. We have to see artistic practice as a format for social activity – and not just as an outdated bourgeois form of gaining distinction. Seen in this way, the artistic 'work' is the starting point for an all-round examination of its own conditions of creation and existence and of its power in the production and reinforcement of pictures, images and dispositions.

Marius Babias

COMMISSIONER
Marius Babias

ARTIST
Daniel Knorr

'SPACE CO-OPTED' At first glance this barely there show of site-specific works is nearly invisible—except for Art Domantay's moldy and irresistible *31 Flavors of Hell* (Baskin-Robbins). But the conceptual twists are terrific. Siobhan Liddell's taut copper threads play counterpoint to Sol LeWitt's single diagonal line. Gretchen Faust's 1989 wall tattoo and Robert Barry's 1970 silver-penciled list trade wordplay with Ricci Albenda's *Algae* decal. Karin Sander's bumpy white wallpaper is as wryly understated as Jonathan Horowitz's white press-tape name or Cary Liebowitz's shy *Cruising Cards*. And Daniel Knorr's modest wall label (from his "Visible Invisible Series") merely lays claim to the whole show. THROUGH JULY 27, Andrew Kreps, 516 West 20th Street, 741-8849. (Levin)

Russia

Russian Pavilion

The exhibition in the Russia Pavilion reveals the dialectic of interaction between the artist and his public. The authors of the installations create the communicative space in such a way that the works of art are only completed with the viewers' participation. A work of art is a reference object, which necessitates negotiations and implies the other. These thoughts are very relevant in Russia, where contemporary art is still a blind spot on the cultural map.

Communication and miscommunication are the principal subjects in the creative work of the Moscow artists involved in the ESCAPE programme. Blending public and private, they offer viewers various modes of 'implication': to look into the privacy of the artists' everyday life, to buy their paraphernalia or pirate copies of works by famous Russian artists, to participate in the ceremony of inventing the motherland. Close communication produces involuntary scepticism and disillusionment. The difficulty of listening to and understanding each other is considered in a delicate video entitled *Quartette*, where the playing of an opus by Beethoven is combined with a sound-track by Shostakovich. The *Vertigo* installation arranges a meeting of the artist and the viewers in a bunker. This has been specially built from rusty metal, and the scene of general mutual alienation seen by a viewer (who has spent quite a time in the queue) raises pessimistic questions. Perhaps this metal-clad building symbolises the aloofness and self-sufficiency of contemporary art.

The interactive video installation *Too Long to Escape* offers viewers an interactive game with the artists, who move toward the public at a speed that is proportional to the number of viewers entering the hall. The attempt to describe the problem arithmetically – the more the viewers, the faster the approach – reveals the relativism and formalism of mass strategies. Along with the irony of the wish to please viewers, the artists raise the question of whether these interactive performances are no more than a simulation of dialogue, which conceals the passive solitude of the viewer.

Galina Myznikova and Sergey Provorov, artists from Nizhniy Novgorod who work with the topical concept of 'public space', do not consider relationships with the public as being so dramatic. They treat viewers as consumers of a specific info-visual product. Their long-term project can be located somewhere between public art and advertising, design and experimental cinema and TV. Unfamiliar with alienation from society, the artists try to remain within, easily combining the positions of a consumer and a sober, cool-headed analyst, judging the situation from the outside. This flexible approach inspires them to work on social projects, suggesting innovative means of communication. Voluntarily dwelling in unstable, marginal areas, where the usual cultural codes are invalid, the artists begin to interact with mass culture instead of opposing it.

This is the case with the *Idiot Wind* installation. Standing in an aero-acoustic space, the viewer becomes the main character in this work of art, feeling the power of art with his own psychosomatic senses. In the first section of the pavilion one can easily touch and try to catch the wind, but then he/she becomes strongly influenced by the increasing power of the windblasts. The force of physical action arouses complex metaphysical feelings, and its visual minimalism suggests numerous mythopoeic connotations of wind, air and the elements.
Liubov Saprykina

COMMISSIONER
Eugeny Zyablov

CURATORS
Olga Lopukhova
Liubov Saprykina

ARTISTS

"Too Long to Escape"
the ESCAPE program
(Valery Ayzenberg, Anton Litvin,
Bogdan Mamonov, Liza
Morozova)

"Idiot Wind"
the PROVMYZA duet
(Galina Myznikova, Sergej
Provorov)

CO-ORDINATION
Julija Abramova

ORGANIZATION AND CARE
Kostantin Larin

www.labiennale.ru

1 The ESCAPE program, *Too Long to Escape*, 2005. Interactive video installation; dimension variable

2-5 Galina Myznikova and Sergej Provorov (the PROVMYZA duet), *Idiot Wind*, 2005. Installation with sound and air

"Too Long To Escape"

Escape - -2005

1

2

3

4

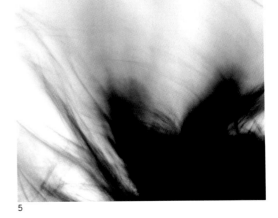

5

Serbia and Montenegro
The Eros of Slight Offence

'The whole business of eroticism is to strike to the inmost core of the living being so that the heart stands still' (Georges Bataille).

The *slight offences* of Jelena Tomašević, Natalija Vujošević and Igor Rakčević are not 'sprigs' of domestic gardens or juicy temptations of minor prohibitions. Nor are they fatal temptations aimed at the strictly constructed and brutally defended system of the *great prohibition*. They are of the order of 'modest trespasses' that 'impartially', with their own wavering logic and seductive strategy, discreetly, non-aggressively, without bitterness, but also free of uncertainty, penetrate unexpected places, nodes of the nervous system of a condition or event in which they sense Eros and the warm delight of power/possibility unleashed by 'minor change'. They seemingly do not 'damage' the condition or event: everything seems unchanged, offering the same, normal, recognisable, tedious 'norm'. It is precisely by fostering the illusion that the situation is immutable, and sustaining the apparently static nature of relations and the 'stability of the system' that a slight offence, though lacking any pretension, subtly but profoundly stirs up the interior forces and flows emerging from every event. The slight offence sets in motion, with waves or svelte leaps, the regrouping of its forces establishing a new constellation of 'old', received values; a new map of occupied space and a crystallisation of active time. In the *course of events*, the most powerful are those unexpected tiny *slips*, brief *submersions*, those slight dislocations or swift *spurts* that pierce the tissue of the event. They develop as vibrant points of authentic fullness, or as foci-fires, 'lateral' buds of the events, 'sliding' constructs or small mobile capsules of time and space, prismatic structures that function and refract the different dimensions of flow and duration, the dimensions of existence, revealing the multitude of its manifestations or its host of identities.

Eros dwells in such *slight offences*. These minute digressions, these barely noticeable shifts, indicate the flaking of a thin crack, a fine tear in the tissue of

COMMISSIONER
Svetlana Racanović

ARTISTS
Igor Rakčević
Jelena Tomašević
Natalija Vujošević

SUPPORTED BY
The Ministry of Culture
of Montenegro

ORGANIZATION
National Museum
of Montenegro, Cetinje

WITH THE SUPPORT OF
Petar Ćuković

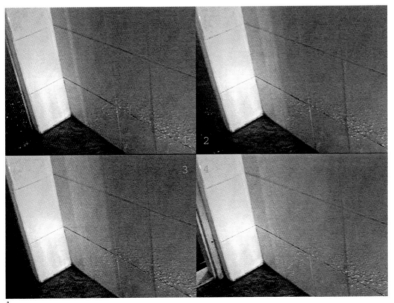

1 Igor Rakčević, *Once Upon a Time*, 2005. Still from video - draft version

events. Forestalling the mind with wonder and strangely titillating the senses, the intuition/promise of a new meaning and new feeling penetrates through this crack, without violence, like a small slit in the clothing that allows nudity to shine and unleashes Eros.

The *slight offences* committed by these artists bear a muted yet active expectancy that does not demand fulfilment. The stimulation, springing from the initial feeling of wonderment at the scene, does not anticipate solution. This is a seductive tactic that, set free from the fate of completion and certainty, not having to obey the regularity of causal relations or have any explicable motivation and logical solution, is not given nor demands definitive gratification. These slight offences generate small delights, such as a *nurtured feeling*, a *levitating pulsation* lacking firm support, clear motives, a 'recognisable feeling' of understandable, predictable duration. Seemingly a superficial intervention, the slight offence, an act of *low intensity* and *delayed effect*, strikes into the heart of a given reality without wounding it or, much less, delivering the *coup de grâce*. The 'regularity' of such scenes is turned into wonderment, into their transposed Otherness; their strangeness that 'hits' the perceived, experienced, desired or unconscious gives absolute clarity and reveals the event's hidden bareness, 'its nudity, exposed, raw, deprived of aura, shadow of its own history'... as 'keen, perfect, self-existing sentiment of duration' (Edgar Allan Poe).

Svetlana Racanović

Translated by Jelena Stanovnik-Champion

2

3

4

5

6

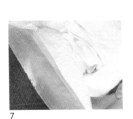

7

Singapore

The work of Lim Tzay Chuen questions notions of aesthetic experience. By compelling viewers to reflect upon their experience of his work, viewers are led to critically re-evaluate perceptions and assumptions as to what constitutes aesthetic experience. This is achieved through intricate and complex engagements with the social, economic, cultural and political processes that define the particular contexts around which his work is situated. Lim's interventions acknowledge the transitory and fragmented nature of space and memory, and it is their engagement with the volatility and uncertainty of situations that is significant. His work rejects the construction and definition of prescribed meanings, particularly pertaining to questions about what constitutes a work of art. Instead, the recognition of an aesthetic event derives from moments of self-discovery, often involving reflexivity and surprise.
Eugene Tan

COMMISSIONER
Khor Kok Wah

CURATOR
Eugene Tan

DEPUTY COMMISSIONER
Paolo De Grandis

ARTIST
Lim Tzay Chuen

CO-ORGANIZERS
National Arts Council (Singapore)
& Singapore Art Museum
Arte Communications, Venice

www.artecommunications.com

02/02/2005

By the time you read
this, I will hopefully
have gone through
with my plans
for Venice.

Tray chman.

Spain

Muntadas. *On Translation*

COMMISSIONER
Bartomeu Marí

ARTIST
Antoni Muntadas

Since 1995 Muntadas has been working on a series of projects under the title *On Translation* developed in museums and cultural institutions. *On Translation* refers to the phenomena of codification, interpretation and transformation of cultural facts approached from diverse perspectives and contexts bringing together urban life, history, narratives and the impact of technology on the construction of the public sphere. Ranging from events of universal scope to local situations, *On Translation* explores the concept of translation and interpretation from an approach that encompasses cultural, linguistic, political and economic issues.

Within this series the *On Translation* pavilion presents a selection of existing works and works conceived especially for the occasion. *On Translation: I Giardini*, for instance, summarises Muntadas' approach to specific places that have become universally recognised spaces as a result of their history and uses. The *On Translation* pavilion propounds a consideration of the 'Biennale machine' through its actual location and its role, not only in the context of contemporary art but as a stage on which the geopolitical and cultural conflicts of our time and their forms of representation are enacted.

On Translation also shifts emphasis towards the figure of the viewer, the citizen, the genuine recipient of the artist's work whose attention is required for the contents of works to be perceived, used and transformed. The statement 'perception requires participation' appears in all presentations of the projects, making spectators the ultimate arbiters of the works.
Bartomeu Marí

ON TRANSLATION
On Translation is a series of works exploring issues of transcription, interpretation and translation.
From language to codes
From subjectivity to objectivity
From agreement to wars
From semiology to cryptography
The role of translation/translators as a visible/invisible fact.
Muntadas, 1995

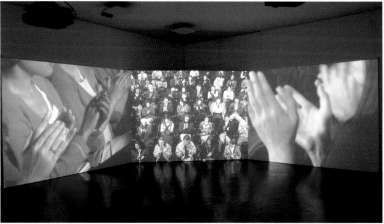

1

1 Antoni Muntadas, *On Translation: El Aplauso*, 1999. Museum am Ostwall Dortmund, Germany 'On Translation: Das Museum', 2003. Photo Sascha Dressler

2 Antoni Muntadas, *On Translation: The Bookstore*, 2001. Museum am Ostwall, Dortmund, Germania, 'On Translation: Das Museum', 2003. Photo Sascha Dressler

3 Antoni Muntadas, *On View*, 2004. Location One, New York, 2004. Photo Jim McGregor

2

3

United States of America

Ed Ruscha. Course of Empire

Inspired by the symmetrical, Jeffersonian layout of the American Pavilion's neo-classical architecture, Ed Ruscha's installation for the 2005 Venice Biennale will comprise ten paintings: five in colour, five in black and white. The colour paintings mirror the black and white in both subject matter and placement. Leaving the pavilion's entry rotunda, 'C', empty, Ruscha will install a combination of pictures, based on his 1992 *Blue Collar* group, as follows:

COMMISSIONER
Linda Norden

DEPUTY COMMISSIONER
Donna De Salvo

COORDINATION
Solomon R. Guggenheim Foundation

ARTIST
Ed Ruscha

1

In the pavilion's left-hand, 'D' and 'E' galleries: the five, original, 1992 'Blue Collar' pictures, black and white canvases depicting urban landscapes.
In the opposite 'A' and 'B' galleries: five new pictures depicting an accelerated, aged version of the same urban landscapes, possibly to the point of deterioration, painted in colour.

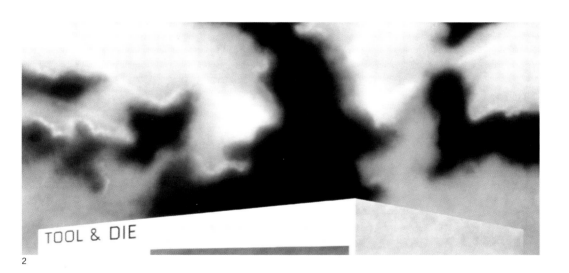

2

Switzerland

Shadows Collide With People

Switzerland is a country of many cultures and many languages living side-by-side within a very small territory. It is therefore fruitful to inquire into what it means to be Swiss and to represent Swiss culture. *Shadows Collide With People* explores that issue. It is a multilingual exhibition in which four artists meet one curator, each with different approaches that shift, diverge and separate again just when unity seems to be emerging.

Gianni Motti was born in 1958 in Sondrio, Italy, and grew up there. He has been living in Geneva for many years. He is a man of the world who moves through the world in a diversity of contexts from politics to athletics and magic. He makes this clear in his actions and installations in visual and experiential terms sometimes playfully, sometimes magically and sometimes with an irresistible immediacy. His language is always the language of others that he distils in his work into images and identities. It is the language of power and impotence, of openness and ignorance, of play and drama, of intervention and appropriation. Gianni Motti crops up like a shadow in order to gave things a shape, a body, an image or an idea.

Shahryar Nashat was born in Iran in 1975 and grew up in Switzerland. The language of his videos and installations often lies beneath what is revealed, although the surface appearance of his productions also has an inescapable presence. He investigates the psychological and political structures of our existence that lie beneath structural evidence, and renders the aesthetic of human weakness or the beauty of fascist architecture beneath the facade of seeing. In the process he demonstrates our longing for identity before identity has even come into play.

Ingrid Wildi, daughter of a Swiss father and Chilean mother, was born in Chile in 1963, where she lived for the first 18 years of her life. She emigrated to Switzerland in the wake of increasing pressures under the Pinochet regime. She has never really felt at home speaking foreign languages and is therefore acutely aware of what it means not to possess a language and, on the other hand, to be foreign to the languages that are spoken where one lives. This is Ingrid Wildi's subject matter in her documentation-oriented video works. What does it mean to speak a foreign language, to live in that context and attempt to chart a personal path through that territory?

Marco Poloni was born in Amsterdam in 1962 and spent the first years of his life in Rome and Mexico City before his family moved to Geneva. Marco Poloni's world is multilingual. This may be one of the reasons why we frequently encounter the system of translation in his photographic works or installations by means of which he makes us feel quite incapable of naming what we see, what we read and what we are confronted with until, ultimately, we can no longer distinguish between reality and fiction. His many languages are like a shadow

COMMISSIONER
Urs Staub

CURATOR
Stefan Banz

DEPUTY COMMISSIONER
Andreas Münch

ARTISTS
Gianni Motti
Shahryar Nashat
Marco Poloni
Ingrid Wildi

www.bak.admin.ch/biennale

1

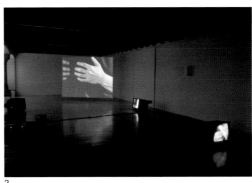

2

3

4

cast upon us. Poloni demonstrates something that is impossible and yet always there – in everyday life, in our heads, as perception, as imagination and as a translated, invented reality.

Shadows Collide With People is a metaphor and refers to the relationship of picture to reality, of art to society. Art is not equivalent to society; art delivers an enduring image of society. And shadows always depict the source of their own existence. But, like shadows, art is also reality. Only when people and shadows, art and society meet, can we perceive the world in all its dimensions and nuances. A shadow alone is inconceivable. Even if we were to see only the shadow, we would recognize in it the foundation of its existence. Similarly, a person without a shadow would be merely a shadow of himself. When shadows collide with people, reality emerges, life emerges.

Stefan Banz

Pipilotti Rist

Pipilotti Rist emerged onto the international art scene in the mid-1990s with mesmerising video installations, such as *Sip My Ocean* (1996). This piece, which incorporates the artist's remake of Chris Isaak's pop song *Wicked Game* (1991), conveys the feelings associated with the joys of falling in love and the devastation of heartbreak. Shot under water, it is composed of colourful images of a woman swimming in the sea and fish moving through calm waters, while a range of toy domestic items – a cup, a plate, a record – sink to the bottom. The narrative and tone of the piece is driven by its strong soundtrack: in Rist's version of the song, longing is countered with desperation.

Rist's earlier *I'm Not the Girl Who Misses Much* (1986) is a single-channel video that recasts a line from John Lennon's *Happiness is a Warm Gun* (1968). Here she dances frenetically while singing in a high-pitched and, at times, almost hysterical voice, both of which are the result of speeding up the footage. Because the artist's early works frequently covered or sampled pop songs, comparisons have been made to music videos; likewise, they have been interpreted as a critique of popular culture. In these two works, for example, her provocative performances can be read as recasting macho rock bravado into witty and ironic feminist manifestos.

Rist's popularity soared with the critical acclaim of *Ever is Over All* (1997), for which she won the Premio 2000 award at the 47th Venice Biennale and is, perhaps, best known. This diptych projection features a young woman dressed in a light blue dress and ruby red shoes, as if having emerged from a fairytale. She strolls carefree along the streets of Zurich carrying a long-stemmed flower cast in metal, which she uses to smash the windows of cars parked along her route. Surprisingly, she receives an approving nod from a passing policewoman. This scene is juxtaposed with images of a Technicolor, larger-than-life garden shot with a swirling camera motion. Set to hypnotic music composed by long-time collaborator Anders Guggisberg, the piece draws viewers into the artist's surreal fantasy.

The importance of music in Rist's work may be influenced by her involvement in the all-female band Les Reines Prochaines (The Next Queens), from 1988 to 1994. However, the artist's influences range widely from visual art and music to architecture and social politics. She regularly cites the work of Nam June Paik and Yoko Ono as points of reference and inspiration for her interest in expanding video into the space of the gallery and engaging viewers in looking at and experiencing art in unconventional ways. Her quirky wit, propensity for experimentation and individual spirit result in unique video installations that intersect with sculpture, poetry and performance.

In Rist's work visual references to the so-called natural and urban worlds collide. Equally important are images of the physical body, which is typically female, frequently naked, and often that of the artist herself. In *Open My Glade* (2000), a large-scale project for New York's Times Square videotron, she flattens her face against the screen, as if attempting to break out of the video perched high above the street. Her deformed features and smeared lipstick are

COMMISSIONERS
Andreas Münch
Urs Staub

ARTIST
Pipilotti Rist
(San Stae Church)

5

both absurd and disturbing. In *Extremities (Smooth, Smooth)* (1999) isolated body parts are projected floating through space, and in *Pickelporno (Pimple Porno)* (1992) the camera pans over a naked, fragmented body as if it were a landscape. In each case Rist approaches physicality with sensuality and whimsy, rather than with voyeurism or clinical detachment.

It would be true to say of Rist's moving imagery, which she refers to as moving paintings on glass, that nothing is fixed – neither the camera movements, the sources of inspiration, nor the art historical references and interpretations. What is consistent, however, is her experimentation with images, sound and presentation formats as well as her playful approach to art-making, resulting in captivating imagery, dreamy narratives, psychedelic colours and beguiling soundtracks.

Rochelle Steiner

Courtesy the Artist and Hauser & Wirth Zürich London

Thailand
Those Dying Wishing to Stay,
Those Living Preparing to Leave

The Vulnerable World

The cycle of birth, life and death is anything but a common matter. Loss and tragedy are indispensable parts of human history. With the high communication technology of this globalised age, we can easily share the same destiny. That includes the threat of local and international terrorism, forest and environmental destruction, food and water shortages, unequal access to modern medicines and medications, and especially the recent unprecedented natural disaster in Asian countries that resulted in the loss of over 200,000 lives.

The beginning of the twenty-first century marks a time when Thai people and their friends around the globe are highly vulnerable and discouraged. The world is now searching for alternative paths for future survival, valid meanings of happiness as well as mental and physical security.

Religion, art and cultural activities have become other answers for a meaningful life. Some contemporary art works have helped treat and heal the creator's mental and physical illness, such as those of Montien Boonma and Araya Rasdjarmrearnsook.

Art for Mental Strength

Montien Boonma (1953-2000) is known for works that successfully blend local and international contemporary art expressions to reflect his exploration of Buddhist philosophy and indigenous Thai wisdom. His large-scale sculptures and installations invoke all human senses. They are not only for the eyes, but also the nose, ears and hands. Viewers are invited to step or push into his works to contemplate and experience them with all the senses. The inter-relationship of the works and the viewer is a crucial part of understanding the artist's projects. His later works consist mainly of Thai herbal pigments traditionally used for medicines.

Boonma's works served as a bridge for the artist's spiritual concentration and mental cure while his wife was suffering from breast cancer. Boonma then quite unexpectedly suffered the same disease and eventually died.

Although it is clear that Boonma sought self-detachment through his works, or 'death before dying', they are also a testimonial to his wish to preserve the life of his loved ones and his own.

Making Contact

Araya Rasdjarmrearnsook (born 1957) has been highly acclaimed for her contemporary art works and writings. Her earlier works are steeped in melancholy and pain caused by irreplaceable loss, solitude and a yearning for the past. They mainly stage the condition between life and death presented in poetic mode combining visual movement, ambient sound and the recital of old verses.

From 1998, Rasdjarmrearnsook's video works started to challenge the ethics and tolerance of her viewers. In one of her video installations, *Reading for Corpses*, the artist is seen seated in a hospital room, reading beside a group of corpses. She was softly reciting excerpts from 'Inao', a well-known traditional Thai poem. The work implies the artist's attempt to communicate with the dead. The recital is their dialogue. The act of reading for others suggests one's giving of time, merit and an intimate relationship like that of a young person taking care of his or her ill elderly relatives.

COMMISSIONER
Apinan Poshyananda

CURATORS
Panya Vijinthanasarn
Sutee Kunavichayanont
Luckana Kunavichayanont

ARTISTS
Montien Boonma
Araya Rasdjarmrearnsook

2

1

3

Those Dying Wishing to Stay, Those Living Preparing to Leave

Although Boonma's works deal mainly with the delicacy of life, we can still experience his effort to control such fragility; the artist's desire to remain in this wonderful world, even for just a few more moments. The selection of Boonma's works in this exhibition reflects art as a process for mental and physical treatment. Meanwhile, Rasdjarmrearnsook has involved herself in the subjects of loss, melancholy and death, as if she is living with death in every breath. To her the comfort of mind seems to lie in the breathless air. Perhaps one's mind has already been buried alive without the body dying. It may also be the artist's hope that an encounter between the living and the dead may pave the way to the artist's personal understanding of the relationship between life and death.

Montien Boonma, Araya Rasdjarmrearnsook

Turkey

Chalayan's approach to the moving image primarily reveals his ability to associate and make territorial and spatial correlations, for designed objects and garments using a surrealist idiom. The cinematic image gives him a fluid and transient medium to surpass the rigidity of the installation – a requisite for displaying his designs. In any case, the raison d'être of his designs has always been more philosophical and conceptual than utilitarian and commercial. Likewise, his fashion shows always had a sense of performance and tended to deviate toward an unnatural aesthetic that explores the different strategies and subversions irreconcilable with the opinions of the fashion world. Half-naked models garbed in traditional Muslim dresses parading down the catwalk (*Between*, 1998) or in dresses made of glass only to be shattered with mallets. At the end of the show are instances of transgressive acts that speak the idiom of contemporary art rather than that of contemporary fashion.

In his films we can discern different layers of narration, with strong connotations to his autobiography as a Turkish Cypriot and as a nomad between worlds. He does not hesitate to 'quote' his ethnicity in his short films when he showcases his quasi-kitsch T-shirt designs that depict an ancient battle fought in a modern holiday resort or when we see a map of Cyprus being assembled out of broken pieces of coffee cups. Yet it would be misleading to read his films as 'ethnic', for they are primarily surrealist and futuristic.

They are surrealist because the fragments of semi-autobiographical narratives used in them are not markers of an identity politics but rather the archaeological remnants of unconscious, hallucinated half-memories. In his films, the fragments of half-remembered realities and reconstructed dreams are enacted as scenes of condensation and displacement (to recall Freud's concept of 'over determination') in a series of rituals that involve bizarre devices (e.g. furniture with modular and alterable functions). The space design and the multifarious mise-en-scène paradoxically reveal a suppressed longing, eroticism and obsession that lie beneath the facade of the futuristic life-style and the graceful and androgynous human figure. Yet, the designed interiors and furniture also create an inherent sense of regularity that, in turn, contributes to an omnipresent balance in the progression and tone of the narrative. This juxtaposition creates an ambiguity and insecurity that is deliberately left unresolved by Chalayan. His works are futuristic in the sense that Tarkovsky's *Solaris* is. *Solaris* is a portrait of man's inequitable, often destructive interaction with his environment. Like Tarkovsky, Chalayan also uses curvilinear structures, confined spaces, or insurmountable landscapes. The title of Chalayan's present work is *Genometrics*, which precisely expands this concept to a Lacanian reading of the signified and the signifier. In this Venice Biennale project he deals with the tantalizing issue of identity as DNA and geographical environment. He opens the argument on how certain identities can or cannot adapt to new environments and generates a research-based narration for his cross-disciplined installation with filmic images and sculptures. There is serious research behind the end product, which is a film displaying the interplay of the real and the imagined with a series of collected clothes and digitally deformed crystallized garments. A DNA extraction process from the clothes of unknown people, an anthropological evaluation of this material and a 3D manipulation all treated through the London sound-scape intricately reveals Chalayan's approach to the ubiquitous dilemma of identity.
Beral Madra

COMMISSIONER
Beral Madra

ARTIST
Hussein Chalayan

COORDINATING PRODUCER
Murat Pilevneli

SPONSOR
TURQUALITY ®
Garanti Bank
shop&miles&club

1-5 Hussein Chalayan, *Place To Passage*, 2003.
Dur.: 12' 10''

1

2

3

4

5

Ukraine
Your Children, Ukraine!

'Don't shout of the entire world – tell about your village, so that the entire world could hear' (Milos Forman).

The concept is very simple: 'Don't shout of the entire world – tell about your village'.

The whole global world consists of separate villages. It would be sad to lose this endless variety, this luxury of nuances, dialects, sounds, tastes and fragrances. Mykola Babak speaks 'in Voronyn dialect': photos, dolls and national pictures of his native village Voronyntsi, in the Chornobayivskyi region of Cherkasy oblast.

'Don't shout of the entire world – tell about your village', – these words by old Forman will shine on the wall in the half dark entrance hall (slide). There won't be almost anything else – and these words fall into the subconscious.

On the walls – authentic black & white photos of children of the 1920s-1950s in Voronyntsi village, the artist's parents in their youthful 50s, christenings, funerals – the whole of life.

It is not a computer – Babak works with the same authentic photographic engineering of those times – he makes another photograph, enlarges it, develops it. He puts the whole – conostasis together from animated photos – as the men of Cherkassy used to do. The photos in real, wooden, 'village' frames of those times are combined in an assemblage with the native pictures and pieces of embroidery from the artist's collection.

Among the photos on display are dolls on a wooden pedestal. 'It's Mara', shows the artist, 'my grandmother was frightening me for disobedience with this doll.'

The sounds – the noise of grass and inflorescence, chirring crickets, the barely-heard melodies of a brass band – are the sounds of childhood.

Hall 2. Video projects – one on each wall. You are in an environment of Kiev in November–December 2004. The children grew older, came to Kiev and made revolution. The separate slide – hundreds of tablets on the square among them – 'Voronyntsi , Cherkashchyna'.

The sound – the voice of Maydan, the music of revolution.

'The future grows from the past', – as is said today in Venice.

Oleksiy Tytarenko

COMMISSIONER
Viktor Hamatov

CURATOR
Oleksiy Tytarenko

ARTIST
Mykola Babak

ORGANIZATION
Ministry of Culture
and Tourism of Ukraine

Mykola Babak, *Your Children,*
Ukraine!, 2004. Photography,
assemblage, object, wooden
frames; 70 × 55 cm,
114 × 90 cm

Hungary
An Experiment in Navigation

An Experiment in Navigation by Balázs Kicsiny

The peculiar existence of Venice is the theme interpreted in the assembled works of Balázs Kicsiny. Instead of the usual national or artistic self-representation, this artist from a landlocked Central European country comments on the position symbolised by Venice, which characterises European thinking: the linear approach to space/time and the ideology of expansion and progress. Balazs Kicsiny was faced with the problem represented by a country without sea for the first time during his stay in Great Britain, where he encountered the cultural background of a western civilisation surrounded by water. He consequently experienced the relation between travel, shipping, trade, colonisation, migration, settling, foreignness, belief and various layers of time.

The idea of the exhibition is to query our common agreement and approach to space, time and orientation, and the potential representation of this in visual, plastic and spatial terms. The series of objects Kicsiny has applied here, like the anchor, the pyjamas, the cassock, the chain, the trunk and even the accessories of deep water diving, can be interpreted as a reference to Venice, a utopian city of European cultural history.

The four artefacts of the exhibition entitled *An Experiment in Navigation* represent the following concepts:
- the paradox of a linear approach to time in *The Cobbler's Apprentice*
- the paradox of the impossibility of experiencing space objectified in *Winterreise*
- the negative allegory of the existence of a home in *Sweet Home*
- the illustration of the controversial nature of profane and sacred aspects of society in *Pump Room*

The starting point of the exhibition itinerary is the video work entitled *The Cobbler's Apprentice*. The moving picture of the video defines and at the same time counterpoints the stillness of the subsequent works, which are layers of present time stiffened in motionlessness. The clock, composed specifically for human figures, indicates the obvious finite-infinite nature of time.

The second station is the first large room on the left, containing Winterreise – a work of art concerned with orientation, localisation and the metaphor of direction and counter direction. It calls one's attention to circumstances in which a fairly large community has to face the past and the future at a time when various fundamental changes are taking place. Directions are queried – what is right and what is wrong or what is good and what is bad: even those basic values. This work of art symbolises leaving a relative coordinate system that has always been thought of as absolute, and the relative loss of one's skills of orientation and certainty of consciousness. The title comes from Schubert's song cycle entitled *Winterreise*, the first line of which is: 'I've arrived as an alien, and now I depart as such'.

The formal solution of Sweet Home is associated with the heart of a beehive. In the middle of the space there is an archetypal figure representing the traveller. This beehive-headed human figure, wrapped in chains and dragging anchors and a trunk, is a negative allegory of the evangelical prodigal-son story, of orientation and domestication. All the motifs of this work – the beehives, the anchors and the chains – are gathered around the sacred and profane symbols

COMMISSIONER
Julia Fabényi

CURATOR
Péter Fitz

ARTIST
Balázs Kicsiny

www.biennale2005.hu

1

of the notion of journey and home, and represent a series of contradictions such as mobility/immobility, home/homelessness, separation/home-coming, familiarity/unfamiliarity.

Pump Room is a representation of paradoxes and notional allegories. It is a depiction of wakefulness and dream, of vulnerability and immunity; it is the state of being defenceless against the elements and of being dependent on water and air. It also embodies the duality of being thrown into the middle of a society and a sense of alienation at the same time.

The works Balázs Kicsiny has assembled here under the name of *An Experiment in Navigation* approach the metaphor of orientation with dramatic iconography.

Péter Fitz

Translated by Brigitta Kovács

2

Uruguay

Deep Connotations in a Feminine Key
Lacy Duarte and Her Work of Art

Lacy Duarte's (1937) artistic career began in 1962. During the 1970s she devoted herself to tapestry; since 1986 she has focused on painting and since 1996 on both painting and installation.

Since 1986 she has favoured the irrational, the emotional self, psycho-sexual problems and personal mythologies in order to express herself in highly chromatic painting. She has also used loud, distorted images in the very violent, neo-expressionist series *Rituales, Mitos, Espejos y Mentiras* (Rituals, Myths, Mirrors and Lies) (1990), in which she embodies solitary feminine beings locked up in enclosed, confined spaces, with boxed-up faces and in attitudes of self-sufficiency.

Lacy Duarte poses problems relating to women's limitations and growing up. In 1996 she radically changed her palette and type of expression, endeavouring to deal with other topics, always subjectively, without abandoning the feminine one. She approaches the world of her rural childhood, particularly the home-made toys made by her mother with loaves and logs, in a subtle, sensitive key. Since then she has devoted herself to exploring the rural world from which she comes, a memory of rural sensations, of poverty at home; very crude, coarse elements, of helplessness in the country.

She also makes three-dimensional works like *Juego de la Memoria: Mulita y Caballito* (Memory Game: Little Armadillo and Little Horse) and she integrates many of these with her installations.

Ceibos y Panes and *Hecha la ley, hecha la trampa*, two fundamental examples of her line of development, combine object creation with painting. Lacy Duarte gives an important role to object-building, to some extent recovering her skill as tapestry maker, though in this case to mould sui generis traps. She depicts a series of units that evoke the coarse, very primitive snares used in the Uruguayan countryside, using natural materials with earthy echoes, such as raw leather, pieces of wood, lianas and tree branches.

She paints sackcloth, using natural elements like prickly pear molasses and vegetal juices. The artist identifies herself with the trapped animals. She raises certain connotations relating to the daily drama of existence and to those traps set for us and the ones we set ourselves. And, while evoking those traps, she still refers to actions connected with aggression in capture, violence in chaining and the pain of confinement.

In another installation, *Las Manos Limpias* (Clean Hands), Lacy Duarte meta-phorically rebuilds the slaughtering of sheep, animals with which we associate suffering and the weak, generating a version of a 'bretes' which means – according to the Spanish dictionary – the 'place where cattle are marked and slaughtered'. This installation reminds us - both explicitly and indirectly – of taming actions, dominance, strength, elimination, limitation and imprisonment.

COMMISSIONER/CURATOR
Alicia Haber

CURATOR
Olga Larnaudie

ARTIST
Lacy Duarte

ORGANIZATION
Ana Campanella
Carlos Frasca
Diego Masi

www.elpais.com.uy/muva/
http://muva.elpais.com.uy/
LACYDUARTE/

Lacy Duarte refers to other butchery and further sufferings. God's lamb. The world's lambs. Life's lambs.

For this Biennial in Venice, in *Territorios/Territorio* she alludes to the rural woman by means of *Las Traperas* (the popular name for very humble, home-made quilts used in the country). In these works in paper on linen she uses knitting and the fantasy of her rural, childhood world, mentioning warmth in shelter; bread toys, with which she connotes feeding and tells of healing and relief; and earth and mud, with which everything concerning maternity and the feminine gains omnipresence.

Alicia Haber

Venezuela
Love, Warmth and Colour of Little Venice

Love, Warmth and Colour of Little Venice
Venezuelan Designs by Santiago Pol

The graphic artist, quite rightly the maker of posters, is a man who helps to construct the identity of cities and thus offers other (reading) alternatives to the architectural space. Nevertheless, the relationship between the designer and his or her natural environment is a symbiosis.

The wall and the paper, the stand and the advertisement, the logo and the institution are all part of the same discourse. One is intertwined with the other, both feed off one another, given the fact that posters, the graphic identity of companies, and even stamps have been conceived, designed and produced for a specific, previously defined climate, colour, light and form of expression.

The urban environment is always changing. At the same time, it is a condition for the artist who transforms it.

Santiago Pol has said many times: 'If Venezuela did not exist, I would not exist as a designer'. His long career as a poster designer rests on his obsession with thinking about, smelling, tasting, touching and listening to the places where he will ultimately place his work. His obsession with representing words, the client's good or bad moods, the noises, temperature and population density of a particular street or place, movie theatre, theatre or the Caracas subway, translates into hundreds of pages drafted by hand in order to synthesise all this in a of the above in a poster.

He is a visual and mass social communicator, eclectic and unpredictable; strongly connected to his daily environment. He carries in his works all the love, warmth and colour of his country, which he examines and studies thoroughly like a graphic mastiff.

His mission is to reach the other, that individual who may walk by without care. That person is a potential target for a visual hit that will inspire reflection.

Pol's Little Venice (The Italian meaning of Venezuela) is not only a disorganised, fertile, complicated, high-contrast country, where he lives. It is a land of pile-dwellings built on its people's emotions. It is also the canvas on which he has worked for over 40 years. He has seen it up and down, inside and out. He has represented this country in different formats and media and created its iconography based on impossible objects. When he speaks through his works about other cultures he does it with the same warmth, colour and love. This makes him a universal Venezuelan citizen; an artist who overcomes linguistic barriers and time constraints in order to reach everyone, at any time.

The exhibit prepared to represent this visual communicator at the Biennale di Venezia summarises the rich, deep relationship between his creativity and the visual and emotional landscape of his country.

Nevertheless, nothing will be available for mere observation, this Little Venice, within the larger Venice, is a graphic experience to be navigated.

Humberto Valdivieso

COMMISSIONER
Vivian Rivas Gingerich

CURATORS
Eduardo Gil
Carlos Pou
Humberto Valdivieso

DEPUTY COMMISSIONER
Katherine Chacón

ARTIST
Santiago Pol

1

2

1 Santiago Pol, *Le Chapeau Melon*, 1999. Lithographic print; 90.3 × 61.5 cm. Courtesy Carlos Suárez

2 Santiago Pol, *Biennale Brno*, 2002. Lithographic print; 64 × 46 cm. Courtesy Bienal de Brno

3 Santiago Pol, *Paris is a Party*, 2001. Lithographic print; 90 × 61 cm. Courtesy AGI

3

Central Asian Academy of Art

Art of Central Asia. The Current Archive

The art of Kazakhstan, Kyrgyzstan and Uzbekistan is probably the last region not clearly defined on the artistic map of the world. The current exhibition – the first Central Asia Pavilion at the Biennale di Venezia – is the first attempt to fill this gap.

The need for this action is motivated not only by the cultural and historical richness, and the ethnic and artistic originality of these countries, but primarily by the fact that this region is a part of modernity. Being subjected to Soviet modernisation, Central Asia was an active participant in the fundamental collisions and historic experience of the twentieth century, while the collisions and experience of the post-communist era have made it a fully fledged participant in the global order. This is also true of art: having been linked to the artistic reform of the Russian historic avant-garde, the art of Central Asia has more recently created its own original context, its own version of the current artistic debate.

The search for identity was the first of the current problems faced by the artists of Central Asia, being from countries that had only recently proclaimed their sovereignty. The mythical-poetic narrative has been actively exploited by artists from different generations: from Rustam Khalfin, the founder and patriarch of the Almaty art scene, to his young follower Almagul Menlibaeva. Appealing to the national-ethnic archetypes – steppa, nomadism, the Sufi tradition, etc. – this narrative however rejected the pretence of authenticity and was presented as a construction; it was created and immediately denied. For example, the personal mythology of Vjaceslav Akhunov also involves the icons of Soviet propaganda, such as the pyramids of busts of Lenin and the icons of western consumerism: the tattered Coca-cola advertisement. The primordial shamanism of Said Atabekov includes post-modern motifs: the Kalashnikov machine gun or the shapes of policemen on the paving.

On the other hand, the national myth is not only the construction of the artists, but also of the new political power, before which artists such as Victor and Elena Vorobyov, for example, take up a position of detached analysis and deconstruction. The mythology of power, as shown by the work of Sergei Maslov, shields the hard reality of survival. But this does not have a national identity: survival is universal. And it is in precisely this opening up to the universal, as Muratbek Dzhumaliev and Gulnara Kasmalieva assert, that the paradoxical positiveness of the dramatic post-Soviet experience lies.

But the artists of Central Asia's understanding of the universal dimension is contradictory, as is their understanding of national identity. For Erbosin Medilbekov the universal is reached by the rejection of identity in self-denial and self-flagellation. For Alessaned Nikolaev, the only one accessible to us, the universal is the globalised cultural industry, which also imposes stereotyped identities. For Roman Maskaliev and Maksim Boronilov identity and the universal are not contradictory, they are blended in the existential and philosophical experience of 'the road'.

These are some of the themes and names that can be found in the current archive of Central Asian art.
Viktor Misiano

COMMISSIONER
Churek Djamgercinova

CURATOR
Viktor Misiano

ARTISTS

KAZAKHSTAN
Rustam Khalfin
& Yulia Tikhonova
Sergey Maslov (1962-2002)
Yelena Vorobyeva
& Viktor Vorobyev
Yerbossyn Meldibekov
Almagul Menlibayeva
Said Atabekov

KYRGYZSTAN
Gulnara Kasmalieva
& Muratbek Djoumaliev
Roman Maskalev
& Maxim Boronilov

UZBEKISTAN
Alexander Nikolaev
Vyacheslav Ahunov
& Sergey Tichina

www.kurama-art.com

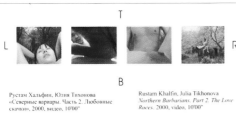

T

L ◻ ◻ ◻ ◻ R

B

Рустам Хальфин, Юлия Тихонова
«Северные варвары. Часть 2. Любовные
скачки», 2000, видео, 10'00"

Rustam Khalfin, Julia Tikhonova
*Northern Barbarians. Part 2. The Love
Races.* 2000, video, 10'00"

1

2

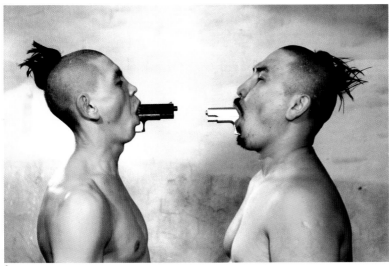

3

1 Rustam Khalfin & Yulia
Tikhonova, *Northern
Barbarians, Part. 2 The Love
Races*, 2000. Video; 10'.

2 Sergey Maslov, *Baikonur - 2*,
2002. Installation, slide, film

3 Yerbossyn Meldibekov,
Pastan, 2002. Video, multiplex

4 Yelena Vorobyeva & Viktor Vorobyev, *Blue period*, 2002-2005. Color photographs (more than 100 color photographs)

5 Almagul Menlibayeva, *Vagon*. Video

6 Said Atabekov, *Neon Paradise*, 2004. Video; 10'. Courtesy the Artist

7 Gulnara Kasmalieva & Muratbek Djoumaliev, *To the future...*, 2005. Author proof. Two screen video film; 6', DVD. Two video projectors (minimum 2000 Ansi lum, audio out), two DVD players, one audio

8-10 Roman Maskalev & Maxim Boronilov, *Paris*, 2004. Video, mp and G4; 23'

4

5

6

7

8

9

10

11

11 Alexander Nikolaev, *I want to Hollywood*, 2004. Video, photography, documents

12 Vyacheslav Ahunov & Sergey Tichina, *Corner*, 2004. DVD; 10'. Courtesy the Artists

12

IILA - Istituto Italo-Latino Americano
The Weft and the Warp

The Weft and the Warp: the canvas. This rather open and stimulating title allows different positions to be represented and the user to communicate with the diversity of beliefs and symbols; with the landscapes (cultural and urban), fears, concerns, dramas and violence; with the poetry (of everyday objects and environments), beauty, creativity, humour and, especially, the art of our continent.

Such variety requires wisdom to coexist; and 'the existence of a thing while another already exists' is the theme broached by Donna Conlon in *Coexistencia*. In 2003 Conlon made a video that is a kind of parade of nations, a protest for peace. The actors are worker ants and the screenplay starts with observation of the behaviour of ants in the forest that 'embraces' her adopted city, Panama.

The threads of the weft and the warp recall the rich tradition of Andean fabrics in the work of Joaquín Sánchez. Bolivia is one of the countries that have most retained the pre-Hispanic and colonial tradition of weaving. Aware of this, Sánchez turns her eye to the folk production still linked to a rural world that is gradually being dismantled, and makes an updated plastic proposal. She proposes local cultural content with the monumental balls of vicuna and llama wool, offering a new interpretation of a still-valid reality in the mixed spirit of the continent, through a fertile dialogue between erudite art and folk art. Her work reveals an intense desire to recover the arts of weaving and insert them into Bolivian art. Burying the threads of the balls in the ground, she speaks to us of 'mother earth', of the union of the arts with the most profound part of being, of creation.

The installation by Guiomar Mesa is also based on forms of folk expression. With his *Palos de lluvia* (Rain Poles), Mesa reveals the profound sense of music – an essential element in demonstrations of the Bolivian soul – pride of race and respect for nature. The rain pole (*palo de lluvia* in Spanish-speaking countries, pāu de chuva in the Portuguese of Brazil) is a native poetic tool made of dried cactus or branches filled with shells or seeds. When they are shaken they emit a delicious and absorbing sound of rain. Guiomar Mesa – a painter who has the rare privilege of having experienced Latin American art and architecture since childhood – takes a bundle of cactus poles, typical of her land, and paints them with faces, bodies, expressions of her race, de-codifying and re-codifying myths and symbols of the collective imagination.

1

CURATOR/COMMISSIONER
Irma Arestizábal

ASSISTANT COMMISSIONER
Alessandra Bonanni

ARTISTS

BOLIVIA
Guiomar Mesa
Joaquín Sánchez

CHILE
Gonzalo Díaz

COLOMBIA
Juan Manuel Echavarría
Oswaldo Macià
Oscar Muñoz

COSTA RICA
Cecilia Paredes
Jaime David Tischler

CUBA
Los Carpinteros

EL SALVADOR
Luis Paredes

GUATEMALA
Luis González Palma

HAITI
Maxence Denis

PANAMA
Donna Conlon

PARAGUAY
Mónica González

PERU
Luz María Bedoya

DOMINICAN REPUBLIC
Polibio Díaz

ORGANIZATION
Paola Pisanelli

WITH THE CONTRIBUTION OF
Centro Cultural del BID - Banco Interamericano de Desarrollo, Washington, USA

www.iila.org (Actividades culturales, Bienal de Venecia)

2   3

The European baroque found fertile ground in the American continent, where it was recontextualised and adapted, acquiring new iconographies, symbologies and values. Faithful to this cultural characteristic, the Guatemalan Luis González Palma proposes a baroque that allows a double reading of fusion and excess, the pleasure of the senses and the presence of the past and history that merge in allegory and metaphor.

In *La luz de la mente* (The Light of the Mind) González Palma has chosen an emblematic historical contrivance to examine the experience of the body, the realistic argument, the constitution of individual and public memory and to oblige us to reflect on the power of the look, on the pleasure of touch and on art as transmitters of thoughts. *The paño de pudor* (Pudenda Covering) of famous crucifixions, generally by artists who have had a major influence on colonial art (El Greco, Velázquez, Zurbarán), by way of originals, copies or etchings brought by the colonisers, are photographed as the single, main object, which takes on new meanings, another symbolic dimension, its own specific volume and its own light.

Making obvious reference to pictorial structures, González Palma photographs life-size models that he himself has made in fabric, starting from the clothes of those portrayed. He prints them on gold to recreate a series of twenty-first-century religious images and stages them in the spaces of the sumptuous piano nobile of the Palazzo Franchetti.

There is also room for the scream in the complex fabric of the Latin American world, when, in a series of videos without conceptual expedients, Juan Manuel Echavarría captures the simple, noble declaration of the inhabitants of the Pacific coast and the Colombian Caribbean, who recount their suffering in song. They are outcast farmers and prisoners of the drugs war that in Colombia has caused the forced exile of more than two million people. These singers, mainly Afro-Colombians, sing of the violence, represent years of conflict in their native Colombia and, in a kind of cathartic act, recount their suffering and their own story, like troubadours who sing their tragedies.

Echavarria gives a metaphorical title to his work, which he calls *Bocas de ceniza* (Mouths of Ashes) the name of the mouths of the río Magdalena, where the bodies of the war victims thrown into its waters converge.

Mixing low- and high-tech, Maxence Denis 'documents' the reality of life and the violence suffered in the capital Port-au-Prince and throughout the country

4

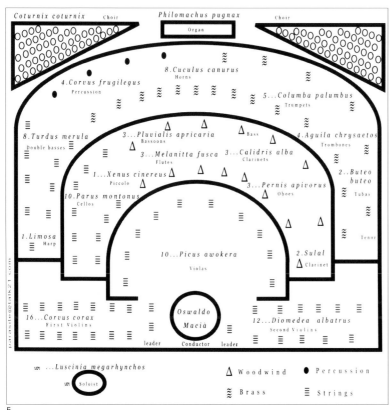

5

in 2004 and still today with his video-installation *Kwa Bawon*. This 'mosaic' of
the traditional and the contemporary is accompanied by a soundtrack
composed by Laurent Lettrée, a blend of sounds, concrete music, noises and
voodoo drums and songs.

The installation is dedicated to Baron Samedi, the 'caretaker' of the cemeteries,

6

7

8

to the victims of the atrocity of civil wars in his suffering country, to the defenders of human rights and to the city of his birth.

The urban environment is crucial to the whole process of codifying contemporary Latin American culture. There is an evident cultural construction that succumbs to the camera and that consciously or unconsciously determines the framing, the focus and the composition. Polibio Díaz portrays and interprets the modus vivendi of the poorest inhabitants of the Dominican Republic in his photographic montages, in sizes similar to the architecture of the places portrayed. These people face a sustainable economic situation thanks only to the incredible vitality and joy that distinguishes them.

By introducing them to the most intimate and public spaces, showing a conception and style of life that become portraits of the national conscience, with a marked assertion of their African background, Polibio Díaz draws us near to Dominican life and the national and cultural identity. We cross the room where visitors are received, the common dormitories, the kitchen. All are covered in ornaments that fill the furniture and walls in a kind of tropical *Wunderkammer*.

Los Carpinteros also portray the customs of their island. They have been analysing life in pre- and post-revolutionary Cuba with intelligent parodies since their first appearance in the 1980s. As they themselves declared at the beginning of their career, there is a need to choose between a form of left-leaning art and folk art. They are not interested in either of these directions. They want to make something completely different from the ruling atmosphere and thus choose to make pieces that at first glance make them seem like restorers. These works are made with impeccable technique, according to the traditional rules of the cabinet maker, with great virtuosity that seeks the perfect metaphor in every piece. They are objects ennobled by good design, that assert themselves in the border area between furniture and architecture, and are

6 Oscar Muñoz, *Re/trato*, 2003. Video still; 28'. Collection of Daros Latinamerica, Zurich

7 Jaime David Tischler, *Domingo y árbol*, 1997 (2002). Enlarged silver print of selenium, sepia and gold toning, starting from a destoyed negative; 120 × 120 cm. Collection of the artist

8 Cecilia Paredes, *Gàrgolas*, 2002. 3 photographs printed on acetate; dimension variable. Collection of the artist

9   10

ironically and elegantly transformed into metaphors of existential problems.
The richness of the flora and fauna of Latin America, the grandiose nature of its spaces and its virgin landscapes have always attracted the traveller and the observer, and have radically marked its inhabitants.

The exuberance of the fauna, which we have already seen in Donna Conlon's video *Coexistencia*, is also present in *Something Going On Above My Head*, the symphony by Oswaldo Macià, who conducts a concert involving 2000 bird calls collected from ornithological archives and audio libraries all over the world. Arranged as if in an orchestra, violins, cellos, flutes, clarinets, oboes, percussion, trumpets, trombones… This sound sculpture uses 16 soundtracks, allowing us to hear 500 African birds, 500 Asiatic birds, 500 European birds and 500 American birds every 30 minutes, creating the sound frame in the gardens of the Palazzo Franchetti on the Grand Canal, at the foot of the Ponte dell'Accademia, where the viewers 'navigate'.

And, speaking of birds, we cannot but pause on the parrot woman who, for an instant, is the artist Cecilia Paredes, following a symbiotic road between man and nature with metaphor, putting us into the skins of animals and plants in danger of extinction, like life itself.

The work presented here is accompanied by a wonderful *guacamayos* feather cape, legacy of Aztec capes and the brother of plumes, necklaces and breast straps. These are the arts and crafts of our pre-Colombian forebears and the peoples that still conserve this sublime art, in a paradigm of unparalleled admiration and respect for nature and ecological balance.

The challenge of the complex space of the palazzo encourages the artist to adapt the other work to it: the gutters merge with the glass of the windows, becoming part of the neo-gothic facade, participating in the movement of the interior space during the day and facing provocatively onto the Grand Canal during the night.

The power and immensity of the American landscape are reflected in *Arroyito* (Stream) by Mónica González, who allows her love of the river, the importance of water in the life of her country and the 'fear that its water-bearing Guaraní will disappear' shine through in this work. These are also evident in the minimal landscapes in the photographs of Luz María Bedoya and Luis Paredes, who manage to capture the horizon of the sea, the immensity of the pampas, the salt lagoon, the desert and the grandiose nature of the sky.

Mónica González takes possession of the Palazzo Franchetti gardens and, 'ascending' from the Grand Canal, moves along an irregular route with her stream of glasses of water on the green of the lawn along the garden paths. Glass, light and water, already used in her previous works, are now seen as an

9 Los Carpinteros, *Siesta*.
Rocking chair and cushions;
335 × 62 × 70.5 cm.
Collection Cisneros

10 Luis Paredes, *Interference*,
2005 (detail). Installation
of photo projection; dimension
variable. Collection of the artist

example of transparency and visual clarity.

Luz María Bedoya brings to Venice an operation she had previously developed in Dublin (Eire), Lima (Peru) and Porto Alegre (Brazil). It consists of leaving messages written on sheets of paper in cracks in the walls of the streets, which 'will end up dissolving into the urban fabric'. The city experienced by the artist is adopted, like a 'labyrinth whose points of inflection are the holes in the walls: they mark the path, a continuity of detours'[1]. A video records the moment the message is inserted, the penetration of the paper in the wall, of language in the city. A simple photograph album documents the result of the action.

The definition of what is Latin American is traditionally based on very tangible spatial references[2]. In Venice Luis Paredes overlays screenings of his *horizontes* – the same image but with inverted values (negative on positive and vice versa). The participant, passing between both, becomes actor and part of the installation and the landscape, separating the two visual values and twisting the sound into a constant tone that gives the projection room its atmosphere.

The work deals with the phenomenon of interference as a voluntary/involuntary act that takes place only because it exists/is. It is an action that interferes actively or passively at every moment and at every level of physical and psychological perception.

The ephemeral nature of time, the universal feeling about time and death is also poetically represented in the works of Oscar Muñoz and Jaime David Tischler, and in many others in the already cited series by Luis González Palma; time as a moving route in which its inexorable and unlocatable movement flows. It is a time, in the art of the twenty-first century, that lacks a single organising perspective, where other visions, other subjects and other themes multiply.

Before Tischler's work we watch the taking flight of an image which, in theory,

11

12

13 Donna Conlon, *Coexistence (Coexistencia)*, 2003. Video DVD, registered on mini-DVs; 5' 26" loop. Collection of the artist

14 Mónica González, *Arroyito*, 1997. Installation made of glasses; approx. lenght 10 m. Collection of the artist. Photo Mónica González, 2002

13

14

should portray a moment for ever, fix it here and now. But the slow disappearance of the photo in the bath full of water underscores the rarefied material nature of that which is visual. The installation acts as if it were a 'time machine', as if the image projected were the 'fluctuating oracle' of that which is slowly decaying to the sound of Yiddish music.

Tischler stamps the photographs from the series *Miedo a la muerte* (Fear of Death) that surround the installation on sepia and gold paper, creating a kind of central 'altar' where time acts.

In the work presented in Venice, Oscar Muñoz inquires into the limits of drawing, or better, the limits of the 'process of drawing'. A hand tries to depict an image with water, used like ink, on a stone heated by the sun. The hand stubbornly repeats the same futile action, as the artist tries to indicate the constant attempt to construct an image, the sketching that continues to reconstruct the lines erased by the heat which, naturally, will never be the same. This is the reason for the title of the work (*Re/trato*). It is both a reflection on the (self) portrait, on intention and on perseverance[3]. A 'portrait' that dissolves, like drawings in the sand with the rising sea water, and goes back to being reconstructed in the looping of the video.

Magnificent warp that strengthens and brings together everything is art. While Luis González Palma is concerned with space and Cecilia Paredes adapts her works to the space of the windows, Gonzalo Díaz, with *Muerte en Venecia* (Death in Venice), makes a genuine intervention on the place assigned to him. With a style I think may be defined as 'obliqueness', Díaz establishes a regime of allusions as the constituent weft of the work and determines the nature of the installation space, ensuring that the building functions as a frame for itself.

Frisco disfecto - Lima

Nother lingdom - Dublin

Funo de die - Lima

Na sabinha delafanada - Porto Alegre

15

15 Luz María Bedoya, *Muro*, 2005. Video and book of pictures; 44'. Collection of the artist

16 Polibio Díaz, *Pasiones interiores*, 2002. Scanned color photograph; 106 × 480 cm. V Bienal del Caribe Prize, 2003. Collection of the artist

The letters that make up the word ARTE are tanks containing goldfish: eight in A, five in R, three in T and 2 in E, according to an inverted segment of the Fibonacci series. In *Muerte en Venecia* (Death in Venice) the work is not only made up of the letters but also the water, which moves thanks to technical purification devices, the swimming of the fish, the red colour, the reflections of the Murano glass chandelier, the light coming in through the windows, the decorations in the room and the reflections that come in from the Grand Canal, which invite us back out, restoring vision, reflection and art to the city.
Irma Arestizábal

[1] Statement made by the artist to Irma Arestizábal.
[2] J.A. Molina, 'Escenarios', *Mapas abiertos*.
[3] Regarding the theme, see J. Roca, *Oscar Muñoz: Re/trato*, catalogue text, Cali, 2004.

16

Collateral events

Atelier aperti
Controluce

Atelier aperti

In connection with the 51st International Art Exhibition, the studios of the Accademia di Belle Arti di Venezia are being opened to the public, presenting a selection of recent works by students and graduates. Painting, sculpture, drawing, design, photography, plastic arts and works made with new digital and multimedia technologies are being presented to the visitor in the places they are made, among the work materials and tools.

Materials and procedures became increasingly decisive in art production over the last century, and in some respects an integral part of the work itself. In contrast with this trend, the logic of presenting the finished 'piece', removed from the process that gave it form, largely dominates in the exhibition process. The studios of the Venice academy, refurbished in 2002 in their new premises, a sixteenth-century charitable institute facing onto the Giudecca canal, are being opened to highlight the procedures that lead from the project and materials to the work, and to show off the different lines of research that every workshop follows. The five studios for painting, six for anatomy, two for sculpture, two for drawing, two for decoration and those for ornamental plastic, restoration and the new art technologies actually follow different directions: from abstract painting to photo-realism, from conceptual art to traditional modelling, from the study of the nude from living models to digital painting, from photography to video. The various procedures and logics that dominate the current art scene are presented in a fascinating update of production techniques and procedures; at times involving total innovation, but more often growing by a process of grafting, underpinned by the ancient, enduring Renaissance and classical roots.

Controluce

Works by students and graduates of the Accademia di Belle Arti are being moved weekly to the Giardini and analysed, along with drawings, designs and materials, as part of a calendar of weekly seminars. The purpose of the meetings is to take the public inside the process of creating a work of contemporary art, which now employs methods and logics that are not adequately understood.

Gloria Vallese

ORGANIZATION
Accademia di Belle Arti
di Venezia
www.accademiavenezia.edu

CURATOR ATELIER APERTI
Gloria Vallese, professor
of history of contemporary art

CURATOR CONTROLUCE
Saverio Simi De Burgis,
professor of history
and methodology of art criticism

1 Martin Emilian Balint, *Alfred Hitchcock's Jellophobia (after the flight of the anorexic ballerinas)*, 2003. Video still

2 Primož Bizjak, *Sarajevo N°2*, 2004. Light-jet print on d-bond; 125 × 157 cm. Courtesy Galleria Andrea Arte Contemporanea, Vicenza

3 Vania Comoretti, *Anima*, 2004. Watercolour, ink and pastel on paper; 49.44 × 56.4 cm. Collection of the Cassa di Risparmio di Venezia. Photo of the artist

4 Elisa Rossi, *Giulia - depilazione*, 2003. Oil on canvas; 50 × 70 cm. Private collection, Vicenza. Courtesy Andrea Arte Contemporanea, Vicenza

1

2

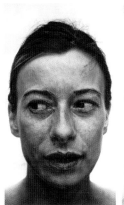

3

4

CHROMOSOMA

Thetis is an engineering company based in the historic Arsenale in Venice. It works in the environment and transport sector, creating innovative technologies and services for the local, national and international market.

Thetis has now been promoting the process of contemporary art for almost a decade – since its opening in the Arsenale – believing there is a similarity between the routes of technological innovation and the experimental ones of art. The Arsenale in Venice offers artists an interesting challenge. Indeed, measuring themselves against the history of a place that has always been a symbol of intelligence and art is a unique and irresistable opportunity.

In these years we have had the pleasure and honour of knowing and working with artists who have made an important contribution to the world of art: Robert Morris, Beverly Pepper and Pinuccio Sciola, to mention just a few.

This year, in line with its philosophy of focusing on young Italian artists, Thetis has the pleasure of hosting the interesting work entitled *Chromosoma* by Enrico Tommaso De Paris
Antonietta Grandesso

Speak of our contemporary way of life, talking of a world that is continuously expanding and constantly changing before our eyes, trying in this way to adapt our minds and souls to the transformations of our daily life and that of the man of the future, changes wrought by social migrations, technology and bio-technologies.

Trying in this fashion to document the so-called 'state of things'; images, sensations, writings that pivot around the man of today thus become stimuli to take action, to suggest the possibility that man may construct a brave new world, a constantly-renewed reality, inventing new metaphors to recognise the new planet.

My work consists in constructing mobiles and fragmented pictorial structures; I organise signals and stimuli in order to construct something with a more scientific than aesthetic, more social than formal character; I feel that, as an artist, this is my function within society.

I explore all aspects of man: rights, needs, dreams and his innate desire for the future. As there are no maps of the future and its outlines are traced by bio-technologies and by the chemical-pharmaceutical and agro-food multi-nationals, it is easy to insert a further vision, to create 'world works'; metaphors that act as conceptual model and not only describe but also predict.

This is because every culture is a synthesis of reality and simulation, a tightly-knit interplay of symbolic references that replace things or round out their essence so that they become an instrument at the service of man.

Today, more than ever before, the world develops at an increasingly faster pace, is modified according to ever more complex schemes that defy representation. Hence the need for open thought, unrestricted by schemes, a 'centre-less' way of thinking like the non-linear logic of electronic languages (flow-chart, feed-back, loop). The messages aim to stimulate the sensitivity with which we must approach the world that surrounds us day-by-day.

The contemporary artist adopts a multiple-logic approach, lives in contact with several material and spiritual realities, with several moments, ways of living,

ORGANIZATION
Thetis
www.thetis.it

CURATOR OF SPAZIO THETIS
Antonietta Grandesso

EXHIBITION CO-ORDINATION
Elena Povellato

IN COLLABORATION WITH
Luca Bich, Mauro Calvone, Francesca Ceradini, Alberto Colombo, Federico De Giuli, Vittorio Del Duca, Massimo Lunardon, Anthony Marasco, Riccardo Mazza, Jean-Claude Oberto, Daniele Perrone, Cristiano Pistis, Alessandro Riva, Alessandro Tosetti

WITH THE CONTRIBUTION OF
Regione Piemonte

WITH THE SUPPORT OF
Ermanno Tedeschi Gallery, Turin
www.etgallery.it
Galleria Traghetto, Venice
www.galleriatraghetto.it

SPECIAL THANKS TO
Edgardo Bianco, Davide Blei, Marco Boglione, Carlo Brignone, Antonella e Carlo Fussotto, Mario Minella, Ernesto Ovazza, Michele Vietti

ARTIST
Enrico Tommaso De Paris

1

2

3

4

constantly changing his point of view in order to increase the energy with which the world imbues him. In his imagination, the artist must exalt the contents of contemporary life and contribute unswerving positivity.... illuminating signals, constructing in-progress works, structures that can be optically reconfigured and are open to various interpretations; there is no beginning or end but a galaxy of meanings; there is no definitive, satisfying univocal key to interpretation; not a random chain of messages but also, not one perspective but many points of view, a representation that speaks loudly of the energy and positivity of the creative power of evolution and of man's potential in the new millennium.

THE *CHROMOSOMA* INSTALLATION IS THE THREE-DIMENSIONAL, POETIC REPRESENTATION OF ONE OF THE MOST IMPORTANT BIOLOGICAL ELEMENTS OF OUR BODY, WHERE THE LIFE OF HUMAN BEINGS DEVELOPS ON A TIME AND STRUCTURAL SCALE, BETWEEN ACTIVE AND PASSIVE GENES. MEMORIES OF OUR FORBEARS (DNA) AND CONTINGENT FACTORS WILL CONSTRUCT THE MAN OF THE FUTURE.
ENRICO T. DE PARIS 2005 ©

Earth's Constructions

The cities, their destiny and their symbolic charge are now the centre of a debate that involves architecture, town planning, cinema, literature and politics. We have learnt that cities rise – as in the early twentieth century utopia of Umberto Boccioni – but can also fall – as was seen in New York in the early twenty first century. There is no better means than painting, in its ability to be contemporary, to grasp and establish in our minds a scenario that is otherwise represented solely by the mass video productions of anonymous, transitory images; incapable of lasting, of narrating.

Croce Taravella has been grandly interpreting the theme of the Painted City for some years now, radicalising the fascination this subject has always had for the imagination of painters. His is a colossal project, implicitly infinite, geographically adventurous: a kind of spectacular planetary recognition of the spirit and the living flesh of places.

So, first of all, the capitals, the big Metropoli: he identifies them and displays them, also to our ability to recognise their essence, like the multi-hued skin of the world. And only the free gesture and his violent way of painting seem to Taravella able to intercept its energy, that inexhaustible flow of actions, movements, thoughts, fears and desires that cross our civilisation.

In contrast to and completion of this, Taravella explores the empty areas of the world, the Deserts. They are imagined as immense areas of decompression, of purification, where nothingness is revealed as a fullness, and the eye and mind re-establish contact with that which there was before history, at the beginning of everything. And which we, confusedly and nostalgically, call origin.

Marco Di Capua

ORGANIZATION
Musei di San Salvatore in Lauro

CURATOR
Sergio Troisi

ARTIST
Croce Taravella

1

2

3

4

1 Croce Taravella, *Mosca 1*,
2005. Mixed technique
on canvas; 133 × 176 cm.
Photo Luciano Schimmenti

2 Croce Taravella, *Patagonia 4*,
2005. Mixed technique
on canvas; 98 × 130 cm.
Photo Luciano Schimmenti

3 Croce Taravella, *Patagonia 2*,
2005. Mixed technique
on canvas; 117 × 157 cm.
Photo Luciano Schimmenti

4 Croce Taravella, *Mosca 3*,
2005. Mixed technique
on canvas; 133 × 176 cm.
Photo Luciano Schimmenti

Emendatio

James Luna: Emendatio

James Luna (b. 1950) is one of the most important and provocative native artists of his generation. Through emotionally compelling performances and installations, he has dramatically expanded the language, territory, and possibilities of Indian art. His work confronts and challenges commonly held perceptions about native Americans. Spoken narratives about the harsh reality of reservation life – infused with humour, irony, and penetrating insight – often incorporate film, music and video. His stories are as specific as his La Jolla reservation in California, yet universal enough to connect with audiences in Tokyo, New York or Saskatoon.

Luna's work for the 2005 Biennale di Venezia is titled *Emendatio*, a Latin word whose English translation is 'emendation'. The definition speaks of 'the act of altering for the better, or correcting what is erroneous or faulty; improvement; removal of errors or corruption'. The work is in three parts: a performance and two installations.

The performance takes place during the first four days of the Biennale in the courtyard garden of the Fondazione Querini Stampalia. The artist employs a ritual structure with visual and audio technological elements. In the performance space, Luna blesses and lays a ritualistic circle of stones, medical vials, syringes and government surplus foods, which speak to the current health plight of many indigenous nations. Luna then begins to dance in place within the circle space on four consecutive hours for four consecutive days as a gesture of sacrifice. Over the course of the performance, Luna adopts a number of distinct personas. The audience is invited to participate in some way, such as offering a prayer, donating an object or perhaps joining in the dance.

The first installation, *Past and Present Apparitions*, challenges the popular notion that there is a discontinuity between the indigenous world of the past and that of the present. A video of Luna and other members of his reservation community, along with photographs contrasting past and present historical images of California Indian life, is projected onto layered screens suspended from the ceiling. Photographs that further question the place of indigenous people in 'popular culture' line the walls. As viewers walk through the installation, they are illuminated by the projections – thus simultaneously conveying the message of *Apparitions* and becoming part of the exhibit itself.

In the second installation, *The Chapel for Pablo Tac*, Luna creates an imagined native place of worship built in honour of Pablo Tac. A Luiseño Indian – the same tribe as Luna – from the San Luis Rey Mission in California, Tac was sent to Rome in 1830 to study for the priesthood, and to be studied by others. Before his death from illness in 1841, Tac produced a written history of the missionisation of his people in California. The installation houses artefacts of the kind that Tac might have possessed or made during his stay at the Vatican, as well as actual Luiseño objects, placed on an altar and in shrine-like vitrines. The interior walls recreate the look of a California mission. Drapes of rabbit fur and deer hide, trimmed with velvet and lace, serve as doors to the chapel. The installation features video images of landscapes and architecture from California and Italy that point up the similarities between the two. Ambient audio includes

ORGANIZATION
Smithsonian's National Museum of the American Indian (NMAI)
www.AmericanIndian.si.edu

CURATORS
Truman Lowe, Curator of Contemporary Art, Smithsonian's National Museum of the American Indian
Paul Chaat Smith, Curator, Smithsonian's National Museum of the American Indian

SPONSOR
Ford Foundation

ARTIST
James Luna

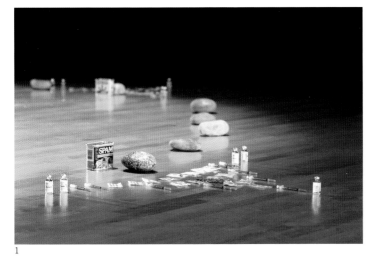

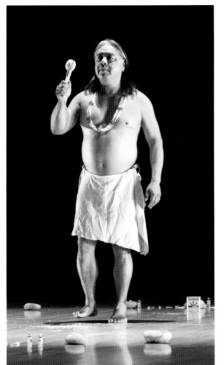

original music and music samples from Luiseño tribal elders, as well as sounds of nature and industry.

Emendatio is a word that Pablo Tac himself may have used when he attempted to correct errors in the way Europeans understood his people. *Emendatio* is a project that collapses the time between 1830 and 2005, and the space between Rome and California. *Emendatio* claims Venice as part of Indian history, and in so doing demonstrates a belief held by James Luna and many other native people: that every place is a native place.

Truman Lowe, Paul Chaat Smith

1-4 James Luna, *Emendatio*, 2005, Rehearsal for the performance. Courtesy the Smithsonian's National Museum of the American Indian. Photos Katherine Fogden

Francesco Vezzoli. *Trilogia della Morte* (Trilogy of Death)

The Fondazione Prada is presenting the *Trilogia della Morte* by Franceso Vezzoli (Brescia 1971) at the Fondazione Giorgio Cini on the occasion of the 51st International Art Exhibition. The work is inspired by some cinematographic works by the Italian poet and director Pier Paolo Pasolini and consists of two installations.

The first is a reconstruction of an old-style movie theatre in which the film entitled *Comizi di Non Amore* (Non Love Meetings, 2004, dvd, 63' 50") is shown continuously. The film was made exclusively for the Fondazione Prada in a television studio following the format of the 'blind date' genre. Here the public are encouraged by a presenter to judge couples of various ages and social backgrounds that are formed before their eyes. The work was conceived as a kind of linguistic reinvention of the documentary *Comizi d'amore* by Pasolini – who in 1964 travelled the length and breadth of Italy asking people of different cultural and social classes questions on love and sex – and is intended to recreate a psychological territory in which the public is urged to speak of themselves and their own point of view on the couple and on love affairs. The difference is that in the case of Pasolini there was a representation of bodies and their sexuality, while with Vezzoli the reference is to the degeneration of culture, the person and sex, which is always based on a relationship of power, between master and slave, television and audience. Inspired by television programmes, *Comizi di Non Amore* is a reality show that has been constructed and edited according to the most classical canons of popular television. Presented by the show-girl Ela Weber in a Rome television studio, the film was made using some of the most acclaimed television technicians, from director to costume manager, producer, stage designer, printer, designer and composer. The female figures, courted by the suitors to form a new couple, are actresses who represent the film world, from Buñuel to Pasolini and from MTV to the soap opera. They are a selection of female cinema icons, including Catherine Deneuve, who in *Belle de jour* (1967) by Luis Buñuel is a woman who embroiders and has very audacious erotic stories, Antonella Lualdi, interviewed by Pasolini in *Comizi d'Amore*, Marianne Faithfull, icon of *Wild Rock*, Terry Schiavo, a former television presenter and media stereotype, and Jeanne Moreau, star of *Jules and Jim* (1961) by François Truffaut, who played Lysiane in *Querelle de Brest* (1982) by Rainer Werner Fassbinder, and is an unforgettable figure in the history of cinema.

The second installation of the *Trilogia della Morte* is entitled *Le 120 sedute di Sodoma* (The 120 Seats of Sodom) and refers to the film *Salò o le 120 giornate di Sodoma* (1975) by Pasolini, a work consisting of 120 black Argyle chairs with embroidered seats designed by Charles Rennie Mackintosh, and by a tapestry *La fine di Canterbury* (The End of Canterbury), woven according to ancient tradition and depicting some erotic scenes from other films by the poet and director. This work will be shown in the early part of the Venetian exhibition while in the latter part it will be replaced by the tapestry *La fine di Edipo Re* (The End of Oedipus the King). The whole speaks both dramatically and ironically to the present and Pasolini's view of Fascism and consumerism.
Germano Celant

ORGANIZATION
Fondazione Prada
www.fondazioneprada.org

ARTISTIC DIRECTOR
Germano Celant

ASSOCIATE CURATOR
Antonella Soldaini

ARTIST
Francesco Vezzoli

1 Francesco Vezzoli, *Le 120 sedute di Sodoma* (The 120 Seats of Sodom), 2004. Laser print on canvas with metallic needlework, Argyle wood chairs; dimension variable; 120 elements, 136 × 47 × 48 cm each. Courtesy Fondazione Prada, Milano. Photo Attilio Maranzano

2-4 Francesco Vezzoli, *Comizi di Non Amore* (Non Love Meetings), 2004. DVD film, 63' 50", colour, stereo sound; dimension variable. Courtesy Fondazione Prada, Milano. Photo Matthias Vriens

1

2

3

4

Games Machine

Annika Eriksson has forged new paths for performative works in various media for a long time. By choosing elements of the undramatic and the quotidian, she has resisted the genre's elevated, theatrical tradition; and by seeking out ways to erase the division between participant and viewer, she has undermined the role-playing of the tradition and the narcissism inherent in the role of the artist. The keenly searching, but also perspicuously questioning conversation has constituted the basis of her work from the video work, *The Collectors*, her loving interpretation of the motivation of various collectors for their passion, to *Arbeitswelt*, the large-scale portrayal of the workplace at a German insurance company. This questioning sometimes creates unease. For the biennial Socle du Monde exhibit in Denmark she did a series of portraits of bus drivers, all with the common denominator of having moved from the country of their birth. Her original intention was to show the pictures – which might best be described as portraits of idols – on the public buses in Copenhagen where the drivers worked. That concept could not be realised, so the pictures were shown only at Hernings Konstmuseum.

Annika Eriksson's works can often be described as condensations and revelations of the underlying relations of a place or situation. But just as often her works are about staging and thereby creating something that is missing – a conversation, an occurrence, arresting the attention of a moment. At Frieze Art Fair, 2004, she created *Do You Want an Audience?*, a 'speakers corner' where singers, entertainers and speakers on many different topics were given space and voice. Her staged situations generate dialogues and grant the observer access to experiences that normally aren't given space in the public sphere.

Games Machine, the work Annika Eriksson has created for IASPIS for the opening of the Venice Biennale, might seem to differ from her earlier work in its conspicuous material and spectacular nature. During a research trip to Venice, she happened upon an amusement hall for young people that had been temporarily set up on the wharf right next to the location of the exhibit. Later, for the opening of the Biennale, she moved the recreation hall back to the exhibit area, and opened the doors to anyone who wanted to play. To get the word out to the area's youth, she had a poster printed that was distributed by other teenagers in the area.

If you can hear beyond the buzzing contemporaneity of the amusement hall, you will recognise the keen sensibility at play in the shaping of a place and an occurrence that so peculiarly characterise Annika Eriksson's works. Here, she reveals an entirely different Venice than the Venice of history and art, a consummately normal place that admits of bored teenagers with nowhere to hang out. She generously creates such a place as a gift to the youth of the area, and offers art observers the possibility of an unexpected encounter, and a glimpse into another world, if we give ourselves a little time to pause on the way to the exhibits of the Biennale.

Sara Arrhenius

ORGANIZATION
IASPIS - International Artists' Studio Program in Sweden
www.iaspis.com

COMMISSIONER
Sara Arrhenius, Director, Bonniers Konsthall, Director of IASPIS from 2001 through 2004

PROJECT MANAGER
Magdalena Malm

ARTIST
Annika Eriksson

1 Annika Eriksson, *Games Machine*, Venice, 2005. Photo Giorgio Boato

2 Annika Eriksson, *Games Machine*, Venice, 2005. Poster. Photo Giorgio Boato

1

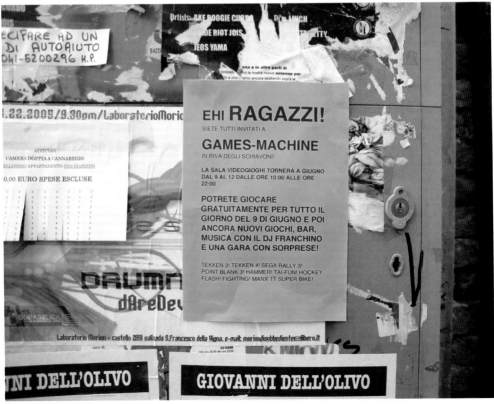

2

Già e non ancora. Artisti per la Liturgia oggi
Arte e Liturgia nel Novecento.
Esperienze europee a confronto

Già e non ancora. Artisti per la Liturgia oggi is the exhibition with which the CEI's national office for culture and the Patriarchate of Venice intend actively participating for the first time in the Biennale. Recognising the need to adapt the spaces and furnishings of churches to the post-council liturgy, 12 emerging artists have been invited to create works for the church of San Lio. This venue is like an original Biennale pavilion where the works are not 'exhibited' but created, with consideration for the historic, artistic and architectural context, and their cultural function.

Churches have always been places of constant transformation and artistic enrichment in their symbiotic relationship with the liturgy and the rites of the Christian community. They are vibrant places in constant transformation, in which art can be expressed in the most up-to-date language, breaking a possibly too long silence and reciprocal diffidence. Devotion and piety are not necessarily linked to stereotypes or consolidated models; education of the believers in new languages and iconographic styles occurs through experience and effort, and not the re-presentation of cliches or standard productions.

Within the limits of this first presentation, the exhibition is a concrete sign that dialogue between the church and the world of artists is alive, that the clients are mature enough to open the doors to new productions, and that research in the sector is supported by study centres and qualified production.

The choice of artists was made by Professors Del Guercio and Bonanno from the academies of Milan and Palermo, Padre Di Bonaventura of the Fondazione Stauros, the artist Padre Tito Amodei and the Sala 1 centre of Rome, all engaged for years in the field of liturgical art.

The liturgy, in tension between the *already* of salvation made by the coming of Christ and the *not yet* of the final salvation of the universe, lends itself to being the place in which art reveals its topicality and its perennial value.

don Gianmatteo Caputo

*Già e non ancora.
Artisti per la Liturgia oggi*
Contemporary sacred art exhibition

ORGANIZATION
Conferenza Episcopale Italiana - Ufficio Nazionale per i Beni Culturali Ecclesiastici,
Patriarcato di Venezia
www.segni-del-9cento.it

CURATOR
don Gianmatteo Caputo

SCIENTIFIC COMMITTEE
mons. Giancarlo Santi - President, Director Ufficio Nazionale per i Beni Culturali Ecclesiastici - Conferenza Episcopale Italiana
don Gianmatteo Caputo, Director Ufficio Promozione Beni Culturali - Patriarcato di Venezia
padre Tito Amodei, Sala 1, Rome
Giovanni Bonanno, Accademia Belle Arti, Palermo
Andrea Del Guercio, Accademia di Brera, Milan
padre Adriano Di Bonaventura, Fondazione Stauros, Isola del Gran Sasso - Teramo

EXHIBITION PROJECT
Maddalena Tomasi

ARTISTS
On invitation
of padre Tito Amodei:
Cosetta Mastragostino
Petric Branislav and Stanisa Dautovic
Luigi Pagano
On invitation
of Giovanni Bonanno:
Antonella Pomara
Elisabetta De Luca
Daniele Franzella
On invitation
of Andrea Del Guercio:
Antonio Spanedda
Stefano Pizzi
Roberto Priod
On invitation of padre Adriano Di Bonaventura:
Giuliano Giuliani
Oleg Supereco
Carlo Marchetti

1

1 Inspection of the artists at the San Lio Church

2 M. Nunes de Almeida, Poblado do Picote Chapel, Portugal, 1956-1958

Arte e Liturgia nel Novecento. Esperienze europee a confronto
Third International Conference

ORGANIZATION
Conferenza Episcopale Italiana - Ufficio Nazionale per i Beni Culturali Ecclesiastici, Patriarcato di Venezia, in collaboration with MART, Museo d'Arte Moderna e Contemporanea di Trento e Rovereto

SCIENTIFIC COMMITTEE
Estèban Fernandez Cobiàn
Frédéric Debuyst
Giorgio Della Longa
Antonio Marchesi
Massimiliano Valdinoci
Walter Zahner

The exhibition and the conference were possible thanks to the support of:
Pontificia Commissione per i beni culturali della Chiesa
MiBAC - Ministero per i Beni e le Attività Culturali
Regione del Veneto
Provincia di Venezia
Comune di Venezia

Arte e Liturgia nel Novecento. Esperienze europee a confronto. The great moments in the history of art are marked by the meeting of great artists with the church, an enlightened client. The artistic works of the past, in that they are contextually present in the liturgical habitat, have played a role that is inseparably linked to the liturgy.

But there has been a break and it has not been left unmentioned. Artistic research is often enclosed in increasingly personal and self-referencing environments, incapable of giving voice to collective feeling. The church has looked with growing diffidence at contemporary art and has kept its distance: the fellowship is broken.

Participants in the great events of the last century, the Liturgical Movement and the Vatican Council II, persuaded the church to make a profound reconsideration of its traditions, practices and customs. The twentieth century saw significant examples of a reaffirmation of the alliance between art and church.

At a time when the failure of models of life based on the ephemeral and on the undisputed domination of technology is clearly evident, there is a growing need to recover the transcendent dimension and spirituality and, consequently, to encounter superior manifestations of human talent. It is undeniable that there is, however, a disturbing absence of the aesthetic dimension in contemporary religious culture and pastoral practices. Church men note the crisis, discuss it and register the positive signs.

What happened in the recently completed century in Europe? In which direction are we going today? After the meetings organised with the Biennale in 2003 and 2004, another opportunity to know ourselves and question ourselves has been given by the third appointment with the European experts. Switzerland, Belgium, Portugal and the Czech Republic are the countries contrasted in this presentation.

Giorgio Della Longa, Antonio Marchesi, Massimiliano Valdinoci

2

God is Great

God is Great

Contemporary scepticism concerning religion and the continuous discoveries of science have made us increasingly more curious about the fundamental essence of creation. The idea and title for the show germinates from two works by John Latham; *The Mysterious Being Known as God*[1], 1981-2005, and the series *God is Great*, 1990-2005[2]. The recent religious and political developments centred on the Middle East give us good reason to focus at this time on the work of these three important British artists, who all concern themselves with the cosmopoetics of this baffling and essential subject. These artists, employing different forms of artistic expression, are concerned with both the origin of creation and the universe we inhabit, as well as the human need for community and belief systems. How do we find a pathway through this confusion? Some artistic enlightenment, through their positioning within the context of this essential and timely subject, is the purpose of this exhibition. John Latham is best known for his art activism of the sixties. Much less understood is his continuing work dealing with time, the universe and the place human beings take up in it. In 1954 Latham was the first painter in England to use spray paint on canvas. He realised that spray paint was not simply a mark of paint; it was a succession of nano-seconds turning into a cloud on the canvas. Latham has devoted a life's work to the creation of a cosmology that aims to unite art and science through his theory of origins. The 'summa' of that theory is contained in Einstein's description of the coming into being of the universe from the state of 'zero space, zero time, infinite heat'. In his 'bookreliefs' of the late fifties Latham presented Darwinian evolution and the appearance of man as part of the history of the universe. Soon he replaced the white canvas with sheets of glass. The glass represents the a-temporal, or not-yet visible, from which the books extrude as events or records of human history.

Anish Kapoor's work expresses the duality of the world and its transcendent potential in concrete form, often using rich colour and, just as readily, the subtlety of pure white surfaces or dense black spaces. Exploring the idea of the primordial 'void', for instance, Kapoor uses reflective surfaces to make sculptures that engulf but also distort his audience and their surroundings. Transformation is a key element within Kapoor's work. He changes our perception of objects and materials by playing with their surfaces or their inherent physical qualities, making them lighter or denser, confounding our preconceptions about matter and space. Kapoor's sculpture when produced on massive scale creates environments in which the viewer becomes a minute participant in a relationship with art that could be seen as an image for our relationship to the world as a whole.

Douglas Gordon manipulates the act of looking in order to express concerns about basic ethical and moral issues that are often incorporated into the fundamentalist canon of God and the Devil. His 1997 projection *Between Darkness and Light (after William Blake)*, for example, pits the Devil against the Virgin Mary using the films *The Exorcist* and *The Song of Bernadette* as vehicles to express the coexistence of good and evil in life. Gordon's film and text pieces address the potential instability of the mind in which the manifestation of darkness and disorientation can be accentuated or alleviated by the psychological imperatives of guilt or redemption to control the psyche. His text pieces articulates in pictorial and sculptural terms slogans that bind people to an anxious existence while offering them a chance for deliverance.
Marianne Brouwer, David Thorp

ORGANIZATION
Outset Contemporary Art Fund
www.outset.org.uk

CURATOR
David Thorp

COORDINATED AND SUPPORTED BY
Lisson Gallery
www.lisson.co.uk

ARTISTS
Douglas Gordon
Anish Kapoor
John Latham

[1] *The Mysterious Being Known as God* is an atemporal score, with a probable time-base in the region of 10-19 seconds.
[2] Including the work *God is Great # 2*, 1991, now in the Tate Collection.

John Latham, *God is Great*, 2005 (four-language version).
Text; dimension variable.
Courtesy the Artist
and Lisson Gallery, London

God is Great

Dio è Grande

Henri Foucault. *Satori*

Henri Foucault. Photography Sculpted

What we usually look for, optically and sensorially, in the photographic representation of bodies and things, is mass rather than contours, weightiness rather than evanescence, volumetric modulation rather than a diaphanous stretching-out of surfaces. Henri Foucault has long been aware that one of photography's undeniable qualities is its ability to magnify matter and to confront, by means other than sculpture, the problem of space, the formation and unending redeployment of representations. Out of this confrontation (which is hard to get beyond) between two approaches – between the slow fashioning of a volume and the lightning speed of the photographic act – there arises the possibility of fusing the concepts of sculpture and photography. *Sosein* and *Satori*, the two series to be presented in Venice, constitute a temporary culmination of this encounter, this radical transcendence.

Photography, then sculpture: this is the order in which the operations are henceforth to take place. To begin with there is the model, the body, which the artist lays out, arranges, then transfers to photosensitive paper after a few seconds' exposure, thereby suppressing details to the benefit of a luminous field and favouring halos with clear-cut outlines. The technique is not gratuitous: this spectral representation of the Real, this ghost of a body, as immediately present as it may be, is given a new dimension by the way Foucault sculpts it. With *Sosein* (begun in 2000), the subsequent action consists of working directly on the photographic paper, perforating it in a repetitive, enlarged, pixel-like pattern; and with the subtraction of matter, as in the sculptural act itself. But there is no chisel to be seen, no gouge, let alone a gradine; just a tool that makes holes and removes material. The photographic plates, superimposed and divergent, present a shimmering effect, a glimmer between the black background and the white of the corporeal impressions. Foucault does not seek to conjure up an illusion of bodies, but to create, in both a literal and a figurative sense, an illusion of sculpture out of this cutting into paper. The body remains a mystery in that it evades matter, and gravity, refusing as it does to clearly embody a 'design' (either drawing or plan). And *Sosein*, after all, means 'being thus'.

The main action involved in the second series, the *Satori*, which was begun in 2002, does not have to do with subtraction, but, on the contrary, addition and accumulation. Photograms of bodies are overrun by thousands of tiny pins with shiny heads, which reconquer the model thanks to the luminous quiverings that ripple over the surface of the glistening metallic epidermis. The title *Satori*, a concept that Roland Barthes borrowed from Zen culture, signifies an illumination of consciousness, a vibration of lucidity.

Illumination, shake-up, shudder: this is the test that photographical material undergoes when it picks up the gauntlet of sculpture. Taking its place in the history of art, it exposes reasoned conflicts between the profundity of things and the illusionist surface of representation. Physically importuned by the real world, it combines stability and weightlessness. Regally reflected, it alternates labour and reverie.

Dominique Païni

PROMOTING INSTITUTIONS
Fondation Pierre Bergé - Yves Saint Laurent
www.ysl-hautecouture.com
AFAA (Association Française d'Action Artistique)
www.afaa.asso.fr

CO-ORDINATION
Galerie Baudoin Lebon
www.baudoin-lebon.com

CURATOR
Dominique Païni

COLLABORATOR
Damien Sausset

SPONSOR
Fondation Pierre Bergé - Yves Saint Laurent
AFAA, Association Française d'Action Artistique
Alliance Française de Venise
Galerie Baudoin Lebon
Editions Léo Scheer
Dominique Belloir - Mirage illimité
François Combeau
Hubert Tisal
Fondazione Antonio Mazzotta

ARTIST
Henri Foucault

Henri Foucault, *Satori n°10*,
2004. Photogram and pins
on stainless steel; 60 × 50 cm

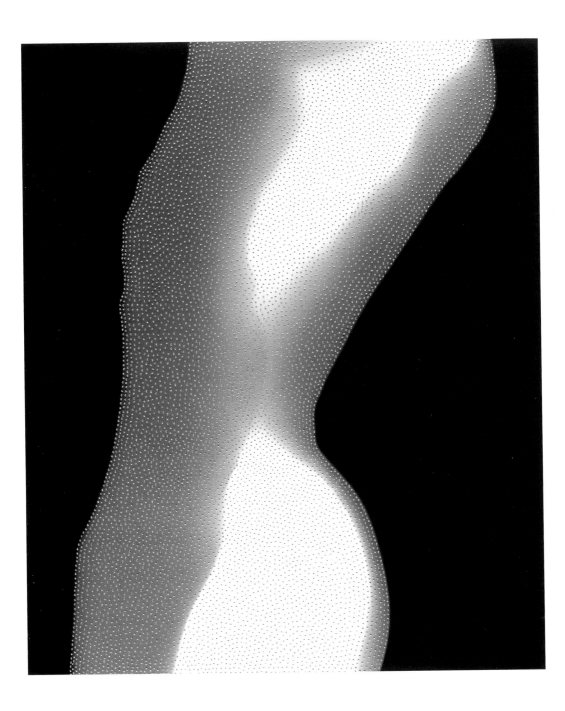

Homespun Tales - Kiki Smith

The Fondazione Querini Stampalia is presenting Kiki Smith's *Homespun Tales*. This project reclaims the domestic space of the palace. It is inspired by the Pinacoteca of the Querini Stampalia as well as American aesthetic traditions ranging from colonial times, tramp and hobo art to the resourcefulness of home makers.

By mimicking and shadowing various subjects represented in the collection, the artist creates her own fractured tale of household yearning and occupation, celebrating domestic life and space. She explores the free inventiveness bred of necessity, creating a narrative that explores emotional interiors, insomnia, bedlam, decorative squalor, possession and the temporal life of squatters.

It is a habitat where faraway pasts and faraway places are inhabited by schoolgirls, guards, domestics, dowagers, dancers, seers and naked lounge ladies.

Kiki Smith

ORGANIZATION
Fondazione Querini Stampalia onlus
www.querinistampalia.it

CURATOR
Chiara Bertola, chief curator Fondazione Querini Stampalia

SPONSOR
MONTBLANC

ARTIST
Kiki Smith

Kiki Smith, *Homespun Tales
project at Fondazione Querini
Stampalia*, 2005

iCon: India Contemporary

As the nation of India continues to become more prominent on the international stage, its culture becomes increasingly relevant to the rest of the world. An amalgam of a wide diversity of ethnicities, cultures, languages, religions, political ideologies and economic strata, the way the people of India negotiate these complexities to form a unified and democratic nation can become a model for how other nations may resolve the anxieties presented by globalisation and post-modernism. *iCon: India Contemporary* presents the work of six artists who represent the vital and engaging art practices to be found in India today. Three artists (Ranbir Kaleka, Nalini Malani and Raqs Media Collective) have been commissioned to create new, large-scale installation projects for the presentation in Venice. In addition, three artists (Atul Dodiya, Anita Dube and Nataraj Sharma) working in painting and sculpture are represented by major new works. The diversity of imagery, subject and technique exhibited by these six artists reflects the concerns of both individuals and society as a whole; the issues raised by their works engage with both an international arts community and different spectrums of India's public. The artists included have been chosen for the rigour and commitment they bring to their practice; their works create bridges of meaning between the global and the local.

ORGANIZATION
Sally and Don Lucas Artists Programs
Montalvo Arts Center
www.montalvoarts.org

CO-ORDINATION
Nuova Icona
Directors: Vittorio Urbani and Camilla Seibezzi
www.nuovaicona.org

EXHIBITION PROJECT
Sally and Don Lucas Artists Programs
Montalvo Arts Center
Coordination in Venice:
Stefania Uberti

WITH THE SUPPORT OF
Bose Pacia, New York
www.bosepacia.com
Nature Morte, New Delhi
www.naturemorte.com

CURATORS
Julie Evans
Gordon Knox
Peter Nagy

ARTISTS
Atul Dodiya
Anita Dube
Ranbir Kaleka
Nalini Malani
Raqs Media Collective
Nataraj Sharma

GOUSERATE

1 Atul Dodiya, *Cracks in Mondrian - Gujarat*, 2004-2005. Acrylic with marble dust on canvas hinged on drainage PVC pipe. Canvas size: 183 × 175 cm; dimension variable

2 Anita Dube, *After Dark (Halleluja Falleluja)*, 2004. Installation with seven elements, styrofoam, bandage, glass, revolving car lights, steel cables, electric wire; dimension variable

3 Ranbir Kaleka, *Man Threading a Needle*, 2001. Video projection & oil on canvas

4 Nataraj Sharma, *Mandu (evening)*, 2003. Oil on canvas. Diptych; 183 × 152.4 cm each

5 Nalini Malani, *Game Pieces*, 2003. Video/shadow play, reverse painted mylar, four video projectors, sound, iron rings, motors

6 Raqs Media Collective, *The Impostor in the Waiting Room*, 2003. Inter-media installation, performance/video still

2

3

4

5

6

"investigation of a journey to the west by micro + polo" artists from hong kong, china

background/ realization/ investigation

investigation of a journey to the west by micro + polo is a double pun on a famous, ancient Chinese mythological tale[1] and Marco Polo's visit to China in the 13th century. The title reflects both the literal and physical nature of the exhibition via a visit to the west in the high technology era of the 21st century by two Hong Kong (China) artists, anothermountainman and CHAN Yuk-keung, also known as 'micro (soft)' and 'polo' (names used to symbolise popular brand names in general). The exhibition is a marvelous, imaginative investigation of travel west in the computer age.

anothermountainman's stylised redwhiteblue rendition of a Hong Kong style tea house is a contemplative reference to the absence of any mention of tea in Marco Polo's travelogue. The work is also a statement on the importance of face-to-face communication in society, which is becoming a lost art in our micro-technological age. The redwhiteblue plastic fabric, a low-cost wrapping material, reflects the transitory and unsettled nature of Hong Kong. Perhaps reestablishing human contact (over a cup of tea) can help society resolve issues and regain its focus.

CHAN's fascination with the imaginative nature of travelogue draws on his own many travel experiences, which, like Polo's, include ventures into foreign lands and cultures. His cityscape installation in the shape of Venice, complete with a 'canal/bridge', reveals CHAN's experiences as a traveller both metaphysically and psychologically. The cityscape is elevated and inverted to provide the viewer a thorough investigation into an imaginary, reinvented world.

The exhibition investigates and explores the blending and divergence of cultures in our societies through the microcosmic vision of the artists. It reflects parallels and differences between Hong Kong and Venice. Both great cities are surrounded by water; but one lives on its history while the other is continually striding into the future.

[1] *Journey to the West*, a classic Chinese mythological novel written around 1570 on the fantasy adventures to the west in search of the Buddhist Sutra by a Tang Dynasty (618-907) priest Sanzang and his three disciples, Monkey King, Pig and Friar Sand.

ORGANIZATION
Hong Kong Arts Development Council, Hong Kong, China
www.hkadc.org.hk

CO-ORDINATION
Arte Communications

COMMISSIONER
MA Fung Kwok

VICE-COMMISSIONERS
Peter K. K. WONG
LEE Kam Yin

CURATOR
Sabrina M.Y. FUNG

ARTISTS
CHAN Yuk-keung
anothermountainman

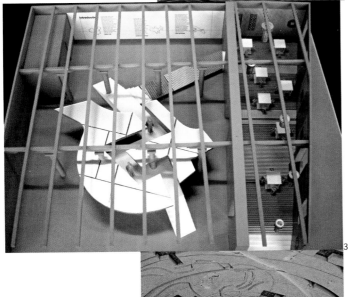

1 anothermountainman,
*Building Hong Kong 14 Let's
talk*, 2005. Mixed media
installation; dimension variable

2 anothermountainman,
*Building Hong Kong 10 Cou
Ma.Kan Hua.*, 2005. Mixed
media installation; dimension
variable

3 anothermountainman, CHAN
Yuk-keung, *investigation of a
journey to the west by micro
+ polo*, 2005

4 CHAN Yuk-keung, *QK*, 2003.
Mixed media installation;
dimension variable

Isola della Poesia

Let Art Have Its Say

In Rotelli, arts respond through the complexity of technique and interdisciplinary cross-fertilisation, capable of restoring that which a single language is so hard put to achieve. Only by proclaiming and explicitly enacting this interdisciplinary cross-fertilisation is it possible to bring about an event capable of drawing even with existence, in terms of real occurrence. The theme of complexity has won full entitlement to a role in the topic and awareness of contemporary art, as in the case of the work of Marco Nereo Rotelli. The poetry space was, then, a metaphorical, invisible space. Rotelli tries to make the dimension of his operation increasingly physical, encouraged by competition with the universe of technology tending increasingly towards abstraction and reproduction.

The artist introduces the body of art into representation: life breaks through the bounds of the page and becomes the locus of a physical event: that of representation, of the mise en scène of space and time, by day and by night.

Contemporary art ponders the problem of overcoming logical discursive communication and aims at multi-sensory communication capable of focusing all the observer's attention outside the cachet of the museum.

Rotelli has taken part in reconquering real space, a physical dimension capable of investing the dimensions of its production.

Achille Bonito Oliva

ORGANIZATION
Incontri internazionali d'arte
www.incontriinternazionalidarte.it
Fondazione Marenostrum
ONLUS
www.fondazionemarenostrum.it

CURATOR
Achille Bonito Oliva

EVENT'S CO-ORDINATION
Anna Maria Orsini

POETIC PROJECT CO-ORDINATION
Federica Guida,
Brunella Buscicchio,
Giovanna Zabotti, Laura Maeran

COLLABORATORS
Luciano Massari,
Matteo Ferretti,
Silvia Camporesi,
Filippo Centenari

ASSISTANTS
Giovanni Fiamminghi, Marco Orlandi, Studio Art Project, Studio Pandolfi, Luca Lombardi, Veronica Romitelli, Francesca d'Ambrosio, Giorgio Tentolini

POETIC CONTRIBUTIONS
Edoardo Sanguineti (Italy), Adonis (Siria), Andrea Zanzotto (Italy), Fawzi Al Delmi (Iraq), Anatolij Naiman (Russia), Roli Opalka (Nigeria), Kikuo Takano (Japan), Yves Bonnefoy (France), Tadeusz Rozewicz (Poland), Ana Blandiana (Romania), XI CHUAN (China), Charles Tomlinson (Great Britain)

SPONSOR
il Mercante di Venezia
Cave di Michelangelo
Miastokina Production
Trend 3D
Borghetto di Chiena
Assicurazioni AXA

SPONSOR TECNICO
ENEL
Luce Pura
Fondazione 3M
Rezina

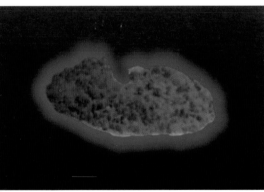

1

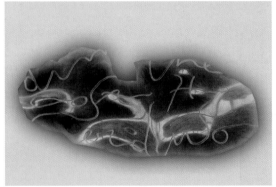

2

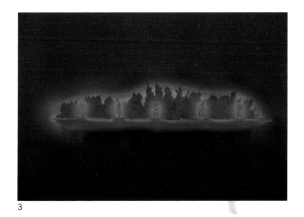

3

WITH THE PATRONAGE OF
Ministero Affari Esteri
CNI UNESCO
Regione Veneto
Comune di Venezia Assessorato
alla Cultura
Presidenza del Consiglio
Comunale di Roma
I.I.R.D
Chile Embassy
I.I.L.A
CoNISMa

LOCATION
Isle of San Secondo

TWINNING
Isla de Pascua, Zante Island,
Eolie Islands, Palmaria Island,
Bodrum Peninsula, Capri
Island, Cousine Island
Seychelles

CONNECTED EVENTS
La vita è sogno
La notte dei poeti, reading
Isola virtuale, curated by
Caterina Davinio, poetry on the
web at www.repubblica.it

The sculpture *Isola della Poesia*,
in white marble from
Michelangelo's quarries, a work
by Luciano Massari, is given
as a present to the Biennale
of Venice

ARTIST
Marco Nereo Rotelli

4

5

1 *Isola della Poesia*, view
from above

2 *Isola di Marmo*

3 *Isola della Poesia*, night view
with 12 screens dedicated
to 12 poets

4 *Isola della Poesia*, day-light
view with 12 screens dedicated
to 12 poets

5 *Isola della Poesia*

6 *La vita è sogno*, raft
on the water, poetic event

6

The "Inner-Soul" Island: the Art of Survival

The island is not only a geographic reality but also a symbolic one. In the collective imagination it synthesises the themes and myths that art has always represented. Survival, return, departure, shipwreck, nostalgia and landing are the interior aspects of an island contemplated by art in multiple forms.

The island of San Servolo in the Venetian lagoon is the theatre within whose water surrounded enclosure an artist will each year represent one of the themes in an emblematic way. *L'arte della sopravvivenza* (The Art of Survival) is the theme considered by Michelangelo Pistoletto through a collective work entitled 'Cittadellarte'. The work is the result of a group collaboration on the theme.

Pistoletto closes the circle of his research starting from the mirror, which reflects reality, with a radical conclusion that implies multiple artifices in an attempt to tangibly modify the social, through new collective linguistic and behavioural models affecting daily life.

Isola Interiore is introduced with an installation by Michelangelo Pistoletto on the tug *Impetus* in the waters of the lagoon in front of the Giardini della Biennale di Venezia: a visual announcement that refers to the island of San Servolo in the distance.

If the island implies an idea of survival in the literary imagination of Defoe, as the colonial supremacy of Robinson Crusoe over nature and men, in that of Pistoletto it infers exchange, equality, coexistence, freedom from need and improvements in the standard of living. Here survival becomes an art, in that it suggests a project focusing on the quality of life and the capacity for the formal elaboration of objects in common use.

The art of survival finally becomes the practicable utopia that does not refer to an impossible elsewhere, but seeks its realisation in the concrete foundation of languages that give reality to the ideal values that permeate it.

Pistoletto moves the collective nature of his 'Cittadellarte' from Biella to the island of San Servolo, making it a creative participant in a tangible dream, that of affecting not quantity, to which the simple concept of survival is tied, but quality, through a collective work that acts on the form of objects in daily use.

The artist also calls in other forces to create a level of genuine cultural and anthropological survival, such as RAM (Radio Arte Mobile of the Zerynthia association) to launch his SOS messages to the international community.

Pistoletto agrees to take on a new identity, passing from individual subject to collective subject of the artistic creation, in order to make the island of San Servolo into a workshop of ideas, above all in permanent synchrony with the international university already there. Art in this way casts off its eternal platonic robes to take on an active identity in contact with things. This is shown by the production of Pistoletto and the other artists in his collective carried out in Marseilles, Arles, Antwerp, Sarajevo, Beirut, Biella and other cities around the world. There have been Mediterranean tables, multi-confessional chapels, doors in the shape of a frame with the words 'art e politica' (art and politics), lagoon boats with 'love difference' written on the sail, glass cabinets for ice cream and red sofas, all confirming that 'Cittadellarte' exists and fights with us. San Servolo becomes the interior island that safeguards the treasures of being, of having, of wanting and knowing.

Achille Bonito Oliva

ORGANIZATION
Venice International University
& Cittadellarte - Fondazione
Pistoletto
www.univiu.org

CURATOR
Achille Bonito Oliva

ASSISTANT
Martina Cavallarin

CONNECTED EVENT
"Impetus 2005"

CO-ORDINATION (CONNECTED EVENT)
Galleria Michela Rizzo, Venice

WITH THE PATRONAGE OF
Ministero Affari Esteri
Provincia di Venezia

WITH THE SUPPORT OF
Fondazione Ermenegildo Zegna
Ministero dell'Ambiente
e della Tutela del Territorio

ARTIST
Michelangelo Pistoletto

TAKING PART IN THE EXHIBITION
Cittadellarte 2005: Francesco
Bernabei, Cristiana Bottigella,
Federica Cerruti, Sara Conforti,
Filippo Fabbrica, Fratelli
Fortuna, Francesca Fossati,
Paolo Naldini, Armona
Pistoletto, Juan Sandoval

1 Michelangelo Pistoletto, *Cappella Multiconfessionale*, 2000. Photo Margherita Spiluttini, Wien

2 Cittadellarte, *Barca - Love Difference*, 2003. Photo Diego Paccagnella, Venice

3 Cittadellarte, *Tavolo Mediterraneo - Love Difference*, 2002. Photo Courtesy Cittadellarte, Biella

4 Cittadellarte, *Gelato - Love Difference*, 2003. Photo Diego Paccagnella, Venice

1

2

3

4

Modigliani a Venezia, tra Livorno e Parigi

The exhibition is divided into four parts:
The history of the Modigliani family in Sardinia, between Livorno and Florence. (1884-1902)
Amedeo Modigliani in Venice. (1903-1905)
Modigliani in Paris. (1906-1920)
The posthumous exhibition of Modigliani at the Biennale di Venezia of 1922 and 1930.

A scientific route illustrated with works by the main artists to whom Modigliani made reference during his training.
All the documentation of the history of the Modigliani family in Italy and France will be presented for the first time, with particular attention paid to his long stay in Venice from 1903 to 1905, after Livorno and Florence.
Amedeo Modigliani's family in Sardinia and the work done by the artist at that time, in 1899 in Cagliari and dedicated to Medea Taci, will receive considerable attention through the presentation of period documents recently found in Italian libraries.
These documents illustrate the life of the Modigliani family from Sardinia in 1884, through to his posthumous marriage in 1924 and the presence of the Hébuterne family.
The exhibition presents documents, period photos and correspondence, gathered from the Archives Légales Amedeo Modigliani in Livorno and Paris, which illustrate the life and work of the artist with reference to his Italian friends.
The Italian friends presented: Ardengo Soffici, Carlo Carrà, Renato Natali, Gino Romiti, Oscar Ghiglia, Aristide Sommati, Manlio Martinelli, Guido Marussig, Mario Crepet, Guido Cadorin, Fabio Mauroner.
An introductory section, consisting of period photos, will illustrate the places and people who played an important role in the artistic training of Amedeo Modigliani in Venice, through to his move to Paris.
B) The French artist friends: Picasso, Max Jacob, Lèon Bakst, Léonard Tsugouhara Foujita, Gabriel Fournier, Jeanne Hébuterne, Moise Kisling, Chana Orloff, Pascin, André Warnod, Théophile-Alexandre Steinlen, Marie Marevna.
The creative path in all its aspects is illustrated with the presentation of works, documents and photos of Amedeo Modigliani from his first days in Livorno to his time in Florence and Venice, through to the French period in Montmarte and then Montparnasse.
Photos of the studios and bistrots of the Paris period punctuate the biographical history of the artist, the models and significant people, from 1906 to 1920, along with the interpreters of the historic and artistic avant-garde, from the Futurists to the Cubists, who made Amedeo Modigliani famous in the Paris School.
Christian Parisot

ORGANIZATION
Modigliani Institut Archives Légales
www.modigliani-amedeo.com

IN COLLABORATION WITH
Biblioteca Nazionale Marciana

CURATOR
Christian Parisot

SCIENTIFIC COMMITTEE
Marino Zorzi, Director of Biblioteca Nazionale Marciana, Venice
Christian Parisot, President of Modigliani Institut Archives Légales, Paris
Sylvie Buisson, Curator of Musée du Montparnasse, Paris
Osvaldo Patani, Art Critic, Milan
Enzo Di Martino, Art Historian, Venice
Franco Tagliapietra, Art Historian, Accademia di Venezia
Italo Zannier, Art Historian, Università Ca' Foscari, Venice
Claudio Gasparoni, Music Critic, Venice
Doretta Davanzo Poli, Art Historian, Venice
Vittoria Masutti, Art Historian, Università di Trento
Gérard-Georges Lemaire, Art Historian, Paris
Giorgio Guido Guastalla, Casa Natale Amedeo Modigliani, Livorno

WITH THE COLLABORATION OF
Carlo Delfino, Sassari

ARTIST
Amedeo Modigliani

1 Amedeo Modigliani, *Testa di atleta di profilo*, 1910. Blue pencil on paper; 39 × 26.5 cm. Courtesy Modigliani Institute

2 Amedeo Modigliani, *Ritratto di giovane seduta*, Venice 1905. Oil on canvas; 68.5 × 42.4 cm. Courtesy Modigliani Institute

3 Marriage declaration between Amedeo Modigliani and Jeanne Hébuterne, 1919. Courtesy Modigliani Institute

4 Ritratto fotografico della modella Lisette Béranger con dedica a Amedeo Modigliani, 1906. Courtesy Modigliani Institute

1

2

3

4

Mona Lisa Goes Space

The Russian-born painter George Pusenkoff has developed an extensive repertoire of images derived from the Internet, digitally manipulated and transferred to canvas by means of classic pictographic technology. The artist's most recurrent motif is the eternal icon of the *Mona Lisa* for which a fragment of the celebrated sitter's face, taken from the Louvre Internet site, is placed in a computerised frame. With this technique, the artist has 'translated' Leonardo's work into a contemporary statement, much as Malevich, Duchamp and Warhol did in their own time.

Pusenkoff has also sent the lady with the mysterious smile on a series of journeys, photographing a single black-and-yellow version at various (and often improbable) locations in his native Russia. As the most reproduced image in art history, *La Gioconda* is already, in a sense, a citizen of the world – a global phenomenon.

Now the artist intends to extend her sphere of influence by sending the traveller into space. On April 15, 2005, a yellow version of *Single Mona Lisa 1:1* has been brought to the International Space Station by Italian astronaut Roberto Vittori. The project has been planned and realised in collaboration with the European Space Agency.

This saga will be documented in the three-part installation which George Pusenkoff has prepared for the Venice Biennale under the motto *Mona Lisa Goes Space*. The first part consists of three oversized aluminium panels bearing the image of the yellow Mona Lisa. These recall her previous 'earthly' journeys but positioned at such an angle that they might almost have tumbled from heaven. Ideally, these would be placed at three contrasting locations: on or near the water, in a residential area (perhaps in the Ghetto) and in a busy pedestrian zone.

Part two, *Mona Lisa Space Station* is a gigantic round tower with a diameter of ten metres, a circumference of 30 and a height of six. The interior is made up of 500 multicoloured images of the *Single Mona Lisa 1:1* each 60 × 60 centimetres. Fabricated entirely of black aluminium, the tower itself resembles a segment of a rocket. Inside, the famous beauty looks down in a rainbow of colours lit from above. First exhibited at Moscow's State Tretjakov Gallery in 2004, where it was curated by Marc Scheps, the work was enthusiastically received by press and public alike.

The tower is constructed entirely of robust, weather-resistant materials and could be installed in virtually any public space in Venice. The third element of *Mona Lisa Goes Space* consists of light-boxes with photographs documenting Mona Lisa's journey into the cosmos with the Italian astronaut Roberto Vittori.

In a very real sense, Pusenkoff's ambitious project – from heaven to earth and back again – comes full circle in Venice. And it underscores the city's continuing role as a cultural crossroads. As ambassador-at-large, the Mona Lisa returns to Italy in her dual function as Renaissance classic and a witness to contemporary scientific progress. As George Pusenkoff has remarked, 'The Mona Lisa's smile in a computer frame is a beacon for the creative unity of art, science and modern technology'.

Seen as a whole, the *Mona Lisa Goes Space* project is a unique example of

ORGANIZATION
Museum Ritter
www.museum-ritter.de

CO-ORGANIZATION
Grandi Stazioni Spa

CURATOR
David Galloway

WITH THE AID OF
ESA
ISA
Roscosmos
Italian Ministry for Foreign Affairs
Italian Embassy in the Russian Federation
Regional Government of Latium

COORDINATION
Associazione Le Muse

TECHNICAL SPONSOR
Grandi Stazioni Spa

TECHNICAL SUPPORT
Eta Beta Produzioni
Ilja Pusenkoff

COLLABORATION
Roberto Vittori
Johanna and Gianfranco Facco Bonetti
Marc Scheps

WITH THE SUPPORT OF
Filas
Ritter Sport
LTW-Neon
Contemporary City

THANKS TO
Pasquale Di Palermo
Pierguido Cavallina
Olga Bisera
Nicolas Chibaeff
Catherine Ivanov-Trotignon
Alain Fournier-Sicre
Alberto Sandretti

ARTIST
George Pusenkoff

1 George Pusenkoff, *Mona Lisa's Space Station*, 2004. Detail of the tower; installation. Tretyakow Gallery, Moscow.

2 George Pusenkoff, photography of the series *Mona Lisa Goes Russia*, 1998, Moscow

3 George Pusenkoff, photography of the series *Mona Lisa Goes Space*, with the Italian spaceman Roberto Vittori, ESA, Koln

1

2

3

international cooperation: its realisation involved a Russian spaceship, the International Space Station, an Italian astronaut, the resources of the Russian and European Space Agencies, the image-generating resources of computer technology and – as a kind of guiding light – the vision of the great Leonardo. *David Galloway*

The Nature of Things. Artists from Northern Ireland

The Nature of Things, presents a view of Northern Ireland that may not be widely known internationally, which is informed by place but not limited by our perceptions of it. It is however impossible to present a view of Northern Ireland without touching on our recent history. Where artists have made reference to 'the troubles' in this exhibition, they do so having lived through ten years of relative civil, if not political stability and from a position of reflection. While not all the artists comment directly on Northern Ireland's political history, there is evident in the work a condition that underpins their shared practice, that is, a desire to promote inclusion, hope and freedom through acceptance, love and beauty and not to continue to promote political cynicism, which feeds anger. It could be said that work about inclusion, understanding and acceptance is the most political work there is, because it is essentially about freedom and freedom can only be achieved through the self, through acceptance of our own nature. In this respect the artists selected are part of a wider conversation, one that is both local and international and one that is rooted in our basic understanding of humanity.

ORGANIZATION
The British Council
www.britishcouncil.org
Arts Council of Northern Ireland
www.artscouncil-ni.org

CURATOR
Hugh Mulholland

ARTISTS
Patrick Bloomer
& Nicholas Keogh
Ian Charlesworth
Factotum
Seamus Harahan
Michael Hogg
Sandra Johnston
Mary McIntyre
William McKeown
Katrina Moorhead
Darren Murray
Aisling O'Beirn
Peter Richards
Alistair Wilson

1

2

3

4

<n kiloton>

Introducing *<n kiloton>* means retracing the stages in the construction / destruction of an image.

Talking of image rather than work seems to restrict the field of research; but a mental path that abandons the idea of the image as representation for a process of elaboration is useful for better expressing the meaning of *<n kiloton>*.

So the hypothesis of Iorio's analysis starts from a metaphor. As in an atom, the electrons/pigments that move and create links are energy. As in an atom, the electrons/pigments determine the physical and chemical characteristics of every element.

In the same manner, the machine becomes a macroscopic unit for representing artistic creation in all its possibilities.

Indeed, Silvia Iorio places the raw material of art inside the bullae: colour, as brilliant, beautiful and stable as can be found.

The colours used, however, are extremely toxic, and because of this they have been taken off the market.

Chrome Red: prolonged inhalation can cause perforation of the nasal septum.

Prussian Blue: has recently been found to cause cerebral dementia.

Cadmium Yellow: an atmosphere containing 25 mg dispersed in a cubic metre of air can cause death in less than two hours.

But *<n kiloton>* is a significant machine and its continuous remixing of colours is not an end in itself. The toxicity, caused by the metallic residues and other highly damaging base components, is integrated with the possibility of causing combustion.

The wheel machine and the ellipses intersect: in these recombinations there is always one pigment that remains outside. There is always one of them (and only one) that does not permit the explosion to take place.

An unfinished tension, a creative, astonishing and always new ex/implosion contains the possibility of destroying or exploding in creativity.

Indeed, the colour of *<n kiloton>* creates and destroys.

Sartre claimed that the image is not a copy nor the materialisation of a personal view of the world. The image is rather an act, it is not a 'thing' but consciousness of something.

Silvia Iorio creates an explosive reaction in power, but centres the discourse on art; on her materials; on her stage of illness... She studies its toxicity, starting from a false myth: the artist paints! Acting in this way, she reflects on the two terms of the same word – colour – to find the paradox of art itself. The art/science relation becomes crucial. Art and science seem to deny the search for a final meaning of the relationship between life and freedom. Silvia Iorio descends to the root of the art question: matter/creativity; and the nucleus of reflection lies precisely in this ancestral dichotomy.

In a certain sense the common Sartre thread of the constitution of the image is ended.

That distancing and return to the real is completed through the ability to conceive a distant view.

But, apart from making itself image, *<n kiloton>* is a contraption, an organum of colour, glass and iron, a demiurge of creation and destruction, whose matrix is the pigment.

The gear motor – that which makes its orbits turn, that which at every throw of the dice recombines ideas, memories, archetypes – consists of a combining

ORGANIZATION
Museum Arterra

CURATOR
Ewald Stastny

PROJECT DIRECTOR
Clarissa Welshman

COLLABORATION
Mirta D'Argenzio

SCIENTIFIC COLLABORATION
Enrico Ravina, Ferdinando Vigo, Federico Canfarini, Generoso Ventre

THANKS TO
Micol Veller, Maurizio Minuti and Mario Codognato

ARTIST
Silvia Iorio

tension, or the opportunity to be either creation or destruction.
Silvia Iorio is the architect of a macroscopic element: unit of measurement between matter and danger.
Clarissa Welshman

Silvia Iorio, *<n kiloton>*, 2005
(detail). Glass,
iron and colour; 5 m.
Photo Cozzi & Scribani snc

NowHere Europe

NowHere Europe is the result of the research project Trans:it. *Moving Culture through Europe*, a recognition across Europe of creative practices in arts, architecture and the urban dimension that are re-defining the concept of shared public space. Beginning with direct field study, the project has produced a cycle of three documentaries, a publication entitled *Il luogo (non) comune. Arte, spazio pubblico ed estetica urbana in Europa* (The (Un)Common Place. Art, Public Space and Urban Aesthetics in Europe) and an exhibition that gathered, in the form of an archive, materials documenting the selected projects. From Norway to Turkey, from Spain to Bulgaria, from Cyprus to Romania, a 'common feeling' has emerged, along with a shared context where artists, institutions and civil societies try out new relationships within which to seek new forms of co-habitation, comprehension and vision of the urban space. A common feeling underlines a European specificity which, to cite Etienne Balibar, 'has the capacity to speak/listen, teach/learn, understand/make understood (in short, to translate); a capacity that can be extended from a strictly linguistic one to a broader cultural level'.

The 'European specificity' which emerges from the artists' projects seems to be articulated in themes that deal with the dichotomy between public and private space in geographically and culturally distant contexts where the boundaries between the social, individual, intimate and shared tend to blur. Artistic practices arise that call into question the traditional institutions of the art system, oscillating between political activism, manifestoes of intentions and direct action on the ground. What emerges from this specificity of approach is a redefinition of the meaning of community through a rediscovery of the urban experience as a learning practice that produces new visions and representations, and an exploration of the collective symbols and memories. In terms of both artistic practice and theoretical reflections, *NowHere Europe* focuses on a new definition of the European cultural identity, characterised by openness and constant redefinition of the self in relation to the other.

Project part of *Trans:it. Moving Culture through Europe*

ORGANIZATION
Fondazione Adriano Olivetti
www.fondazioneadrianolivetti.it

IN COLLABORATION WITH
European Cultural Foundation
Fondation de France
Fondation Evens
The J.F. Costopoulos Foundation
Soprintendenza Speciale per il Polo Museale Veneziano

CURATOR
Bartolomeo Pietromarchi

ADVISORY BOARD
Ruxandra Balaci
Iara Boubnova
Anselm Franke
Germana Jaulin
Katerina Koskina
Marco Scotini
Nina Vagić

1 Osservatorio Nomade,
Immaginare Corviale,
2003-2005.

2 Can Altay, *We are Papermen*,
2003. Video still

ARTISTS
Mario Airò
Can Altay
Patrick Andrè
An Architektur
Atelier van Lieshout
Baktruppen
Shigeru Ban
Massimo Bartolini
Matej Bejenaru
Luchezar Boyadjiev
Eva Brunner-Szabo
Campement Urbain
Mircea Cantor
Montserrat Cortadellas Bacaria
Matali Crasset
Călin Dan
Esra Ersen
Gelatin
Ion Grigorescu
Gülsün Karamustafa
Kimsooja
Iosif Király
Athanasia Kyriakakos
Aydan Murtezaoglu
Lucy Orta
Osservatorio Nomade
Maria Papadimitriou
Oda Projesi
Bülent Şangar
School of Missing Studies
Škart
Sean Snyder
Simon Starling
Socrates Stratis
Anne-Violaine Taconet
Gert Tschögl
Urban Void
Jeanne van Heeswijk
Erik van Lieshout
Mona Vatamanu & Florin Tudor
Zafos Xagoraris

PROJECTS
Artistic Interruptions
Idensitat
Nouveaux Commanditaires,
France
Nuovi Committenti

1

2

Personal Living Space

Oscillating between soft, subtle mindscapes and densely littered violent undertones, the artist seeks mental clarity with a similar mandate as in the heyday of modern contemporary art. 'We take a fresh look at things familiar to us, yet uprooted from their ordinary context and reflect upon contemporary existence'.

The artist is beyond ordinary artistic confines in that her end result gives the effect of not just merely existing, but being alive in the room with you. These objects always have something surprising about them, whether it is in size, material or texture.

This is wonderfully illustrated in Kazoun's work. Her pieces are made of everyday materials, such as fabric, threads, stuffing and rubbish bags; they are sewn and pieced together to create bulbous, organ-like shapes and nightmarish landscapes. The artist feels that there is an emotional bond, certain memories that are attached to items we use everyday. As someone who feels quite alien in today's world, it is a way for her to curtail the social sigma placed on her for being both female and of Arab descent. 'There is temporary satisfaction in my work, in its organic forms and the world made with skin like materials stitched together. I sew them to perfection. I am in physical pain because of the labour of their making and I embrace it, it is the labour of giving birth. The boundary between art, art making and life is very thin, as is the boundary between pleasure and pain. Slipping to the other side is very easy. Human balance stands on a thread. I am more sane than the sane.'
Lynn Del sol

I am a modern 'Queen' of sorts. I sit on my throne and eunuch fan-bearers provide cool air for me to breathe, air cooled by their tall feathers. Their constant repetitive movements sink me into a languorous trans state and have done so many times. The heat becomes bearable. I can create anything in my mind. I can tell you a story a night. I can tell you intricate weavings of different cultures. I will weave for you, if you let me.
Think!
The culture of listening is disappearing! Can you hear me when I am talking?
We are being educated to the culture of applause. Where is the culture of listening? Words choked by silence become meaningless because of their clash with stoned, emotionless and inexpressive faces. Who finds the time, the will, the disposition and the patience to listen? Such is our culture. Silence becomes turmoil and darkness starts to talk.
'Silence is not just criminal but suicidal. If they come for you in the morning they will come for us that night.'
I am responsible for the culture that I eat. It is shaping me.
Do you long for the warmth of my words reader? I am and I will speak on behalf of all the guilty, the unfortunate, the miserable, the oppressed, the tired, the needy, the hungry, the lonely, the sad, the beggars, the fighters, the strong, the

ORGANIZATION
Mjellby Konstmuseum
www.halmstad.se/mjellby

Arte Communications
www.artecommunications.com

CURATOR
Jackie Winsor

CO-CURATORS
Arwa Seifeddine
Lynn Del sol

COORDINATORS
Paivi Tirkkonen
Carlotta Scarpa

THANKS TO
Berengo Fine Arts

ARTIST
Marya Kazoun

Marya Kazoun, *Personal Living Space*, 2005. Model; plaster, balsa sticks, chicken bones, beads, mirror, metal; 2.70 × 20 × 15 m. Photo Sammy Haddad

mighty and the courageous. I carry their load on my shoulders. I will confront You-me one day, and you will have to look, to listen reader. My name is Marya. You cannot and you will not escape then. You will not hide behind the biased media anymore. You will not hide behind your shadow and Your-my sheltered life anymore.

The Dark doesn't speak with banal useless consolatory words but with broken words. It speaks wit words equal to lacerations and deadly wounds. The 'Spectre' speaks. He talks about a permanent state of exile.

I want to tell you about intellectual orgies, spools of memories, lust and perversions, and yarns of coded content. I want to tell you about the (informally) intangible, the missing areas and the repair.

I put lipstick to work. I learn this privilege of 'The right to play', slowly as do one thousand children living in a refugee camp in Uganda. We are learning to 'play'. I want to play with you reader.

Marya Kazoun

PINK HOUSE
"Generation Europe" pavilion in Venice

'Generation Europe' is an international programme and network established by Latvian artists Kristaps Gulbis, Aigars Bikse and the Centre for Art Management and Information in collaboration with international partners and Open Society 'Delna', a Latvian branch of 'Transparency International'. The primary aim of 'Generation Europe' is the creation of experimental projects to seek innovative solutions for breaking down elitism in artistic and cultural space through openness and accessibility.

The 'Generation Europe' partners are: Birmingham Institute of Art & Design University of Central England (UCE), United Kingdom; Ludwig Museum Budapest - Museum of Contemporary Art, Hungary; Bremen 2010, Germany; British Council, United Kingdom; Latvian Art Academy, Latvia.

PINK HOUSE - 'Generation Europe' pavilion in Venice
A new situation has developed in Eastern European countries since accession to the European Union. As a result mutual relations between civil groups who reside on the territories of different independent countries is changing, the local units that organise themselves around particular interest groups are differentiating. Mutual obligations and liabilities have completely altered in type and character. Irrespective of various cooperation and competition restrictions in some member states that the EU Constitution concedes to implement, people living in Eastern Europe have managed to become relatively equal citizens of the European Union. Fifteen years after the collapse of totalitarianism, the introduction of a consumer society at lightning speed, the establishment of aggressive capitalist relations and the privatisation of state property, can these citizens become aware of their equality or inequality under the new circumstances? There will always be people who are apt to adjust to changes and there will always be people who are incapable of doing so and will therefore feel discomfort. To what extent are these changes existential, and is it true that only the frame of reference has changed in the same terms of conformity and subordination or the relations of equality and inequality as in the past?

The European cultural space is based on the values and understanding of the mutual relations of the ancient Greeks and Christianity. They represent the mechanisms in the human mind that restrict natural competitiveness, uncompromising expressions of the survival instinct and aspiration for power, which, as the society develops, constantly interchanges with its opposing side – members of the society are predisposed to autonomy, equality, independence and freedom. The motives of relations, solutions and cultural perceptions are also determined by local and more ancient traditions.

Our pavilion is located in Marghera. Our purpose is to reveal the situation and show that such a marvellous pearl as Venice, a city-museum, where the qualities of cultural heritage are emphasised, has a totally different part that also represents today's real and true Venice.

Pink House is an inflatable building in the form of a Greek temple; the building has retained the shape of a temple only externally and it indicates its origin in a very simplified manner. The shape refers to cultural symbols and signs of a departed culture that has lost its content and meaning. The trivial colour emphasizes how a sign, extracted from the context, becomes a part of popular culture. For any social process, interrelation or interactivity to take place it should be related to a certain form of ideology (a structure that explains what is

ORGANIZATION
The Centre for Art Management and Information - MMIC
www.mmic.lv
www.pinkhouse.lv

CURATORS
Kristaps Gulbis
Aigars Bikse

COLLABORATORS
Andris Brinkmanis
Ilze Egle
Ilze Stala
Artis Rutks
Andris Dinsbergs

WITH THE SUPPORT OF
European Union - Directorate General Education and Culture
Latvian Ministry of Culture, Latvia
Riga City Council, Latvia
Centro Intermodale Adriatico Spa, Italy

PINK HOUSE. Marghera,
Venice

in fact happening). Previously this sign (a temple) perhaps legitimised a certain form of ideology that introduced order to the political relations of power, while at present the sign has become slogan-like and turned into an exhibit that is sold and purchased in souvenir kiosks. We want to show that a similar situation exists in Europe – a disabled person bears representations and social constructions that operate automatically and unconsciously for a long time and that frequently have no actual coverage; social stereotypes are made international without challenging or questioning their status quo.

Mud fights. A woman is fighting with a man. Personal equality in all spheres is understood as an axiom; it is not a problem itself, there are no discussions about that – its non-existence is regarded as a problem. People tend to be equal before power, but power is anonymous – the power of the market, of success or of society's opinion, the power of 'common sense' or even more likely – the power of generally accepted insanity; to a person it creates an identity that can be exposed, forms an understanding about who he or she is because 'he or she' is a part of a certain power (of gender, an organisation, a nation, a political party, a union etc.). This (mud) fighting is a way of paying attention to the fact that equality is impossible. The human aspiration to restrict competition reaches new borders again and again, and this aspiration tends to overcome these borders, too. Therefore, this fight is endless at personal, social and political levels. We would like to point out that at present Eastern Europe and Western Europe are not equal partners.

You are welcome to sign up for mud fights on www.pinkhouse.lv
Aigars Bikse, Kristaps Gulbis

European Commission  Direction générale de l'éducation et de la culture

PLAY THE GLASS

Forever fascinated by the celebrated alchemical union of sand and fire, Masuda Hiromi is an artist who has for 20 years assiduously frequented the furnaces of Murano, where the encounter between her Oriental delicacy and the strength of the master glassblower gives rise to artistic creations that offer us moments of sweetness, suffering and even anger.

Following her first exhibition in 2002 at 'OPEN', accompanied by the wonderful text of Pierre Restany ('Masuda's works are similar to three-dimensional musical scores representing a melodic concatenation of the material'), she is taking part in the Venice Biennale for the first time in a joint effort that associated her with the two curators, María de Corral and Rosa Martínez.

The exhibition *PLAY THE GLASS*, unravelling in the Scoletta di San Giovanni Battista e del Santissimo Sacramento, produces a prehistoric space marked by spherical forms that are duplicated in an urgent rhythm, recognisable as a prefigural manifestation, something coming before form and hence closely linked to an emotion. The form is frail, of cellular origin, devoid of subjection, full of inspiration and highly spirited vital thrust. Her art certainly preserves that 'artistic will', a philosophical cornerstone from which Schopenhauer derived all the theoretical thinking at the base of 'Einfühlung' (empathy), an art that is no longer depiction of reality but in empathy with reality.

With the *PLAY THE GLASS adirato* installation, Masuda celebrates the unconscious, instinct, the remote stirrings of the human soul and, to borrow her own words: '[...] Instinct is like a substance that leavens in the brain, giving life to an enormous bubble. The bigger the bubble grows, the more the substance becomes slimy'.

Instinct is something which has its roots in the unconscious and its expression manifests itself outside in an immediate and unconditioned manner, without following any precise rules, producing signs that are completely innovative. A passionate outburst, the sudden emergence of violent emotions and hidden sentiments, of dimensions and recondite thoughts are the characteristics of the thinking and poetics of the artist. The art of Masuda Hiromi strives for the most intimate essence of things, where no outlines or the exact 'rules' of forms are imposed.

The obscurity of *adirato* ('angry') prepares one for the reflected light in the 'mirrored' bubbles of the second installation, which form elements of connection or eyes with infinite potential, capturing bodies and objects and linking them in a single space, able to express a simultaneity of presences in the one image and

ORGANIZATION
Arte Communications
www.artecommunications.com

CURATOR
Paolo De Grandis

ARTIST ASSISTANT
Tsuchida Yasuhiko

COLLABORATOR
Carlotta Scarpa

PATRONAGES
Regione del Veneto
Provincia di Venezia
Comune di Venezia
The Japan Foundation
General Consulate of Japan
Mim- Museum In Motion-
Castello di San Pietro in Cerro,
Piacenza
Fondazione D'ARS
Official event of the year
in commemoration of "2005
Japan-EU Year of People-to-
People Exchanges"

SPONSOR
Copromet Spa, Piacenza
Palazzo del vetro, Franco
Schiavon, Murano
Masukan Co Ltd
Istituto italo-giapponese
Nichiigakuin

ARTIST
Masuda Hiromi

1

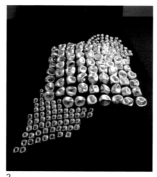

2

3

4

5

6

7

8

9

cause one or more worlds to co-exist in the same place and time.

Throughout history, the mirror has been a recurrent symbol of the literary and iconographic stock of images, loaded with references to the ambiguous appeal of doubles, of a faithful, illusory reproduction as a perfectly congruent yet depthless image: it comforts, helps, frightens and destroys.

The reflection recalls the paradox of identity, the contradiction between appearance and essence, and supplies the pretext for a dialogue with oneself.

In this way, the artist created a 'mental climate' that takes form from the flashing relationship between a predefined spaces and the presences appearing in them. These attract and sometimes disturb us, because an aggressive presence is manifested within them, or perhaps just because they reflect the fear of perception of our ego, creating a sort of impasse.

Masuda creates a series of dreamlike visions which, in the awareness of being unable to seize everything, offer us the unknown that the artist has within herself. She incarnates this in something that remains obscure, and tries to express it without using clear-cut forms. This is the depiction of the inexpressible.

Paolo De Grandis

1 Masuda Hiromi, *PLAY THE GLASS adirato II*, 1991. Installation: blown glass and mixed technique; 200 × 600 cm. Photo Stefania Giorgi

2 Masuda Hiromi, *PLAY THE GLASS passione*, 1994. Installation: blown glass and mixed technique; 300 × 300 cm. Photo Dan Wada

3 Masuda Hiromi, *PLAY THE GLASS requiem*, 1998. Installation: blown glass and mixed technique; 700 × 500 cm. Photo Dan Wada

4 Masuda Hiromi, *PLAY THE GLASS mille acque*, 1999. Installation: blown glass and mixed technique; 800 × 400 cm. Photo Saito Sadamu

5 Masuda Hiromi, *PLAY THE GLASS vento di venezia II*, 2002. Installation: blown glass and mixed technique; 600 × 700 cm. Photo Mirco Toffolo R.

6 Masuda Hiromi, *PLAY THE GLASS onda di venezia II*, 2002. Installation: blown glass and mixed technique; 900 × 600 cm. Photo Mirco Toffolo R.

7 Masuda Hiromi, *PLAY THE GLASS con tenerezza*, 2003. Installation: blown glass and mixed technique; 2500 × 2500 cm. Photo Ubaura Chie

8 Masuda Hiromi, *PLAY THE GLASS fonte*, 2004. Installation: blown glass and mixed technique; 500 × 500 cm. Photo Stefania Giorgi

9 Masuda Hiromi, *PLAY THE GLASS sotto voce*, 2004. Installation: blown glass and mixed technique; 2500 × 3000 cm. Photo Stefania Giorgi

Poles Apart / Poles Together.
An Outdoor Installation on the Grand Canal

The Venice Biennale has always reflected the individuality of the artist in unity not only with the world of art but with the world at large. *Poles Apart / Poles Together* stems from an idea which the Venetian poet John Gian, the Israeli curator Doron Polak, and the Spanish-born, New York-based curator Juan Puntes have derived from the Biennale's central message and meaning: that creativity and the artist are individual, but that art itself is communal and unifying. At least at its best, public art can be authentically populist without being an affront to the authority of art critics. With this in mind, *Poles Apart / Poles Together* seeks to unite a large number of artists' individual works into a communal effort through a local theme with international resonance. In this project, one hundred and one known international artists will employ one of the traditional features of the Venetian landscape to create environments that generate a sense of outdoor intimacy and surprise. By relating the conventional to the creative they will demonstrate how the traditional and commonplace can foster innovative approaches to art making.

What can be more common to Venice than water and its many features? Some of the most ubiquitous of those features, overlooked because of their very ordinariness, are the mooring poles (pilings) throughout Venice's waterways. The proposed project converts these myriad poles – plain and weathered timbers – into fresh blossoms on the water, by sheathing them in images and textures, making each a unique piece of art, and without damage to the original or the ability to restore it to its traditional state. Single poles or clusters of several poles along the Grand Canal will be developed thematically by individual artists, but the project in its totality will involve the cumulative creative work of an array of artists, representing a dynamic, publicly accessible, and aesthetically exciting addition to the Biennale.

Venice, the city of canals, whose access to the world's waterways has always made it look beyond its horizons, can draw focus to its cosmopolitan character through such an installation. What more appropriate adjunct to the Biennale could there be than temporary embellishment of the Grand Canal with international works of public art for the sake of pure aesthetic sensation? With

ORGANIZATION
The International Artists' Museum
www.lodzbiennale.pl/html/konst rukcja/museum.htm

White Box
www.whiteboxny.org

CURATORS
Doron Polak, International Artists' Museum
Juan Puntes, White Box

CO-CURATORS
Esti Drori
Raul Zamudio

ASSISTANT TO THE CURATOR
Ruth Perez-Chaves

IN COLLABORATION WITH
Comune di Venezia
Paolo Cacciari, councillor
Alberta Basaglia, Fabio Bozzato, Rossana Papini, Centro Pace e politiche giovanili

PROJECT DESIGNER AND ART DIRECTOR
Amir Cohen (Idya.com)

PROJECT DESIGN PARTNER
John Isaacs (John Isaacs Design, New York)

PROJECT CO-ORDINATOR
Doron Hanoch, Carla Stellweg (White Box)

Artistic consultant:
Ayelet Danielle Aldouby
Ethan Cohen
Ieva Kalnina (Riga City Council Department of Culture, Latvia)
European artistic co-ordinator:
Barbara Basile (Mietart, Berlin)
Industrial design:
Reuven Givati (Sdom Design Group, Israel)
Concept consultant and honorary board:
Michael Sterenberg
International Artists' Museum
Executive Director:
Ryszard Wasko
International Artists' Museum
President:
Emmett Williams

WITH THE SUPPORT OF
Angel Orensanz Foundation, New York
Atelier 14, New York

1

1-2 *Poles Apart / Poles Together. An Outoor Installation on the Grand Canal*. A project of White Box and the International Artists' Museum

ARTISTS
Ora Abrahami, Vito Acconci, Siemon Allen, Carlos Amorales, Anastasi/Bradshaw, Conrad Atkinson, Hanna Barak, Stefan Becker, Barbara Benish, Orit Ben-Shitrit, Elena Berriolo, Dara Birenbaum, Francie Bishop Good, Kristians Brekte, Aisha Burnes, Mimmo Catania, Loris Cecchini, Charlie Citron, Orly Cogan, Agnes Denes, Norma Drimmer, Jimmie Durham, Aziz Elhihi, El Perro, Erre, Jan Fabre, Emilio Fantin, Flavio Favelli, Dorit Feldman, Kendell Geers, John Gian, Leon Golub, Eugina Gortchakova, Gruppo ALE, Doron Hanoch, Huang Yong Ping, Scott Hug, Peter Hutton, Jian Jun Zhang, Juanjun Xi, Mary Judge, Rajkamal Kahlon, Dani Karavan, Laszlo Kerekes, Jon Kessler, Kimsooja, Adam Klimczak, Kaisu Koivistu, Igor Kopystianski, L. Laganovskis, Lee Ming Wei, Denica Lehocka, Matt Leines, Les Levine, Sol Lewitt, Marcos Lopez, Ivan Macha, Teemu Mäki, Enrique Marty, Tomasz Matuszak, Eraldo Mauro, Dominic McGill, Rajul Mehta, Matt Mullican, Ivan Navarro, Joshua Neustein, Ann Noel, Richard Nonas, Dennis Oppenheim, Angel Orensanz, Yigal Ozeri, Philip Pavia, Vickie Pierre, Giovanni Rizzoli, Martha Rosler, Riiko Sakkinen, Jack Sal, Avelino Sala, Krish Salmanis, Karin Sander, Eduardo Sarabia, Ray Smith, Michael Snow, Nancy Spero, Suzi Sureck, Javier Tellez, Richard Thomas, Barthélémy Toguo, Momoyo Torimitsu, Bernar Venet, David Wakstein, Ryszard Wasko, Ouattara Watts, Lawrence Weiner, Roger Welch, Bernard Williams, Emmett Williams, Wu Shan-Zhuan, Xu Bing, Zhang Huan, Zhu Ming

2

dazzling effect, *Poles Apart / Poles Together*, like the lagoon itself, will reach out across peoples and space and beyond parochialism.
Juan Puntes, Doron Polak

Reaction

Reaction is an event featuring ten of the most noted European performers, in Campo Santo Stefano in the old city of Venice and Piazzale Candiani in Mestre, metropolitan Venice, during the opening days of the Biennale. The locations were chosen on the basis of the diversity of the intended audience. The aims of the project include the desire to create a new connective tissue between the specific and contingent reality of the international audience of the Biennale and the daily life of the residents and of those who would otherwise not approach the art world. An open opportunity will be provided for dialogue and contrast through the themes and subjects of contemporary culture.

The individual projects making up the initiative are works in progress *par excellence*, where the dimension of the comparison and dialectic reign supreme and whose outcome will only be noted in the unfolding of each performance. There will be constant and open development, but which above all is unpredictable through to the end.

The project guidelines may lead to the desire to revive a direct, unmediated relationship between the artist and the public. The attempt at communication thus takes on the most varied forms in order to make the interlocutor participant and construct a shared meaning. This is not an easy task, but the art of performance seemed already by its nature particularly suited to the sharing of a universal language and the artists ready, in terms of talent and experience, for such an audacious gesture.

Camilla Seibezzi

ORGANIZATION
Comune di Venezia Assessorato alla Cultura e Spettacolo Centro Culturale Candiani
Provincia di Venezia
www.culturaspettacolovenezia.it
Plug
www.plug-space.org
Nuova Icona
www.nuovaicona.org
Fnv

IN COLLABORATION WITH
FRAME - Finnish Fund for Art Exchange
W.A.I. - Wales Arts International

CURATORS
Camilla Seibezzi (Plug)
Vittorio Urbani (Nuova Icona)
Lorenzo Cinotti and Laura Scarpa (Fnv)

CO-ORDINATION
Sandro Mescola
Silvio Fuso

ARTISTS
John Court
Helinä Hukkataival
Eddie Ladd
Désirée Palmen
Marc Rees
André Stitt
Roi Vaara
ZimmerFrei (Anna Rispoli, Anna de Manincor, Massimo Carozzi)

1 Eddie Ladd, *Sawn-off Scarface*. Performance. Photo Max Moser

2 André Stitt, *I love You*, 2004. Performance

3 Helinä Hukkataival, *Towards the Pure (negative)*. Performance, Tampere, Finland, 2002. Photo Mia Ristimäki

4 ZimmerFrei, *Panorama*, 2004

5 Désirée Palmen, *BUS*, 2002. C-print; 100 × 150 cm

6 Marc Rees, *Norman Behaviour*, 2005. Performance

7 Roi Vaara, *Shoe Shining*, the first scene from *One And the Same*, Navinki, International Performance Festival, Minsk, Belarus, 2004. Photo Marjo Levlin

8 John Court, *Marking space*, Liverpool Biennial, 2004. Performance of 8 hours. Paper, 3000 pencil black leads

3

4

5

6

7

8

Real Presence - Floating Sites

Real Presence - Generation 2001

I remember when I was preparing the Biennale in 1999, the bombing of Belgrade stopped the evening before the opening. We were all relieved.

Now assisting the opening of *Real Presence*, another successful initiative by Biljana and her beautiful daughter Dobrila, I saw the night before the opening what intelligent and stupid bombs did to the city.

What Biljana and Dobrila wanted and achieved wasn't an addition to the already overloaded art agenda, it was a piece of life given to the capital of an impoverished nation. It was fantastic to see how hundreds of young artists from all over the world approached the Tito Museum, ready after a first meeting to spread out in the city, taking it over, as ideal territory for their works, actions and performances.

I was lucky to be there.

The oldest Biennale in the world, the Venice Biennale, is nowadays not only an art exhibition but an occasion for many new and old nations to show their interest in a complex and many layered Europe.

But the Biennale cannot just passively wait for the others. It has to go where the Real Presences are and be part of their energies.

Thank you Biljana and Dobrila for what you have given to young artists, showing them that Belgrade is alive.
Harald Szeemann

Real Presence - Floating Sites

In 2001, after the democratic change in Serbian, the idea of a big meeting of young artists was born. We asked the new generations from all over Europe to come to Belgrade and witness with their presence the beginning of a new period, freer and more propitious for the nation emerging from ten years of isolation. *Real Presence* was thus born to be a bridge able to rise above the splinters of the past and constitute an open channel for the dynamic flow of ideas and energy for the future. Over the years it has been transformed into a powerful construction, in a kind of spontaneous and fluid behavioural architecture, a constantly evolving communicative network. Thanks to hundreds of 'real presences' that crossed Belgrade, we can now begin another adventure in Venice, which involves numerous young people ready to make their entry into the world of art.

Real Presence is a dynamic and nimble workshop that develops through actions, performances, expressions of attitudes and behaviours, which since the first stage, during the opening of the Biennale, has translated into workshops and in the second into the creation of works, hosted in the spaces of the IUAV. The meeting in both stages is aimed at launching the multiple aspects of creativity that unravel between art and real life.
Dobrila Denegri

Art is learnt but that does not mean it can be taught. This seems true mainly because, with academies and universities using the method of the short workshop, teaching can no longer be likened to a kind of long moral subjugation on the part of a teacher. What has been lost on one hand – the symbiotic but

ORGANIZATION
nKA / ICA Belgrade
University IUAV of Venice
Academy of Fine Art, Wien
Academy of Fine Art, Ljubljana
Staatliche Hochschule für
Bildende Künste, Frankfurt

CURATORS
Biljana Tomic, Director nKA / ICA
Dobrila Denegri, Independent Curator

IN COLLABORATION WITH
Angela Vettese, Director, Art Department, IUAV, Venice
Stephan Schmidt-Wulffen, Rector, Academy of Fine Art, Wien
Bojan Gorenec, Vice-President, Academy of Fine Art, Ljubljana
Daniel Birnbaum, Rector, Staatliche Hochschule für Bildende Künste, Frankfurt

SPONSOR
Ministry for Foreign Affairs RSM, Ministry of Culture RS, City Council Belgrade, European Cultural Foundation, Amsterdam, Pro Helvetia, Belgrade
Telecom, Grafix, ITM, Coca Cola, Don Café, Belgrade, US Still-Sartid, Smederevo, Participating Academies and Art Schools

Albania, Academy of Fine Arts, Tiranë
Austria, Academy of Fine Art, Vienna, University of Applied Arts, Vienna
Belgium, Academie Royale des Beaux-Arts de Bruxelles
Bulgaria, Academy of Fine Art, Sofia
Denmark, Royal Danish Academy of Fine Arts, Copenhagen
Spain, Academy of Fine Arts, Madrid
Estonia, Academy of Fine Arts, Tallin
Finland, Academy of Fine Arts, Helsinki
France, École Nationale Superieure Des Beaux-Arts, Paris
Germany, Staatliche Hochschule für Bildende Künste, Frankfurt, Academy of Fine Arts, Berlin, Academy of Fine Arts, Munich, Kunstakademie, Düsseldorf
Holland, Dutch Art Institute - AKI 2, Enschede, Gerrit Rietveld Academie, Amsterdam
Iceland, Academy of Fine Arts, Reykjavik
Italy, IUAV, Venice
Macedonia, Academy of Fine Arts, Skopje
Norway, Academy of Fine Arts, Oslo
Portugal, Maumaus - Escola de Artes Visuais, Lisbon
Romania, University of Arts, Bucarest
Serbia and Montenegro, Academy of Fine Arts, Belgrade, Academy of Fine Arts, Cetinje
Singapore, Lasalle-Sia College of The Arts
Slovenia, Academy of Fine Arts, Ljubljana
South Africa, Technikon, Pretoria
Sweden, Konstfack, Stockholm, Umeå Art Academy
Switzerland, Hochschule für Gestaltung Kunst, Zurich

hierarchical relationship between young and old artist – is however being gained on the other: it seems clear that another type of educational relationship is taking shape, the completely horizontal one between young artists/students. What they take from the school they bring to a debate among themselves.

The great merit of *Real Presence* has been to encourage largely international meetings of a vast emotional intensity. The initiative was invented after the Balkan war by Biljana Tomic. It is a story of meetings of young people from different art schools, a way of encouraging the rebirth of Belgrade and at the same time the European artistic identity. In the *tabula rasa* of a city that is both wounded and accused of wounding, the old continent has been conceived as a place of transit, of dialectic and of macro regions.

From Belgrade to Frankfurt to Venice, *Real Presence* overcomes the banalities of the virtual and asserts that there are moments, particularly the one of education, when one's own physical presence must be real, physical, able to give rise to passions, to falling in love and to discussions, once again passing hatred and real peace.

Angela Vettese

Scotland & Venice 2005: Selective Memory

The *Scotland & Venice 2005: Selective Memory* exhibition will focus on the individual practices of Alex Pollard and Cathy Wilkes and the collaborative practice of Joanne Tatham and Tom O'Sullivan. These practices have made a significant impact on the development of the cultural ecology of Scotland and they are valued for their contributions to the field. The internationalism by which contemporary art from Scotland is understood and by which its makers understand themselves reveals a critical mass that has been developed through a combination of traditional formats of practice and expanded practices. As well as producing traditional artworks, artists in Scotland are recognised for forms of practice that create circumstances, respond to voids, develop strategic dialogues, support networks, initiate collaborations, co-ordinate self-generated initiatives and discover new contexts for the dissemination of works by themselves and their peers.

The three artists' practices chosen for the *Scotland & Venice 2005: Selective Memory* exhibition at the Venice Biennale 2005 express one perspective of the cultural ecology which has developed within contemporary art from Scotland in recent years, and in particular art from the city of Glasgow.

Pollard, Tatham and O'Sullivan and Wilkes are reflective of current activity within Scotland and show a particular interest in art-historical references beyond the fields of minimalism and conceptualism that were indicative to the development of contemporary art from Scotland throughout the 1990s.

This second representation of contemporary art from Scotland at the Venice Biennale, *Scotland & Venice 2005: Selective Memory*, focuses on practices that reflect an interest in the pursuit and construction of meaning through studio-based and practice-led activities. Alex Pollard, Joanne Tatham and Tom O'Sullivan and Cathy Wilkes have dedicated their practices to the development of value systems that are influenced by and at the same time advance the propositions of art historical movements and their vocabularies. Ranging from the application of vernacular and marginalised languages to re-focusing attention on neglected feminist iconography, to establishing recurring visual motifs and symbols, these artists are genuinely concerned with examining the construction of meaning as a significant act of artistic labour.

ORGANIZATION
The Scottish Arts Council
The National Galleries
of Scotland
The British Council
www.scotlandandvenicebiennale.com

CURATORS
Jason E. Bowman
Rachel Bradley

PROJECT MANAGER
Jean Cameron

TECHNICAL CO-ORDINATION
Troels Bruun, M + B Studio

ARTISTS
Alex Pollard
Joanne Tatham
& Tom O'Sullivan
Cathy Wilkes

OFF-SITE PROJECT
Joanne Tatham
& Tom O'Sullivan

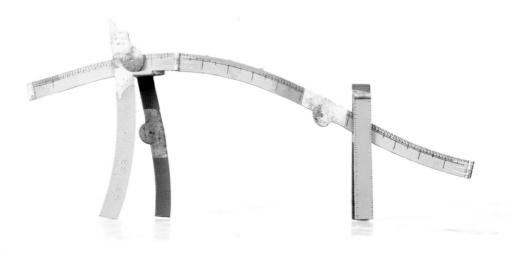

2

3

An awareness of the need to negotiate with the viewer is inherent to the work of these artists. Their individual works require the viewer to recognise that what they are encountering are works that arise from what could be described as a 'life-long' path of research and production or continuous practice, rather than an illustration of a succession of completed bodies of work.

Scot*land* & *Venice 2005: Selective Memory* is a concept-driven project concerned with the notion of artistic behaviour and the conditions and environments within which these artists configure their individualistic practices. Central to the selection of the three artistic practices is the criteria by which they continuously cultivate their practices as self-determined loci that provide them with the resources to consistently research, develop, edit, and produce art works and projects.

A further exhibition of more works by the artists will be shown at The Scottish National Gallery of Modern Art, Edinburgh from December 2005.

Jason E. Bowman, Rachel Bradley

The Shape of Time

'Let us suppose that the idea of art can be expanded to embrace the whole range of man-made things, including all tools and writing in addition to the useless, beautiful and poetic things of the world. By this view the universe of man-made things simply coincides with the history of art.' These are the first two sentences of *The Shape of Time*, written by my father, George Kubler, in 1962. My *Shape of Time* sculptures evolved from Kubler's theory that works of art represent cultures and cross cultures, acting as significant markers in the history of civilisation.

'Works of art are like gateways, where the visitor can enter the space of the painter or the time of the poet, to experience whatever rich domain the artist has fashioned.' Through *GATEWAY*'s Romanesque arch, viewers look into a dome-like environment symbolising sacred space. This opening functions as an intermediary between real space and the imagined space of the artist's construct.

CHACMOOL is my interpretation of Toltec-Maya recumbent deities that inspired Henry Moore's reclining figures. Defying gender characteristics, *CHACMOOL* simply reclines upon sturdy arms which form a stylised Moorish arch to contrast with the arches of *GATEWAY*. Having inspired Henry Moore, the Chacmool motivated me to reactivate a 'formal sequence'.

Like an angular, multifaceted eye, *PENUMBRA* symbolises the space 'between actuality and the future, where the dim shapes of possible events are perceived'. Unlike the other *Shape of Time* sculptures, whose maquettes were carved in the Virgin Islands, PENUMBRA was fabricated with an interior structure so viewers can sense how hard it is to accept new knowledge.

To represent St Thomas Aquinas' notion of the AEVUM, or 'the duration of human souls and other divine beings… intermediate, between time and eternity', I borrowed from an extinct culture to carve a dual-chambered vessel resembling the Canopic urns used by Etruscans to contain ashes of the dead.

Since concepts in *The Shape of Time* continue to inform my work, I have expanded on the idea of 'time and eternity' by carving *AEVUM II*. In direct contrast with the first *AEVUM*, which is an enclosing form, *AEVUM* II is open at both ends to collect light and radiate toward 'eternity'.

I hope the sculptures I am exhibiting in Venice are compatible with the contention that 'artistic inventions alter the sensibility of mankind', if only through their spirit of inquiry and authoritative presence.

Cornelia Kubler Kavanagh

The art of Cornelia Kubler Kavanagh does not reproduce nature; her sculptures are within nature and it is this distinguishing mark that immediately attracted me to her work, presented at the seventh 'OPEN'.

The natural beauty of the US Virgin Islands and the throbbing material determine in her a striving for an autonomous language that abandons figuration for a volumetric and plastic softness that is constantly evolving on a journey of discovery of the intimate geometries unravelling and rewinding the dialectic tension of space and time. Formal synthesis and a return to primary values are translated into a geomorphic, archetypal tendency, in which the masses that lie between the abstract and organic are rendered harmonious and compact, as though an incessant energy flowed through them. But it is light that plays a key role, sliding over the sinuous, smooth surfaces and disappearing in the straying of a

ORGANIZATION
Virgin Islands Council
on the Arts

IN COLLABORATION WITH
Arte Communications
www.artecommunications.com

COMMISSIONERS
Betty L. Mahoney, Executive
Director, Virgin Islands Council
on the Arts
The Honorable Lorraine L.
Berry, Senate President, 26th
Legislature of the U.S. Virgin
Islands

CURATOR
Paolo De Grandis

COLLABORATORS
Thomas F. Reese, PHD,
Executive Director, Stone Center
for Latin American Studies,
Tulane University;
Victor M. Cassidy, art critic
and journalist

WITH THE PATRONAGE OF
Legislature of the U.S. Virgin
Islands

SPONSOR
Pamela C. Richards,
Commissioner, U.S. Virgin
Islands Department of Tourism

ARTIST
Cornelia Kubler Kavanagh

1

2

3

4

5

curve, before being projected outwards by the dazzling finish of the works.
What is sculpture today?
I stop to look at her work…
I understand…
and… I contemplate new expressive frontiers that aim directly at the heart and the mind.
Paolo De Grandis

Celebrated for beautiful beaches, magnificent vistas and crystal-clear waters, the US Virgin Islands have long been a source of artistic inspiration. Camille Pisarro first honed his artistic skills on St Thomas in the nineteenth century. Since then, thousand of artists have come to the islands for artistic exploration. One such artist is sculptor Cornelia Kubler Kavanagh, who works out of a studio in St. Thomas. Although her sculptures are generally found in corporate and private collections on the US mainland, Mrs Kavanagh develops most of her creative ideas in the islands, where the climate and beauty of the natural surroundings have become the primary source of her creativity.
Betty L. Mahoney

1 Cornelia Kubler Kavanagh, *AEVUM II*, 2004. Polished bronze; 96.5 × 91.4 × 30.3 cm

2 Cornelia Kubler Kavanagh, *PENUMBRA*, 2002. Bronze; 68.6 × 63.5 × 61 cm

3 Cornelia Kubler Kavanagh, *GATEWAY*, 2002. Bronze; 94 × 50.8 × 76.2 cm

4 Cornelia Kubler Kavanagh, *CHACMOOL*, 2001. Bronze; 81.3 × 76.2 × 116.8 cm

5 Cornelia Kubler Kavanagh, *AEVUM*, 2001. Bronze; 81.3 × 76.2 × 76.2 cm

Somewhere Else. Artists from Wales

This is the second visit to the Venice Biennale for the artists from Wales, following the powerful and evocative exhibition *Further* in 2003, which included the work of Bethan Huws, Simon Pope, Paul Seawright and Cerith Wyn Evans. The exhibition *Somewhere Else* is at the same superb site as in 2003 – the Ex Birreria on Giudecca. *Somewhere Else* will include new commissions by three artists – Peter Finnemore, Laura Ford and Paul Granjon. In addition to the exhibition we also have a residency, an exciting partnership between Wales at Venice and Cywaith Cymru. Artworks Wales. The artist selected for the residency by open submission is Bedwyr Williams, who will spend 14 weeks on the island of Giudecca based at a studio in the garden of the Ex Birreria.

Although all four artists are known respectively for work in specific media – photography, sculpture, new-media and performance, somehow these descriptions do not adequately give a sense of their work. All of the artists simultaneously work with and against their chosen medium – this is telling as it reveals broader concerns and strategies at the core of each one's artistic practice. For example Peter Finnemore's artistic practice takes place in and around his home and garden, and features the artist, his family, friends and pets, but any description should also include the words performance and collaboration as well as photography and video. Laura Ford's work has sometimes been described as 'soft' sculpture, but this loaded term does not make sense of the diversity of materials she uses – everything from plaster, fabric, bronze and found objects to ceramics – neither does it give a sense of the uncanny creatures she creates. Paul Granjon is sometimes referred to as a new-media artist, but his works are as low as they are high tech, they have been exhibited in the gallery but he is equally happy performing with tu-tu the robotic dog. In his work, Bedwyr Williams shifts from karaoke to drawing, from gallery to stand-up comedy and deliberately retains his position as an outsider who infiltrates. This strategy of infiltration is employed by

ORGANIZATION
Arts Council of Wales
www.walesvenicebiennale.org

IN COLLABORATION WITH
Nuova Icona (Camilla Seibezzi and Vittorio Urbani)

COMMISSIONER
Michael Nixon

CURATOR
Karen MacKinnon

PROJECT MANAGER
Nia Roberts

SUPPORTED BY
Arts Council of Wales
Arts & Business Cymru
British Council
Castle Fine Arts
Contemporary Art Society for Wales
Cywaith Cymru . Artworks Wales
The Henry Moore Foundation
Swansea Institute of Higher Education a Member of the University of Wales
Tŷ Nant
Wales Arts International
Wales Trade International
Welsh Assembly Government
Welsh Development Agency Food Directorate

ARTISTS
Peter Finnemore
Laura Ford
Paul Granjon
Bedwyr Williams - Residency

1 Peter Finnemore, *Ringo Gringo*, 2005. Digital film still

2 Laura Ford, *Beast*, 2005. Installation, sacking, wood and mixed media. Somewhere Else: Artists from Wales, Venice. Photo Laura Ford

3 Paul Granjon, *Smartbot (work in progress)*, 2005. Mobile robot. Photo Paul Granjon

4 Bedwyr Williams, *Bastamask*, 2005. Computer image. Residency, Somewhere Else: Artists from Wales, Venice. Photo Bedwyr Williams

2   3

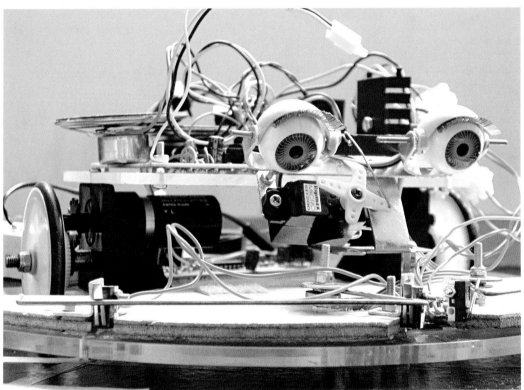

4

all of the artists in different ways in order to see and show things more clearly. Whether they are exploring the complexities of culture, identity, nationhood, social institutions and/or questioning the "grand narratives" of science or technology, all, through their work take a sideways look, a view from the periphery. From that ever-elusive somewhere else, somewhere outside the inside, they reveal a clearer sense of our contemporary condition. Although their work raises serious issues they all use humour and play to entertain, to draw us in and to create spaces in which to think about the complex ways in which our world is constructed and how art might help make sense of where we are in these difficult times.
Karen MacKinnon

The Spectre of Freedom. Il Fantasma della Libertà

The Spectre of Freedom is inspired by the late Spanish surrealist director Luis Buñuel's famous film, *Le fantôme de la Liberté* (1974).

In his film, Buñuel explored the concept of human freedom as an illusive spectre. Although freedom may seem at hand, it is more often a 'ghostly entity,' ethereal and unreachable. As the film critic Marco Lanzagorta has put it, 'Buñuel showcases the severe limitations of human freedom in a world full of seemingly arbitrary social codes and norms.'

The concept of freedom as a spectre will be adapted to reveal the contemporary human condition in an era of globalisation.

Human history has now moved into the dawn of the third millennium, and the role of freedom as a treasured idea and a core value of civilisation is now facing threats on a global scale.

Numerous crises endanger the global community, including human disasters, terrorist threats and the unjust war waged by the hegemonic US and its alliance against Iraq. Natural catastrophes have also been witnessed and experienced, such as those brought on by global warming, the SARS epidemic that threatened to cripple the world economy, and the devastating earthquakes that have relentlessly pounded Asia.

Capitalism is the pavement of the new global economy that we all drive on, but it seems that the ride is even bumpier than before, with an economic crisis in one area often setting off a vicious chain reaction around the world.

Globalisation, apart from being a force in the expansion of capitalism and the formation of a post-industrial consumer society, has also acted to spur the growth of international media conglomerates. Today's media society seems to announce that the 'society of the spectacle,' is already upon us. Citizens living in 'the spectacle' seem to have endless freedom to choose, yet a bombardment of images created by the post-modern consumer society has permeated their thinking, subtly influencing and manipulating their preferences, choices and judgments.

The Spectre of Freedom is not only an attempt to translate Buñuel's surrealist vision of freedom into the context of today's world, it also represents a questioning of the spectacle being created by the media of our times. The word 'spectre' carries a sentiment of death, but it also denotes a haunting quality, like a shadow that is always attached to human subjectivity. Deep inside the human psyche, the pursuit of freedom has constantly appeared as both a 'conscious' goal and an eternal 'unconscious' desire that constantly lingers in our subconscious.

The Spectre of Freedom will showcase four of Taiwan's best contemporary artists, including Chung-li KAO (b. 1958), Kuang-yu TSUI (b. 1974), Hsin-i Eva LIN (b. 1974) and I-chen KUO (b. 1979). Chung-li KAO will exhibit a body of works comprised of projector-based, 8 mm film installations. Their principal form is hand-painted animation merged with historical images. Recurrent brawling, confrontation and wrestling are frequent themes of KAO. Kuang-yu TSUI will also show a body of works based on single channel videos. Most of TSUI's works are self-taped performances, taking metropolis as his major arena. TSUI's works are mimetic parodies of contemporary humanity in the globalised consumer societies. Hsin-i Eva LIN will launch an interactive, net-based installation, titled *De-strike*. Using 'Artist on Strike' as a pretext to target the nature and essence of the act of strike, the artist intends to persuade the

ORGANIZATION
Taipei Fine Arts Museum of Taiwan
www.tfam.gov.tw

COORDINATION
Arte Communications

COMMISSIONER
Tsai-lang HUANG

VICE-COMMISSIONER
Paolo De Grandis

CURATOR
Chia Chi Jason WANG

ARTISTS
Chung-li KAO
I-chen KUO
Hsin-i Eva LIN
Kuang-yu TSUI

1 Chung-li KAO, *Arise*, 2005. Frame from animation
Chung-li KAO, *Anti.mei.ology 002*, 1999-2001. 8mm film projector-based installation

2 I-chen KUO, *Invade the TFAM*, 2004. Video installation

3 Hsin-i Eva LIN, *De-strike*, 2005. Net installation (Image taken from the "De-Strike" flypost and webpage)

4 Kuang-yu TSUI, *The Shortcut to the Systematic Life: Superficial Life*, 2002. Single channel video; 10' 02" loop

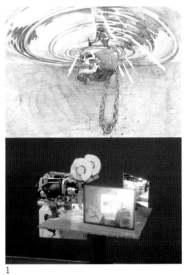

1

2

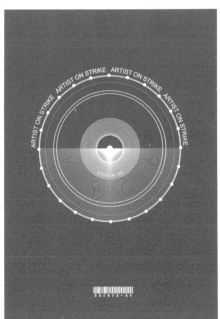

3

4

spectators to join her in the strike by sitting in, standing in, or actively interacting with the internet devices she provides. Seemingly enhancing the metaphoric image of *The Spectre of Freedom*, the fourth artist I-chen KUO will present a video installation by projecting a huge moving image of an aircraft onto the vault of the Palazzo delle Prigioni. This phantasmic, hovering shadow will haunt the exhibition space like a spectre, evoking a major impression of threat and apprehension.

Chia Chi Jason WANG

Unspoken Destinies

Unspoken Destinies creates an image of the inequalities, cultural and economic circumstances and power relations within societies that are used to justify historical events and human exploitation.

Carlos Bunga was introduced to the wider international art public by Manifesta 5 in San Sebastian in 2004, with his project built inside Rafael Moneo's Kursaal. Its temporary cardboard structure and its falling apart as a result of a series of strategic cuts expressed the artists' interest in the rapid degradation of things and the performative nature of urban spatial relationships. The same performative working method characterises Carlos Bunga's recent video work *Mother* from 2005.

'Who is my father?' is one of the questions a grown-up son, visiting his illiterate mother with a video camera, asks about his mother's life before his birth, and about the reasons she ended up moving from Angola to Portugal. After her initial blank refusal, the mother finally tells her story, which gives the viewer some sense of the life she has experienced. She describes how she lived in her home country, her family and the hardships and horrors she had to face to escape in order to save the lives of her white-skinned, then two-year-old, daughter and her unborn baby, the son.

The narrative, filmed in a single shoot, challenges the mystification that is often associated with unusual human destinies by highlighting the role of racism, murderous violence, self-justification using rationalist reasoning, or the institutionalised prostitution that accepts the idea of exploitation and the use of women's bodies as a commodity.

By portraying humanity, ethnicity and history, Jaakko Heikkilä's photo essay, Lucid Rooms, is a strong metaphor for cultural and religious conflicts – as well

ORGANIZATION
FRAME - Finnish Fund
for Art Exchange
www.frame-fund.fi

IN COLLABORATION WITH
Nuova Icona (Vittorio Urbani,
director and Camilla Seibezzi,
curator)
www.nuovaicona.org

CURATOR
Marketta Seppälä

ARTISTS
Carlos Bunga
Jaakko Heikkilä

1

2

3

4

1-4 Carlos Bunga, *Mother*, 2003. DVD PAL; 40'; video still. Courtesy the Artist

6

5

7

as for the significance of chance. It is dedicated to a remembrance of the genocide committed during the time of the Ottoman Empire against the Armenian population in the shadow of World War 1.

It is estimated that one and a half million Armenians out of a total population of 2 million perished between 1915 and 1923. Well over one million were deported in 1915. Despite the moral outrage of the international community, attention was largely directed to the war in continental Europe and no firm action was taken against the Ottoman Empire. Today, despite having embarked on membership negotiations with the European Union, the Turkish government still denies that the Armenian Genocide ever occurred.

Jaakko Heikkilä started his ongoing project with Armenian communities in Armenia in April 2004 and is continuing it in Los Angeles and Venice in 2005. His work reveals an intense involvement with members of local communities, which has helped him gain their trust and document their collective memories of past horrors and the profound, ineffable stories of their lives.

Marketta Seppälä

Index
of the artists
and exhibited
works
Participating
countries

Lida Abdul, 16
Born in Kabul, Afghanistan,
in 1973. Lives and works
in Kabul, Afghanistan,
and Los Angeles, USA.
www.lidaabdul.com

EXHIBITED WORKS
▪ Video performance, 2005.
Courtesy the Artist

Sona Abgarian, 90
Born in Berd, Republic
of Armenia, in 1979. Lives
and works in Yerevan, Republic
of Armenia.
www.accea.info

EXHIBITED WORKS
▪ *Tomorrow at the Same Time*,
2005. Video, DVD

Vahram Aghasyan, 90
Born in Yerevan, Republic
of Armenia, in 1974. Lives
and works in Yerevan, Republic
of Armenia.
www.accea.info

EXHIBITED WORKS
▪ *The Factories in Heaven*,
2005. Video, DVD

**Vyacheslav Ahunov
& Sergey Tichina**, 138
Vyacheslav Ahunov: born
in Och, Kyrgyzstan, in 1948.
Sergey Tichina: born
in Tashkent, Uzbekistan, in 1960.
They live and work
in Tashkent, Uzbekistan.

EXHIBITED WORKS
▪ *Corner*, 2004. DVD; 10'.
Courtesy the Artists
▪ *Ascent*, 2004. DVD; 11'.
Courtesy the Artists
▪ *Clay Fish*, 2004. DVD; 9'.
Courtesy the Artists

Helena Almeida, 86
Born in Lisbon, Portugal,
in 1934. Lives and works
in Lisbon, Portugal.

EXHIBITED WORKS
▪ *Eu estou aqui*, 2005. Black
& white photographic print.
Courtesy the Artist

Carolina Raquel Antich, 66
Born in Rosario, Argentina,
in 1970. Lives and works
in Venice, Italy.

EXHIBITED WORKS
▪ *Noia*, 2005. Acrylic on
canvas; 150 × 150 cm
▪ *La rana*, 2005. Watercolour
on paper; 24 × 18 cm
▪ Design of the space
at the Italian Pavilion

Said Atabekov, 138
Born in Shymkent, Uzbekistan,
in 1965. Lives and works
in Shymkent, Uzbekistan.

EXHIBITED WORKS
▪ *Neon Paradise*, 2004. Video;
10'. Courtesy the Artist

Mykola Babak, 130
Born in Voronyntsi, Cherkasy,
Ukraine. Lives and works
in Cherkasy, Ukraine.

EXHIBITED WORKS
▪ *Your Children, Ukraine!*,
2004. Photography,
assemblage, object, wooden
frames; 70 × 55 cm, 114 × 90
cm. Private collection.
Courtesy the Artist

Miriam Bäckström, 82
Born in Stockholm, Sweden,
in 1967. Lives and works
in Stockholm, Sweden.

EXHIBITED WORKS
▪ *Unplified Pavillion*, 2005. Site
specific sound installation
▪ *All images of an anonymous
person*, 2005. Artist book. In
collaboration with Moderna
Museet

Young-Whan Bae, 100
Born in Seoul, Republic
of Korea, in 1967. Lives
and works in Seoul, Republic
of Korea.

EXHIBITED WORKS
▪ *Heart*, 1999. Installation
on the public wall of a public
toilet (tile, pils, cotton balls,
bomd, mercurochrome).
Courtesy the Artist
▪ *Homeless Project - Homeless
Diary*, 2000. Packetbook, 99
pages long (including covers);
10.5 × 14.5 cm
▪ *Pop song*, 2002. Installation,
projection, sound; dimension
variable

Yiso Bahc, 100
Born in Busan, Republic
of Korea, in 1957. Died
in Seoul, Republic of Korea,
in 2004.

EXHIBITED WORKS
▪ *Wide World Wide*, 2003.
Acrylic and oil on canvas,
paper labels and light fixtures;
242 × 415 cm. Courtesy
Mr Daeyeol Ku and friends
of Yiso Bach

Izrail Basov, 94
Born in Mstislavl, Moghilev,
Republic of Belarus, in 1918.
Died in Minsk, Republic
of Belarus, in 1994.

EXHIBITED WORKS
▪ *The Conversation*, 1993.
Oil on canvas; 57 × 77 cm.
Courtesy The Estate
▪ *A Red Landscape*, 1993.
Oil on canvas; 57 × 70 cm.
Courtesy The Estate
▪ *At Dawn*, 1993. Oil
on canvas; 65 × 74 cm.
Courtesy The Estate

Luz María Bedoya, 142
Born in Talara, Peru, in 1969.
Lives and works in Lima, Peru.

EXHIBITED WORKS
▪ *Muro*, 2005. 44' video.
Book of pictures

Fouad Bellamine, 76
Born in Fez, Morocco,
in 1950. Lives and works
Rabat, Morocco.

EXHIBITED WORKS
▪ *Untitled*, 2004. Mixed media
on canvas; 140 × 160 cm
▪ *Untitled*, 2003. Mixed media
on canvas; 140 × 160 cm
▪ *Untitled*, 2004. Mixed media
on canvas; 140 × 160 cm
▪ *Untitled*, 2004. Mixed media
on canvas; 140 × 160 cm
▪ *Untitled*, 2004. Mixed media
on canvas; 140 × 160 cm

Rebecca Belmore, 32
Born in Upsala, Ontario,
Canada, in 1960. Lives
and works in Vancouver,
Canada.

EXHIBITED WORKS
▪ *Fountain*, 2005. Performance
based video/sculpture
installation. Courtesy the Artist

Guy Ben-Ner, 64
Born in Tel Aviv, Israel,
in 1969. Lives and works
in New York, USA.

EXHIBITED WORKS
▪ *Treehouse Kit*, 2005. Wooden
furniture, carpet, video
projection; 800 × 800 × 600
cm. Courtesy the Artist

Manfredi Beninati, 66
Born in Palermo, Italy,
in 1970. Lives in Campagnano
Romano, Rome, Italy.

EXHIBITED WORKS
▪ *Prendere appunti
per un sogno da iniziare
di pomeriggio e continuare
la notte (e che non si cancella
al risveglio) ovvero svegliarsi
su una spiaggia sotto il sole
cocente*, 2005. Installation

Mohamed Bennani Moha, 76
Born in Tétouan, Morocco,
in 1943. Lives and works
in Paris, France, and Rabat,
Morocco.

EXHIBITED WORKS
▪ *Acrylique sur toile 2*, 2004.
200 × 180 cm
▪ *Acrylique et matière sur toile
3*, 2004. 200 × 180 cm
▪ *Acrylique sur toile 4*, 2004.
200 × 180 cm
▪ *Acrylique sur toile 5*, 2004.
200 × 180 cm
▪ *Bronze 1*. 70 × 20 cm
▪ *Bronze 2*. 70 × 20 cm

Montien Boonma, 126
Born in Bangkok, Thailand,
in 1953. Lives and works
in Chiangmai and Bangkok,
Thailand.

EXHIBITED WORKS
▪ *Room*, 1994. Pinewood; dimesion variable
▪ *Temple of the Mind: Sala for the Mind*, 1995. Herbal medicine, wood, brass; dimesion variable. Collection of the National Gallery of Australia, Canberra
▪ *Zodiac Houses (Das Haus der Sternzeichen)*, 1998-1999. Steel, transparency, wood, herb, cinnabar; dimesion variable. Collection of the Museum of Contemporary Art, Bangkok

Maxim Boronilov see **Roman Maskalev & Maxim Boronilov**

Stephen Brandes, 58
Born in Wolverhampton, UK, in 1966. Lives and works in Cork, Ireland.

EXHIBITED WORKS
▪ *Various untitled works*, 2005. Dimension variable. Courtesy the Artist and the Rubicon Gallery, Dublin

Pasko Burdelez, 34
Born in Dubrovnik, Croatia, in 1969. Lives and works in Dubrovnik, Croatia.

EXHIBITED WORKS
▪ *Bez naziva / Untitled*, 2004. Performance and video documentation of the performance; dimension variable. Courtesy the Artist

Los Carpinteros (Marco Antonio Castillo Valdés, Dagoberto Rodríguez Sánchez, Alexandre Jesús Arrechea Zambrano), 142
Marco Antonio Castillo Valdés: born in Cuba in 1971. Dagoberto Rodríguez Sánchez: born in Cuba in 1969. Alexandre Jesús Arrechea Zambrano: born in Trinidad, Cuba, in 1970. At the moment he is no more part of the group. They live and work in Cuba.

EXHIBITED WORKS
▪ *Siesta*. Rocking chair and cushions; 335 × 62 × 70.5 cm. Courtesy Cisneros
▪ *Granada a mano (Granada de mano)*, 2004. Wood; 190 × 110 × 110 cm. Edition of 5 + artist's proof. Courtesy Galeria Fortes Vilaça, São Paulo, Brasil. Photo Eduardo Ortega © 2004

Loris Cecchini, 66
Born in Milan, Italy, in 1969. Lives and works in Milan and Prato, Italy.

EXHIBITED WORKS
▪ *Monologue Patterns (Crisalide)*, 2005. Installation, steel structure, plexiglas, optical lighting, 3 M film, artificial plant; 480 Ø × 280 cm

Hussein Chalayan, 128
Born in Nicosia/Lefkosia (Cyprus), Turkey, in 1970. Lives and works in London, UK, Istanbul, Turkey, and New York, USA.
www.husseinchalayan.com.tr

EXHIBITED WORKS
▪ *Genometrics*, 2005. Video installation and mechanical figure realized in a space approx. 10 × 20 m. Courtesy the Artist

Chelpa Ferro (Luiz Zerbini, Barrão, Sérgio Mekler), 30
Luiz Zerbini: born in São Paulo, Brazil, in 1959.
Barrão: born in Rio de Janeiro, Brazil, in 1959.
Sérgio Mekler: born in Rio de Janeiro, Brazil, in 1963. They live and work in Rio de Janeiro, Brazil.

EXHIBITED WORKS
▪ *Untitled*, 2005. Installation, mixed media; dimension variable. Collection of the artists and Galeria Vermelho, São Paulo

Donna Conlon, 142
Born in Atlanta, Georgia, USA, in 1966. Lives and works in the City of Panama, Republic of Panama.

EXHIBITED WORKS
▪ *Coexistence (Coexistencia)*, 2003. DVD video, registered on mini-DV; 5' 26''. Courtesy the Artist

Honoré δ'O, 28
Born in Oudernaarde, Belgium, in 1961. Lives and works in Gent, Belgium.

EXHIBITED WORKS
▪ *The Quest*, 2005. Mixed media (wood, PVC, video); 2100 × 1600 × 580 cm

Maxence Denis, 142
Born in Port-au-Prince, Haiti, in 1968. Lives and works in Paris, France.

EXHIBITED WORKS
▪ *Kwa Bawon*, 2003. Audiovisual installation, films and sound registrations of different running times; metal and wood structure, 7 monitors; sound track Laurent Lettrèe; 190 × 156 cm. Courtesy the Artist

Jeroen de Rijke and Willem de Rooij, 80
Jeroen de Rijke: born in Brouwershaven, The Netherlands, in 1970. Willem de Rooij: born in Beverwijk, The Netherlands, in 1969.

They live and work in Amsterdam, The Netherlands.

EXHIBITED WORKS
▪ Work made on the occasion of the 51. Biennale di Venezia, 2005

Gonzalo Díaz, 142
Born in Santiago, Chile, in 1947. Lives and works in Santiago, Chile.

EXHIBITED WORKS
▪ *Muerte en Venecia Lettera A*, 2005. Installation. Letters A, R, T, E form of polycarbonate, acrylic glass; 28 × 98 cm. Courtesy the Artist
▪ *Muerte en Venecia Lettera R*, 2005. Installation. Letters A, R, T, E form of polycarbonate, acrylic glass; 28 × 75 cm. Courtesy the Artist
▪ *Muerte en Venecia Lettera T*, 2005. Installation. Letters A, R, T, E form of polycarbonate, acrylic glass; 28 × 91 cm. Courtesy the Artist
▪ *Muerte en Venecia Lettera E*, 2005. Installation. Letters A, R, T, E form of polycarbonate, acrylic glass; 28 × 91 cm. Courtesy the Artist

Polibio Díaz, 142
Born in Barahona, Dominican Republic, in 1952. Lives and works in Gazcue, Santo Domingo.

EXHIBITED WORKS
▪ *Pasiones interiores*, 2002. Scanned color photograph; 106 × 480 cm. 5. Bienal del Caribe Prize, 2003. Courtesy the Artist
▪ *Sin titulo*, 2002. Scanned color photograph; 100 × 450 cm. Courtesy the Artist
▪ *Después de la siesta*, 2002-2005. Scanned color photograph; 100 × 450 cm. Courtesy the Artist

Muratbek Djoumaliev see **Gulnara Kasmalieva & Muratbek Djoumaliev**

Lacy Duarte, 134
Born in Mataojo, Salto, Uruguay, in 1937. Lives and works in Salto, Uruguay.

EXHIBITED WORKS
▪ *10 Trapezas*, 2004-2005. Mixed techinque; 100 × 130 cm. Courtesy the Artist
▪ *3 Paintings*, 2004-2005. Mixed techinque; 130 × 130 cm. Courtesy the Artist
▪ *Installation*, 2004-2005. Mixed technique; dimension variable. Courtesy the Artist

Zlatan Dumanić, 34
Born in Split, Croatia, in 1951. Lives and works in Split, Croatia.

EXHIBITED WORKS
▪ *Igra / the Play*, 2003. Weld-painted tin-zinc, rice; 25 × 119 × 16 cm. Courtesy the Artist
▪ *Simbol / the Symbol*, 2004. Weld-painted tin-zinc; 26.5 × 141 × 27.5 cm. Courtesy the Artist
▪ *Slavlje / the Celebration*, 2005. Weld-painted tin-zinc, fruits, vinegar flies; 27 × 100 × 14 cm. Courtesy the Artist

Juan Manuel Echavarría, 142
Born in Medellin, Colombia, in 1947. Lives and works in Bogota, Colombia.

EXHIBITED WORKS
▪ *Bocas de ceniza*. Video still; frame from the video, *Rafael Moreno* 2003, from the series *Bocas de ceniza*. Seven chants, video; 2' 30'' each. Collection of Daros Latinamerica, Zurich

the ESCAPE program, 112
(Valery Ayzenberg, Anton Litvin, Bogdan Mamonov, Liza Morozova)
Valerij Ayzenberg: born in Ukraine in 1947. Lives and works in Moscow, Russia, New York, USA, and Tel Aviv, Israel.
Anton Litvin: born in Moscow, Russia, in 1967. Lives and works in Moscow, Russia.
Bogdan Mamonov: born in Moscow, Russia, in 1964. Lives and works in Moscow, Russia.
Liza Morozova: born in Moscow, Russia, in 1973. Lives and works in Moscow, Russia.

EXHIBITED WORKS
▪ *Too Long to Escape*, 2005. Interactive video installation; dimension variable. Courtesy the Artists

et al, 78
They are born in Aotearoa, New Zealand. They live and work in Auckland, New Zealand.
www.etal.info
www.thefundamentalpractice.org
www.creativenz.govt.nz/venice

EXHIBITED WORKS
▪ *the fundamental practice*, 2005. Site specific installation; various media including audio, video, computers, and constructed objects; dimension variable
Factotum www.factotum.org.uk

Matias Faldbakken, 82
Born in Hobro, Denmark, in 1973. Lives and works in Oslo, Norway.

EXHIBITED WORKS
▪ *Black Screen*, 2005. DVD video, color, no sound; approx. 1'. Courtesy Standard, Oslo
▪ *Black Screen book*, 2005. Catalogue, colour and black & white

Lara Favaretto, 66
Born in Treviso, Italy, in 1973.
Lives and works in Turin, Italy.

EXHIBITED WORKS
• *La terra è troppo grande*,
2005. Video installation, loop,
black & white DVD

Bita Fayyazi Azad, 56
Born in Teheran, Iran, in 1962.
Lives and works in Teheran,
Iran.

EXHIBITED WORKS
• *Kismet*, 2005. 50 sculptures
of aluminium casted life-size
new-born babies positioned
within a purpose built structure
made from aluminium plate
sheets; 200 × 200 × 400 cm.
Courtesy the Artist

Stano Filko, 88
Born in Vel'ká, Slovak Republic,
in 1937. Lives and works
in Bratislava, Slovak Republic.

EXHIBITED WORKS
• *Model sveta - Quadrophonia /
Model of World -
Quadrophonia*, 2005

Vadim Fiškin, 104
Born in Penza, Russia,
in 1965. Lives and works
in Ljubljana, Slovenia.
www.dum-club.si/vaf/

EXHIBITED WORKS
• *Another Speedy Day*, 2003-
2005. Light system, electronic
clock; dimension variable.
Courtesy the Artist

Alen Floričić, 34
Born in Pula, Croatia, in 1968.
Lives and works in Rabac,
Croatia.

EXHIBITED WORKS
• *Bez naziva N° 03/04 /
Untitled N° 03/04*, 2004.
Three channel video installation;
dimension variable; 1' 53"
(each video), loop. Courtesy
the Artist

Gabríela Friðriksdóttir, 62
Born in Reykjavik, Iceland,
in 1971. Lives and works
in Brussels, Belgium.
www.gabriela.is

EXHIBITED WORKS
• *Versations/Tetralogia*, 2005.
Pen drawing: Gabríela
Friðriksdóttir; design: M/Mparis;
photographs: D100/ 6Mpxls
each

Mark Garry, 58
Born in Westmeath, Ireland,
in 1972. Lives and works
in Dublin, Ireland.

EXHIBITED WORKS
• *Site specific installation*,
2005. Mixed media. Courtesy
the Artist

Gilbert & George, 50
Gilbert: born in the Dolomites,
Italy, in 1943.
George: born in Devon, UK,
in 1942.
They live and work in London,
UK.

EXHIBITED WORKS
• *Perversive Pictures*, 2004.
Mixed media; dimension
variable. © Gilbert & George.
Courtesy Sonnabend Gallery,
New York / Lahmann Maupin,
New York
• *Twenty London ei Pictures*,
2003. Mixed media; dimension
variable. © Gilbert & George.
Courtesy Galerie Thaddens
Ropac, Paris
• *Thirteen Hooligan Pictures*,
2004. Mixed media; dimension
variable. © Gilbert & George.
Courtesy Bernier / Eliades,
Athens

Gimhongsok, 100
Born in Seoul, Republic
of Korea, in 1964.
Lives and works in the Republic
of Korea.

EXHIBITED WORKS
• *Love*, 2004. Steel;
150 × 145 cm
• *Literal Reality*, 2004. Polyeter
resin; dimension variable

Mónica González, 142
Born in Asunción, Paraguay,
in 1952. Lives and works
in San Bernardino
and Asunción, Paraguay.

EXHIBITED WORKS
• *Arroyito*, 1997. Installation
made of glasses; approx. lenght
10 m. Courtesy the Artist

Group F5, 70
(Līga Marcinkeviča, Ieva
Rubeze, Mārtiņš Ratniks,
Ervins Broks)
Līga Marcinkeviča: born
in Skrunda, Latvia, in 1975.
Ieva Rubeze: born in Liepāja,
Latvia, in 1977.
Mārtiņš Ratniks: born
in Saulkrasti, Latvia, in 1975.
Ervins Broks: born in Riga,
Latvia, in 1975.
They live and work in Riga,
Latvia.

EXHIBITED WORKS
• *Dark Bulb*, 2005. Installation
(video object). Courtesy Group
F5

George Hadjimichalis, 52
Born in Athens, Greece,
in 1954. Lives and works
in Athens and Sfedouri
(Aegina), Greece.
www.ghadjimichalis.gr

EXHIBITED WORKS
• *Hospital, The Building,
the Plan, the View from
the Windows, the Ward*,

2004-2005. Installation; mixed
media; dimension variable.
Courtesy the Artist

Diana Hakobian, 90
Born in Yerevan, Republic
of Armenia, in 1974. Lives
and works in Yerevan, Republic
of Armenia.
www.accea.info

EXHIBITED WORKS
• *The Logic of Power*, 2005.
Video, DVD

**Salah El Din Ahmed Mohamed
Hammad**, 38
Born in Cairo, Egypt, in 1961.
Lives and works in Cairo, Egypt.

EXHIBITED WORKS
• *Migration*, 2005. Construction
wood, granite, marble, metal,
sand, bowling, effect sound
(music); 4 × 5 m

Yung Ho Chang, 106
Born in Beijing, People's
Republic of China, in 1956.
Lives and works in Beijin,
People's Republic of China,
and Boston, USA.

EXHIBITED WORKS
• *Bamboo Shoots*, 2005.
Bamboo, galvanized iron wire,
hemp cord, iron tube;
52.5 × 29 × 8 m

Carsten Höller, 82
Born in Brussels, Belgium,
in 1961. Lives and works
in Stockholm, Sweden.

Noor Ibrahim, 54
Born in Magelang, Indonesia,
in 1966. Lives and works
in Djiakarta, Indonesia.

EXHIBITED WORKS
• *Fossilised Behavior*, 2005.
Mixed media; 600 × 400 cm

Miyako Ishiuchi, 48
Born in Gunma, Japan,
in 1947. Lives and works
in Tokyo, Japan.

EXHIBITED WORKS
• *Mother's 2002-2005 - Traces
of future*, 2002-2005. 33
photographs, video installation.
Collection of the artist

Choi Jeong-Hwa, 100
Born in Seoul, Republic of Korea,
in 1961. Lives and works
in Seoul, Republic of Korea.

EXHIBITED WORKS
• *Dragon Flower*, 2003.
Installation (waterproof cloth,
motor, ventilator; timer);
45 × 300 cm
• *Happy Togheter*, 2004.
Installation (waterproof cloth,
motor, ventilator; timer);
100 × 1500 cm
• *Site of Desire*, 2005.
Installation; plastic baskets

Ham Jin, 100
Born in Seoul, Republic
of Korea, in 1978. Lives
and works in Seoul, Republic
of Korea.

EXHIBITED WORKS
• *Aewan Love # 2*, 2004. C-
print photograph of a sculpture
made of polymer clay, fly and
mixed media; 155 × 125.5 cm.
Courtesy the Artist
• *Aewan Love # 3*, 2004. C-
print photograph of a sculpture
made of polymer clay, fly and
mixed media; 155 × 125.5 cm.
Courtesy the Artist

Yeondoo Jung, 100
Born in Jinju, Republic
of Korea, in 1969.
Lives and works in Seoul,
Republic of Korea.

EXHIBITED WORKS
• *Evergreen Tower*, 2001.
Multi-side projection, 32
images; dimension variable.
Courtesy Artsonje Center, Seoul
/ JGS Foundation, NY / Fukuoka
Asia Museum, Fukuoka, Japan

**Gulnara Kasmalieva
& Muratbek Djoumaliev**, 138
Muratbek Djoumaliev: born
in Bishkek, Kyrgyzstan,
in 1965.
Gulnara Kasmalieva: born
in Frunze (Bishkek), Kyrgyzstan,
in 1960.
They live and work in Bishkek,
Kyrgyzstan.

EXHIBITED WORKS
• *To the future...*, 2005. Author
proof. Two screen video film, 6';
DVD; two video projectors
(minimum 2000 Ansi lum,
audio out); two DVD players;
one audio. Courtesy the Artist

Tigran Khachatrian, 90
Born in Yerevan, Republic
of Armenia, in 1980. Lives
and works in Yerevan, Republic
of Armenia.
www.accea.info

EXHIBITED WORKS
• *Theodicy*, 2005. Video, DVD

**Rustam Khalfin & Yulia
Tikhonova**, 138
Born in Tashkent, Uzbekistan,
in 1949. Lives and works
in Almaty, Kazakhstan.

EXHIBITED WORKS
• *The Pinch*, 1990. Drawing;
14.5 × 20 cm. Courtesy
the Artist
• *Northern Barbarians, Part. 2
The Love Races*, 2000. Video;
10'. Courtesy the Artist
• *Pulota*, 1990. Drawing; 12.8
× 19 cm. Courtesy the Artist

Leonid Khobotov, 94
Born in Rechitsa, Republic
of Belarus, in 1950. Lives

and works in Minsk, Republic of Belarus.

EXHIBITED WORKS
• *Dream*, 1999. Oil on canvas; 50 × 195 cm. Courtesy the Artist
• *Refractions*, 1999. Oil on canvas; 140 × 145 cm. Courtesy the Artist
• *Marine*, 2000. Oil on canvas; 150 × 315 cm. Courtesy the Artist

Balázs Kicsiny, 132
Born in Salgótarján, Hungary, in 1958. Lives and works in Budapest, Hungary, and London, UK

EXHIBITED WORKS
• *Cobbler's Apprentice*, 2005. Video installation
• *Winterreise*, 2005. Installation, life-size figures, plastic, mixed media
• *Sweet Home*, 2005. Installation, life-size figure, mixed media
• *Pump Room*, 2005. Installation, 12 life-size figures, mixed media

Beom Kim, 100
Born in Seoul, Republic of Korea, in 1963. Lives and works in Seoul, Republic of Korea.

EXHIBITED WORKS
• *An Iron in the form of a Radio, a Kettle in the form of an Iron, ads a Radio in the form of a Kettle*, 2002. Mixed media. Collection of the National Museum of Contemporary Art, Kuachon, Republic of Korea
• *Patient # 403*, 2001. Mixed media; 40 × 34 cm. Collection of the Ho-Am Art Museum, Seoul, Republic of Korea

Sora Kim, 100
Born in Seoul, Republic of Korea, in 1963. Lives and works in Seoul, Republic of Korea.

EXHIBITED WORKS
• *1,650 CYN*, 2002. Installation; mixed media; dimension variable
• *Ephemeral Market*, 2002. Installation; mixed media; dimension variable
• *CapitalPlus Credit Union*, 2002. Project; mixed media; dimension variable

Daniel Knorr, 110
Born in Bucarest, Romania, in 1968. Lives and works in Berlin, Germany.

EXHIBITED WORKS
• *European Influenza*, 2005. Mixed media; dimension variable. Courtesy the Artist

Eva Koch, 36
Born in Denmark. Lives and works in Copenhagen, Denmark.
www.evakoch.net

EXHIBITED WORKS
• *Approach*, 2005. Video and sound installation. Courtesy Gallery Asbæk, Copenhagen

Joachim Koester, 36
Born in Copenhagen, Denmark, in 1962. Lives and works in Copenhagen, Denmark, and New York, USA.

EXHIBITED WORKS
• *Message from Andrée*, 2005. 16 mm film loop. Courtesy Gallery Nicolai Wallner, Copenhagen

Peter Land, 36
Born in Århus, Denmark, in 1966. Lives and works in Copenhagen, Denmark.

EXHIBITED WORKS
• *Legepladsen / Play ground*, 2005. Sculpture. Courtesy Nicolai Wallner

Lim Tzay Chuen, 116
Born in Singapore in 1972. Lives and works in Singapore.

Ann Lislegaard, 36
Born in Norway in 1962. Lives and works in Copenhagen, Denmark, and New York, USA.

EXHIBITED WORKS
• *u.t.*, 2005 (work in progress). Animated video installation

Jorge Macchi, 22
Born in Buenos Aires, Argentina, in 1963. Lives and works in Buenos Aires, Argentina.

EXHIBITED WORKS
• Jorge Macchi in collaboration with Edgardo Rudnitzky, *La Ascensión*, 2005. Installation; trampoline-CD, sound installation; 1200 × 1400 × 800 cm

Oswaldo Macià, 142
Born in Cartagena, Colombia, in 1960. Lives and works in London, UK.

EXHIBITED WORKS
• *Something Going On Above My Head*, 1995-1999. Sound-sculpture with 16 sound-channels; 30'

Jan Mančuška, 88
Born in Bratislava, Slovak Republic, in 1972. Lives and works in Prague, Czech Republic.

EXHIBITED WORKS
• *Model sveta - Quadrophonia / Model of World - Quadrophonia*, 2005

Roman Maskalev & Maxim Boronilov, 138
Roman Maskalev: born in Bishkek, Kyrgyzstan, in 1977. Lives and works in Bishkek, Kyrgyzstan. Maxim Boronilov: born in the region of Chui, Kyrgyzstan, in 1980. Lives and works in Lebedinovka, Kyrgyzstan.

EXHIBITED WORKS
• *Paris*, 2004. Video, MP and G4; 23'. Courtesy the Artists

Sergey Maslov, 138
Born in Samara, Russia, in 1962. Died in 2002.

EXHIBITED WORKS
• *Baikonur - 2*, 2002. Installation, slide, film

Antoni Maznevski, 42
Born in Skopje, FYROM, in 1963. Lives and works in Skopie, FYROM.

EXHIBITED WORKS
• *Mozart's Boat*, 2004. Installation; ready-made wooden boat; dimensions: 100 × 650 × 200 cm, and 10-15 wooden bows of different dimensions. Courtesy the Artist

Ronan McCrea, 58
Born in Dublin, Ireland, in 1969. Lives and works in Dublin, Ireland.

EXHIBITED WORKS
• *Sequences, Scenarios & Locations*, 2004-2005. Slide installation; dimension variable. Courtesy the Artist

Jonas Mekas, 72
Born in Semeniskiai, Lithuania, in 1922. Lives and works in New York, USA.

EXHIBITED WORKS
• *Rillettes*, 2000. Slides-photo diapositives. Courtesy the Artist
• *Notes on Utopia*, 2002-2004. Video DVD. Courtesy the Artist
• *Home Videos*, 1987-2004. Video DVD. Courtesy the Artist
• *Frozen film Frames*, 1990-2005. Paper. Courtesy the Artist
• *Videos About Jonas*, 1970-2005. DVD. Courtesy the Artist
• *DVD videos*. Courtesy the Artist

Yerbossyn Meldibekov, 138
Born in Tulkubas, Kazakhstan, in 1964. Lives and works in Timiryazev, Kazakhstan.

EXHIBITED WORKS
• *Pastan*, 2002. Video, multiplex. Courtesy the Artist

Almagul Menlibayeva, 138
Born in Almaty, Kazakhstan, in 1969. Lives and works in Berlin, Germany.

EXHIBITED WORKS
• *On the military range*. DVD, color, sound; 7'. Courtesy the Artist

Guiomar Mesa, 142
Born in La Paz, Bolivia, in 1961. Lives and works in La Paz, Bolivia.

EXHIBITED WORKS
• *Palos de Agua*, 2005. Installation; cactus piles painted in oils; 200 × 250 cm. Courtesy the Artist

Annette Messager, 44
Born in Berck-sur-Mer, France, in 1943. Lives and works in Malakoff, France.

EXHIBITED WORKS
• *Casino*, 2005. Installation; mixed media; dimension variable

Panayiotis Michael, 98
Born in Nicosia, Republic of Cyprus, in 1966. Lives and works in Nicosia, Republic of Cyprus.
www.artrageousgroup.com

EXHIBITED WORKS
• *I Promise, You Will Love Me Forever*, 2005. Drawing collage; dimension variable. Courtesy the Artist

Mandana Moghaddam, 56
Born in Teheran, Iran, in 1962. Lives and works in Teheran, Iran, and Göteborg, Sweden.
www.mandana-m.com

EXHIBITED WORKS
• *Chelgis II*, 2005. Installation, sculptures, iron rod, cement, iron wire, human hair (woman); 200 × 150 × 100 cm. Courtesy the Artist

Sungshic Moon, 100
Born in Gimchun, Republic of Korea, in 1980. Lives and works in Seoul, Republic of Korea.

EXHIBITED WORKS
• *Garden in the Forest*, 2003. Black and white ink on paper; 42 × 30 cm. Courtesy the Artist
• *Talkin Trees*, 2004. Watercolor on paper; 38 × 56 cm. Courtesy the Artist
• *Rectangular Garden*, 2004. Acrylic on canvas; 334 × 112 cm. Courtesy the Artist

Gianni Motti, 122
Born in Sondrio, Italy, in 1958. Lives and works in Geneva, Switzerland.

EXHIBITED WORKS
• *Rael*, 2005. Multi-media installation; dimension variable. Courtesy the Artist

EXHIBITED WORKS
• *Isolator*, 1997-2005.
Photographs and videos.
Courtesy the Artist

Igor Rakčević, 114
Born in Podgorica, Serbia
and Montenegro, in 1971.
Lives and works in Podgorica,
Serbia and Montenegro.

EXHIBITED WORKS
• *Once Upon a Time*, 2005.
Video

Araya Rasdjarmrearnsook, 126
Born in Trad, Thailand,
in 1957. Lives and works
in Chiangmai, Thailand.

EXHIBITED WORKS
• *Reading for Corpses*, 2002.
Video installation; dimension
variable. Collection of the artist
• *Reading for Corpses*, 2001.
Video installation; dimension
variable. Collection of the artist

Caio Reisewitz, 30
Born in São Paulo, Brazil,
in 1967. Lives and works
in São Paulo, Brazil.

EXHIBITED WORKS
• *Real Gabinete Português
de Leitura 1*, Rio de Janeiro,
2004. C-print; 235 × 190 cm.
Collection of the artist. Courtesy
Galeria Brito Cimino, São Paulo
• *Real Gabinete Português
de Leitura 2*, Rio de Janeiro,
2004. C-print; 190 × 235 cm.
Collection of the artist. Courtesy
Galeria Brito Cimino, São Paulo
• *Gabinete do Prefeito de São
Paulo (Palácio do
Anhangabaú)*, 2004. C-print;
190 × 235 cm. Collection
of the artist. Courtesy Galeria
Brito Cimino, São Paulo
• *Fundação Bienal de São
Paulo (Pavilhão Ciccillo
Matarazzo)*, 2005. C-print;
235 × 190 cm. Collection
of the artist. Courtesy Galeria
Brito Cimino, São Paulo
• *Ministério das Relações
Exteriores (Palácio do
Itamaraty)*, 2005. C-print;
190 × 235 cm. Collection
of the artist. Courtesy Galeria
Brito Cimino, São Paulo
• *Igreja de São Francisco
da Penitência*, 2004. C-print;
235 × 190 cm. Collection
of the artist. Courtesy Galeria
Brito Cimino, São Paulo

Jewyo Rhii, 100
Born in Seoul, Republic
of Korea, in 1971. Lives
and works in Amsterdam,
The Netherlands.

EXHIBITED WORKS
• *Moon drawing*, 2004. Wall
drawing; dimension variable
• *The Half of Basemente -
Homage to Yiso Bahc*, 2004.
Installation; dimension variable

Pipilotti Rist, 124
Born in Grabs, Switzerland,
in 1962. Lives and works
in Zurich, Switzerland.

Edgardo Rudnitzky, 22
Born in Buenos Aires,
Argentina, in 1956. Lives
and works in Berlin, Germany.

EXHIBITED WORKS
• Jorge Macchi in collaboration
with Edgardo Rudnitzky, *La
Ascensión*, 2005. Installation:
trampoline-CD, sound
installation; 1200 × 1400
× 800 cm

Ed Ruscha, 120
Born in Omaha, Nebraska,
USA, in 1937. Lives and works
in Venice, California, USA.

EXHIBITED WORKS
• *Blue Collar Trade School*,
1992. Acrylic on canvas;
294.64 × 132.08 cm.
Courtesy Neda Young
• *Blue Collar Telephone*, 1992.
Acrylic on canvas; 305.2
× 137.5 cm. Courtesy Refert
Art Collection, Museum
für Kommunikation, Frankfurt,
Germany
• *Blue Collar Tires*, 1992.
Acrylic on canvas; 304.8
× 137.16 cm. Courtesy Museo
Nacional Centro de Arte Reina
Sofía, Madrid, Spain
• *Blue Collar Tool & Die*, 1992.
Acrylic on canvas; 294.64 ×
132.08 cm. Courtesy Fondation
Belgacom Brussels, Belgium
• *The Old Trade School
Building*, 2005. Acrylic on
canvas; 304.8 × 137.16 cm.
Courtesy the Artist
• *The Old Tires Building*, 2005.
Acrylic on canvas; 304.8
× 137.16 cm. Courtesy
the Artist
• *Site of a Former Telephone
Booth*, 2005. Acrylic on
canvas; 304.8 × 137.16 cm.
Courtesy the Artist
• *Blue Collar Tech Chem*,
1992. Acrylic on canvas;
276.86 × 122.88 cm. Courtesy
the Artist
• *The Old Tech Chem Building*,
2003. Acrylic on canvas;
276.86 × 122.88 cm. Courtesy
the Artist
• *The Old Tool & Die Building*,
2004. Acrylic on canvas;
294.64 × 132.08 cm. Courtesy
the Artist

Joaquín Sánchez, 142
(artistic name)
Fredy Ramón Sanchez
Born in Eusebio Ayala,
Paraguay, in 1975. Lives
and works in La Paz, Bolivia.

EXHIBITED WORKS
• *Ovillos*, 2005. Installation
of llama and alpaca wool
with metal stuctures;

Ø 200 cm. Courtesy the Artist
• *Ovillos*, 2005. Installation
of llama and alpaca wool
with metal stuctures.
Ø 180 cm. Courtesy the Artist
• *Ovillos*, 2005. Installation
of llama and alpaca wool
with metal stuctures;
Ø 150 cm. Courtesy the Artist

Yani Mariani Sastranegara, 54
Born in Rangkasbitung,
Indonesia, in 1955. Lives
and works in Jl. Sumatra
Tangerang, Indonesia.

EXHIBITED WORKS
• *Lazuardi*, 2005. Mixed
media penter, combstone;
250 × 250 × 300 cm

Tomo Savić Gecan, 34
Born in Zagreb, Croatia,
in 1967. Lives and works
in Amsterdam, The
Netherlands.

EXHIBITED WORKS
• *Bez naziva / Untitled*, 2003-
2005. Interactive space
installation. Courtesy Isabella
Bortolozzi Gallery, Berlin

Hans Schabus, 26
Born in Watschig, Austria,
in 1970. Lives and works
in Vienna, Austria.

EXHIBITED WORKS
• *Installation*, 2005. 3500
× 1700 cm. Courtesy the Artist

Thomas Scheibitz, 46
Born in Radeberg, Germany,
in 1968. Lives and works
in Berlin, Germany.
www.thomasscheibitz.de

EXHIBITED WORKS
• *16 Sculptures*, 2004-2005.
Wood, MDF, paint, metal;
between 80 × 80 × 80 cm and
285 × 450 cm. Courtesy the
Artist; Tanya Bonakdar Gallery,
New York; Produzentengalerie,
Hamburg; Monika Sprüth
Galerie, Cologne
• *7 Paintings*, 2004-2005. Oil
on canvas; between 220 × 160
cm and 285 × 450 cm.
Courtesy the Artist; Tanya
Bonakdar Gallery, New York;
Produzentengalerie, Hamburg;
Monika Sprüth Galerie, Cologne

Tino Sehgal, 46
Born in London, UK, in 1976.
Lives and works in Berlin,
Germany.

EXHIBITED WORKS
• *This is exchange*, 2003
• *This is so contemporary*,
2004

Park Sejin, 100
Born in Gwangju, Republic
of Korea, in 1977. Lives
and works in Seoul, Republic
of Korea.

• *Landscape*, 1993-2002.
Acrylic on canvas; 30 × 40 cm.
Courtesy the Artist
• *The Helipad*, 2001. Cherry
and mixed media on paper;
108 × 146 cm. Collection
of The Korean Culture & Arts
Foundation, Seoul, Korea
• *Labor*, 2004. Rose and mixed
media on paper; 164 × 150 cm

Valery Shkarubo, 94
Born in Borisov, Republic
of Belarus, in 1957. Lives
and works in Minsk, Republic
of Belarus.

EXHIBITED WORKS
• *Invasion*, 2002. Oil
on canvas; 110 × 150 cm.
Courtesy the Artist
• *Wild Tree*, 2002. Oil
on canvas; 90 × 120 cm.
Courtesy the Artist
• *White Snow*, 2003. Oil
on canvas; 95 × 115 cm.
Courtesy the Artist

Boris Šincek, 34
Born in Osijek, Croatia,
in 1971. Lives and works
in Osijek, Croatia.

EXHIBITED WORKS
• *Pucanj / Shooting*, 2002.
Video documentation
of the performance

Konstantia Sofokleous, 98
Born in Limassol, Republic
of Cyprus, in 1974. Lives
and works in Limassol,
Republic of Cyprus.
www.Konstantiasofokleous.com

EXHIBITED WORKS
• *Alice's Adventures
in Wonderland*, 2003. 2D
animated movie, drawings,
charcoal, colour crayons
on paper. Courtesy the Artist
• *Children's Poem*, 2004-
2005. 2D animated movie,
drawings, charcoal, colour
crayons on paper. Courtesy
the Artist

Sun Yuan & Peng Yu, 106
Sun Yuang: born in Beijing,
People's Republic of China,
in 1972.
They live and work in Beijing,
People's Republic of China.

EXHIBITED WORKS
• *Unidentified Flying Objects*,
2005. UFO; 6 × 2.5 × 6 m

Nakhee Sung, 100
Born in Seoul, Republic
of Korea, in 1971. Lives
and works in Seoul, Republic
of Korea.

EXHIBITED WORKS
• *# 2 (Zhaüs)*, 2003. Wall
drawing with vinyl sheet,
marker, paint, and spray paint;
dimension variable

• *# 6 (Shangai)*, 2003. Wall drawing with vinyl sheet, marker, paint, and spray paint; dimension variable

Ricky Swallow, 24
Born in San Remo, Victoria, Australia, in 1974. Lives and works in London, UK.

EXHIBITED WORKS
• *Come Together*, 2002. Laminated jelutong; 63.5 × 81.3 × 66 cm. Collection of Peter Norton, Santa Monica, USA
• *Field Recording / Highland Park Hydra*, 2003. Laminated jelutong; 104 × 40 × 105 cm. Private collection Janet de Botton, London, UK
• *KillingTime*, 2003-2004. Laminated jelutong and maple; 184 × 118 × 108 cm. Courtesy Art Gallery of New South Wales Collection, Australia
• *The Arrangement*, 2004. Laminated lime wood; 46 × 24 × 51 cm. Courtesy the Artist and Moder Art, London, UK
• (title to be confirmed), 2004-2005. Laminated jelutong and maple; 102 × 20 × 102 cm. Courtesy the Artist and Darren Knight Gallery, Sydney, Australia
• *The Exact Dimendions of Staying Behind*, 2004-2005. Laminated lime wood; 110 × 105 × 70 cm. Courtesy the Artist and Modern Art, London, UK

Nagui Farid Tadros, 38
Born in Cairo, Egypt, in 1964. Lives and works in Cairo, Egypt.

EXHIBITED WORKS
• *Another Time*, 2005. 14 pieces in one composition

Fathiya Tahiri, 76
Born in Rabat, Morocco, in 1959. Lives and works in Morocco.

EXHIBITED WORKS
• *Langue au chat*, 2003. Oil on canvas; 200 × 140 cm
• *Rupture*, 2003. Oil on wood and ostrich skin; 200 × 140 cm
• *Naissance*, 2003. Oil on canvas; 200 × 140 cm
• *Tout feu tout flamme*, 2004. Oil on canvas; 200 × 140 cm
• *Clown*, 2005. Oil on canvas; 200 × 140 cm
• *Sculptures. Équilibre*. Bronze and massive silver; 80 × 50 cm
• *Boîte à pandore*; Bronze and massive silver; 80 × 50 cm

Sergey Tichina see **Vyacheslav Ahunov & Sergey Tichina**

Yulia Tikhonova see **Rustam Khalfin & Yulia Tikhonova**

Jaime-David Tischler, 142
Born in San José, Costa Rica, in 1960. Lives and works in San José, Costa Rica.

EXHIBITED WORKS
• *La máquina del tiempo*, 2005. Video installation and decomposing negatives. Collection of the artist
• *Epitafio*, 1997 (2002). 120 × 120 × 10 cm. Collection of the artist
• *Domingo y árbol*, 1997 (2002). Enlarged silver print of selenium, sepia and gold toning, starting from a destroyed negative; 120 × 120 cm. Courtesy the Artist
• *Miedo a la Muerte*, 1997 (2002). Enlarged silver print of selenium, sepia and gold toning, starting from a destroyed negative; 120 × 120 cm. Courtesy the Artist
• *El Cielo Protector II* (diptych), 1997 (2002). Enlarged silver print of selenium, sepia and gold toning, starting from a destroyed negative; 120 × 120 cm. Courtesy the Artist

Igor Tishin, 94
Born in Vasilpolye Gomel, Republic of Belarus, in 1958. Lives and works in Brussels, Belgium.

EXHIBITED WORKS
• *The Nanny's Wish*, 2000. Oil on canvas; 174 × 125 cm. Courtesy the Artist
• *Red Rose*, 2001. Oil on canvas; 140 × 120 cm. Courtesy the Artist
• *Face and Surface*, 2001. Oil on canvas; 100 × 110 cm. Courtesy the Artist

Jelena Tomašević, 114
Born in Podgorica, Serbia and Montenegro, in 1974. Lives and works in Podgorica, Serbia and Montenegro.

EXHIBITED WORKS
• *Joy of Life*, 2004. Mixed media (façade colours, acrylic, sellotape on canvas); 41 × 64 cm
• *Joy of Life*, 2003. Mixed media (façade colours, acrylic, sellotape on canvas); 47 × 75 cm. Private collection
• *Joy of Life*, 2004. Mixed media (façade colours, acrylic, sellotape on canvas); 46 × 74 cm

Goran Trbuljak, 34
Born in Varaždin, Croatia, in 1948. Lives and works in Zagreb, Croatia.

EXHIBITED WORKS
• *The need to add a footnote to a text is more important than whatever might be in the footnote 30 years later*, 1976-2005. Episcope text projection;

21 × 30 cm. Courtesy the Artist
• *What is not in the text is also not in the footnote*, 2005. Episcope text projection; 63 × 90 cm. Courtesy the Artist
• *The need to add a footnote to a text is more important than whatever might be in the footnote 30 years later*.
• *What is not in the text is also not in the footnote*, 2005. Colored metal plate; 50 × 60 cm. Courtesy the Artist

Vladimir Tsesler and Sergey Voichenko, 94
Vladimir Tsesler: born in Sluzk, Republic of Belarus, in 1951. Lives and works in Minsk, Republic of Belarus. Sergey Voichenko: born in Mariupol, Zhdanov, Ukraine, in 1955. Died in Minsk, Republic of Belarus, in 2004.

EXHIBITED WORKS
• *Spiral*, 1995. Acrylic paste in relief and oil on canvas; 103 × 130 cm. Courtesy the Artists
• *Models and Factory*, 1999. Acrylic paste in relief and oil on canvas; 103 × 175 cm. Courtesy the Artists
• *Project of the XII Century from 2000*, 2000. Wood sculptures, resin, polyester, marble, steel, bronze; 28.5 × 21 cm. Courtesy the Artists

Ruslan Vashkevich, 94
Born in Minsk, Republic of Belarus, in 1966. Lives and works in Minsk, Republic of Belarus.

EXHIBITED WORKS
• *Colorblind Tryptich*, 2002. Oil on canvas; 90 × 120 cm. Courtesy the Artist
• *Colorblind Tryptich*, 2002. Oil on canvas; 100 × 120 cm. Courtesy the Artist
• *Colorblind Tryptich*, 2002. Oil on canvas; 55 × 120 cm. Courtesy the Artist
• *Deep Forest Kiss*, 2003. Oil on canvas; 80 × 100 cm. Courtesy the Artist
• *Murder in Paradise*, 2004. Oil on canvas; 130 × 130 cm. Courtesy the Artist

Gitte Villesen, 36
Born in Billund, Denmark. Lives and works in Copenhagen, Denmark, and Berlin, Germany.

EXHIBITED WORKS
• *Helene*, 2005. Video installation. Courtesy Gallery Nicolai Wallner, Copenhagen

Sergey Voichenko see **Vladimir Tsesler e Sergey Voichenko**

Yelena Vorobyeva e Viktor Vorobyev, 138
Yelena Vorobyeva: born in Nebit-Dag, Turkmenistan, in 1959. Viktor Vorobyev: born in Pavlodar, Kazakhstan, in 1959. They work together since 1994. They live and work in Almaty, Kazakhstan.

EXHIBITED WORKS
• *Blue period*, 2002-2005. Color photographs (more than 100 color photographs). Courtesy the Artist

Natalija Vujošević, 114
Born in Podgorica, Serbia and Montenegro, in 1974. Lives and works in Podgorica, Serbia and Montenegro.

EXHIBITED WORKS
• *U slučaju da te više ne sretnem*, 2005. Video and sound installation (three simultaneous video projections)

M. Rahim Walizada, 18
Born in Bagalan, Afghanistan, in 1963. Lives and works in Kabul, Afghanistan.

EXHIBITED WORKS
• *Chuk Palu 1*. Wool, cotton, vegetable color (madder root, indigo, tumelic yellow); 2 × 3 m. Courtesy the Artist
• *Chuk Palu 2*. Wool, cotton, vegetable color (madder root, indigo, tumelic yellow, walnut, onion); 2 × 3 m. Courtesy the Artist
• *Chuk Palu 3*. Wool, cotton, vegetable color (madder root, indigo, walnut and onion peels); 3 × 2 cm. Courtesy the Artist

Walker and Walker, 58
(Joe Walker and Pat Walker)
Both born in Dublin, Ireland, in 1962. They live and work in Dublin, Ireland.

EXHIBITED WORKS
• *Nightfall*, 2004. 16mm film; 7'. Courtesy the Artists

Liu Wei, 106
Born in Beijing, People's Republic of China, in 1972. Lives and works in Beijing, People's Republic of China.

EXHIBITED WORKS
• *Star*, 2005. *Monolights*, 2005. Digital cameras, motion detectors; dimension variable

Entang Wiharso, 54
Born in Tegal, Central Java, Indonesia, in 1967. Lives and works in Yogyakarta, Indonesia.

EXHIBITED WORKS
• *Forbidden Exotic Fruits*, 2005. Painting and sculpture; mixed media; 600 × 200 × 300 cm

Ingrid Wildi, 122
Born in Santiago, Chile,
in 1963. Lives and works
in Geneva, Switzerland.

EXHIBITED WORKS
▪ *Autoportrait oblique*, 2005,
Video installation; dimension
variable. Courtesy the Artist

Sislej Xhafa, 20
Born in Peja, Kosovo, Serbia
and Montenegro, in 1970.
Lives and works in New York,
USA.

EXHIBITED WORKS
▪ *Ceremonial Crying System PV*,
2004. Iron, PVC, water; 8 Ø
× 23 h m. Courtesy the Artist
and Magazzino d'Arte Moderna,
Roma

Andrei Zadorine, 94
Born in Mariupol, Zhdanov,
Ukraine, in 1955.

EXHIBITED WORKS
▪ *School Class*, 2002. Oil
on canvas; 100 × 130 cm.
Courtesy the Artist
▪ *Nectarine*, 2004. Oil
on canvas; 40 × 50 cm.
Courtesy the Artist
▪ *Untitled*, 2004. Oil
on canvas; 115 × 145 cm.
Courtesy the Artist

Natalya Zaloznaya, 94
Born in Vasilpolye Minsk,
Republic of Belarus, in 1960.
Lives and works in Brussels,
Belgium.

EXHIBITED WORKS
▪ *Meridian*, 1999. Oil
on canvas, paper; 120 × 150
cm. Courtesy the Artist
▪ *Drawer with Self-portrait*,
2000. Oil on canvas; 97 × 130
cm. Courtesy the Artist
▪ *Usual Thought*, 2004. Oil
on canvas; 140 × 200 cm.
Courtesy the Artist

Xu Zhen, 106
Born in Shanghai, People's
Republic of China, in 1977.
Lives and works in Shanghai,
People's Republic of China.

EXHIBITED WORKS
▪ *Shout*, 2005. DVD, DVD
player, projector; dimension
variable

Artur Zmijewski, 84
Born in Warsaw, Poland,
in 1966. Lives and works
in Warsaw, Poland.

EXHIBITED WORKS
▪ *Repetition*, 2005. Video film.
Courtesy the Artist

Index
of the artists
Collateral
events

Mario Airò, 189
Born in Pavia, Italy, in 1961.
Lives and works in Radda
nel Chianti, Italy.

Can Altay, 189
Born in Ankara, Turkey,
in 1975. Lives and works
in Ankara, Turkey.

An Architektur, 189
Collective founded in Berlin,
Germany, in 1995. Active
in Berlin, Germany.

Patrick Andrè, 189
Born in Dijon, France,
in 1966. Lives and works
in Paris, France.

anothermountainman, 174
Born in Hong Kong, People's
Republic of China, in 1960.
Lives and works in Hong Kong,
People's Republic of China.

Atelier van Lieshout, 189
Collective founded in
Rotterdam, The Netherlands,
in 1995. Active in Rotterdam,
The Netherlands.

Baktruppen, 189
Collective of Norwegian artists
founded in 1986 by Tone
Avenstroup and Øyvind Berg
and composed by Erik Balke,
Øyvind Berg, Ingvild Holm,
Trine Falch Johannessen,
Jørgen Knudsen, Per Henrik
Svalastog, Bo Krister Wallström
and Worm Winther. Active
in Oslo, Norway.

Shigeru Ban, 189
Born in Tokyo, Japan, in 1957.
Lives and works in Tokyo,
Japan.

Massimo Bartolini, 189
Born in Cecina, Italy, in 1962.
Lives and works in Cecina, Italy.

Matei Bejenaru, 189
Born in Suceava, Romania,
in 1963. Lives and works
in Iassy, Romania.

Patrick Bloomer
& Nicholas Keogh, 184
They work together since 1999.
Patrick Bloomer: born
in Banbridge, Northern Ireland,
UK, in 1974.
Nicholas Keogh: born
in Rostrevor, Northern Ireland,
UK, in 1974.
They live and work in Belfast,
Northern Ireland, UK.

Luchezar Boyadjiev, 189
Born in Sofia, Bulgaria,
in 1957. Lives and works
in Sofia, Bulgaria.

Petric Branislav
and Stanisa Dautovic, 164
Petric Branislav: Born
in Zemun, Serbia and
Montenegro, in 1959. Lives
and works in Rome, Italy.
Stanisa Dautovic: born
in Belgrade, Serbia
and Montenegro, in 1964.
Lives and works in Novi Sad,
Serbia and Montenegro.

Eva Brunner-Szabo, 189
Born in Oberwaz, Austria,
in 1961. Lives and works
in Vienna and Burgenland,
Austria.

Carlos Bunga, 210
Born in Porto, Portugal,
in 1976. Lives and works
in Lisbon, Portugal.

Campement Urbain, 189
Collective founded in Paris,
France, in 1997. Active
in Paris, France.

Mircea Cantor, 189
Born in Transilvania, Romania,
in 1977. Lives and works
in Paris, France.

CHAN Yuk-keung, 174
Born in Hong Kong, People's
Republic of China, in 1959.
Lives and works in Hong Kong,
People's Republic of China.

Ian Charlesworth, 184
Born in 1970. Lives and works
in Belfast, Northern Ireland,
UK.

Montserrat Cortadellas Bacaria,
189
Born in Reus, Spain, in 1958.
Lives and works in Reus, Spain.

John Court, 198
Born in Bromley, UK, in 1969.
Lives and works in Tornio,
Finland.

Matali Crasset, 189
Born in Chalons-en Champagne,
France, in 1965. Lives
and works in Paris, France.

Cālin Dan, 189
Born in Arad, Romania,
in 1955. Lives and works
in Bucharest, Romania.

Stanisa Dautovic see
Petric Branislav
and Stanisa Dautovic

Elisabetta De Luca, 164
Born in Altofonte (PA), Italy,
in 1975. Lives and works in
Palermo, Italy.

Enrico Tommaso De Paris, 154
Born in Mel (BL), Italy,

in 1960. Lives and works
in Turin and Venice, Italy.

Atul Dodiya, 172
Born in Mumbai, India,
in 1959. Lives and works
in Mumbai, India.

Anita Dube, 172
Born in Lucknow, Uttar
Pradesh, India, in 1958. Lives
and works in New Delhi, India.

Annika Eriksson, 162
Born in Malmö, Sweden,
in 1956. Lives and works
in Berlin, Germany.

Esra Ersen, 189
Born in Ankara, Turkey,
in 1970. Lives and works
in Istanbul, Turkey.

Factotum, 184
www.factotum.org.uk

Peter Finnemore, 206
Born in Llanelli, Wales, UK,
in 1963. Lives and works
in Gwendraeth Valley,
Carmarthenshire, Wales, UK.

Laura Ford, 206
Born in Cardiff, Wales, UK,
in 1961. Lives and works
in London, UK.

Henri Foucault, 168
Born in Versailles, France,
in 1954. Lives and works
in Paris, France.
www.henri-foucault.com

Daniele Franzella, 164
Born in Palermo, Italy, in 1978.
Lives and works in Palermo, Italy.

Gelatin, 189
Collective founded in Vienna,
Austria, in 1995
and composed by Wolfgang
Gantner, Ali Janka, Florian
Reither and Tobias Urban.
Active in Vienna, Austria.

Giuliano Giuliani, 164
Born in Ascoli Piceno, Italy,
in 1954. Lives and works
in Colle San Marco (AP), Italy.

Douglas Gordon, 166
Born in Glasgow, UK, in 1966.
Lives and works in Glasgow,
UK, and New York, USA.

Paul Granjon, 206
Born in Lyon, France, in 1965.
Lives and works in Cardiff,
Wales, UK.

Ion Grigorescu, 189
Born in Bucharest, Romania,
in 1945. Lives and works
in Bucharest, Romania.

Seamus Harahan, 184
Born in London, UK, in 1968.
Lives and works in Belfast,
Northern Ireland, UK.

Jaakko Heikkilä, 210
Born in Kemi, Finland,
in 1956. Lives and works
in Kukkola, Finland.

Masuda Hiromi, 194
Born in Yokohama, Japan,
in 1942. Lives and works
in Tokyo, Japan.

Michael Hogg, 184
Born in Belfast, Northern
Ireland, UK, in 1957. Lives
and works in Belfast, Northern
Ireland, UK.

Helinä Hukkataival, 198
Born in Helsinki, Finland,
in 1941. Lives and works
in Tampere, Finland.

Silvia Iorio, 186
Born in Rome, Italy, in 1977.
Lives and works in Rome, Italy.

Sandra Johnston, 184
Born in Co. Down, Northern
Ireland, UK, in 1968. Lives
and works in Belfast, Northern
Ireland, UK.

Ranbir Kaleka, 172
Born in Patiala, Punjab, India,
in 1953. Lives and works
in Delhi, India.

Chung-li KAO, 208
Born in Taipei, Taiwan,
in 1958. Lives and works
in Taipei, Taiwan.

Anish Kapoor, 166
Born in Bombay, India,
in 1954. Lives and works
in London, UK.

Gülsün Karamustafa, 189
Born in Istanbul, Turkey,
in 1946. Lives and works
in Istanbul, Turkey.

Marya Kazoun, 190
Born in Beirut, Lebanon,
in 1976. Lives and works
in New York, USA.

Nicholas Keogh see
Patrick Bloomer
& Nicholas Keogh

Kimsooja, 189
Born in Taegu, Repubublic
of Korea, in 1957. Lives
and works in New York, USA.

Iosif Király, 189
Born in Resita, Romania,
in 1957. Lives and works
in Bucarest, Romania.

Cornelia Kubler Kavanagh, 204
Born in New Haven,
Connecticut USA, in 1940.
Lives and works in St. Thomas,
Virgin Islands, USA.
www.corneliakavanagh.com.

I-chen KUO, 208
Born in Kaohsiung, Taiwan,
in 1979. Lives and works
in Taipei, Taiwan.

Athanasia Kyriakakos, 189
Born in Baltimore, USA,
in 1968. Lives and works
in Athens, Greece.

Eddie Ladd, 198
Born in Aberteifi, Cymru, Wales,
UK, in 1964. Lives and works
in Cardiff, Wales, UK.

John Latham, 166
Born in Africa in 1921. Lives
and works in London, UK.

Hsin-i Eva LIN, 208
Born in Taipei, Taiwan,
in 1974. Lives and works
in Taipei, Taiwan.

James Luna, 158
Born in Orange, California,
USA, in 1950. Lives and works
in the Indian Reserve La Jolla,
San Diego County, California,
USA.

Nalini Malani, 172
Born in Karachi, Pakistan,
in 1946. Lives and works
in Mumbai, India.

Carlo Marchetti, 164
Born in Ossida (AP), Italy,
in 1956. Lives and works in
San Benedetto del Tronto (AP).

Cosetta Mastragostino, 164
Born in Mafalda (CB), Italy,
in 1949. Lives and works
in Rome, Italy.

Mary McIntyre, 184
Born in Coleraine, Northern
Ireland, UK, in 1966. Lives
and works in Belfast, Northern
Ireland, UK.

William McKeown, 184
Born in Co. Tyrone, Northern
Iremand, UK, in 1962. Lives
and works in Dublin, Ireland.

Amedeo Modigliani, 180
Born in Livorno, Italy, in 1884.
Died in Paris, France, in 1920.

Katrina Moorhead, 184
Born in Coleraine, Northern
Ireland, UK, in 1971. Lives
and works in the USA
and Northern Ireland.

Darren Murray, 184
Born in Co. Antrim, Northern
Ireland, UK, in 1977.
Lives and works in Belfast,
Northern Ireland, UK.

Aydan Murtezaoglu, 189
Born in Istanbul, Turkey,
in 1961. Lives and works
in Istanbul, Turkey.

Aisling O'Beirn, 184
Born in Galway, Ireland,
in 1968. Lives and works
in Belfast, Northern Ireland, UK.

Tom O'Sullivan see
Joanne Tatham
& Tom O'Sullivan

Oda Projesi, 189
Collective founded in Galata,
Turkey, in 1997. Active
in Istanbul, Turkey.

Lucy Orta, 189
Born in Sutton Coldfield, UK,
in 1966. Lives and works
in Paris, France.

Osservatorio Nomade, 189
Collective founded by Stalker
in Rome, Italy, in 2002.
Active in Rome, Italy.

Luigi Pagano, 164
Born in Scafati (SA), Italy,
in 1963. Lives and works
in Scafati (SA), Italy.

Désirée Palmen, 198
Born in Maasbracht,
The Netherlands, in 1963.
Lives and works in Rotterdam,
The Netherlands.

Maria Papadimitriou, 189
Born in Athens, Greece,
in 1957. Lives and works
in Volos and Athens, Greece.

Michelangelo Pistoletto, 178
Born in Biella, Italy, in 1933.
Lives and works in Turin
and Biella, Italy.

Stefano Pizzi, 164
Born in Pavia, Italy, in 1955.
Lives and works in Milan, Italy.

Alex Pollard, 202
Born in Brighton, UK,
in 1977. Lives and works
in Glasgow, Scotland, UK.

Antonella Pomara, 164
Born in Palermo, Italy,
in 1976. Lives and works
in Palermo, Italy.

Roberto Priod, 164
Born in Aosta, Italy, in 1961.
Lives and works in Aosta
and Turin, Italy.

George Pusenkoff, 182
Born in Krasnopolje, Republic
of Belarus, in 1953. Lives
and works in Köln, Germany,
and Moscow, Russia.
www.pusenkoff.de

Raqs Media Collective, 172
Collective founded in 1991
and composed by:
Jeebesh Bagchi, born in Delhi,
India, in 1965.
Monica Narula, born in Delhi,
India, in 1969.
Shuddhabrata Sengupta, born
in Delhi, India, in 1968.
Active in Delhi, India.

Marc Rees, 198
Born in Swansea, South Wales,
UK, in 1966. Lives and works
in Cardiff, Wales, UK.

Peter Richards, 184
Born in Cardiff, UK, in 1970.
Lives and works in Belfast,
Northern Ireland, UK.

Marco Nereo Rotelli, 177
Born in Venice, Italy, in 1955.
Lives and works in Milan, Italy,
and Paris, France.

Bülent Şangar, 189
Born in Eskişehir, Turkey,
in 1965. Lives and works
in Istanbul, Turkey.

School of Missing Studies, 189
International collective founded
in 2003. Active in Belgrade,
Munich, Rotterdam, Zürich
and New York.

Nataraj Sharma, 172
Born in Mysore, Karnataka,
India, in 1958. Lives and works
in Baroda, India.

Škart, 189
Collective founded in Belgrade,
Serbia and Montenegro,
in 1990. Active in Belgrade,
Serbia and Montenegro.

Kiki Smith, 170
Born in Nuremberg, Germany,
in 1954. lives and works
in New York, USA.

Sean Snyder, 189
Born in Virginia Beach, USA,
in 1972. Lives and works
in Berlin, Germany.

Antonio Spanedda, 164
Born in Novara, Italy,
in 1961. Lives in Novara
and works in Milan, Italy.

Simon Starling, 189
Born in Epsom, Surrey, UK,
in 1967. Lives and works
in Glasgow, Scotland, UK.

André Stitt, 198
Born in Belfast, Northern
Ireland, UK, in 1958. Lives
and works in Cardiff, Wales,
UK.

Socrates Stratis, 189
Born in Nicosia, Republic
of Cyprus, in 1964. Lives
and works in Nicosia, Republic
of Cyprus.

Oleg Supereco, 164
Born in Moscow, Russia,
in 1974. Lives and works
in Casale sul Sile (TV), Italy.

Anne-Violaine Taconet, 189
Born in Abondance, France,
in 1949. Lives and works
in Paris, France.

Croce Taravella, 156
Born in Polizzi Generosa (PA),
Italy, in 1964. Lives and works
in Castellana Sicula (PA)
and Rome, Italy.
www.crocetaravella.com

Joanne Tatham
& Tom O'Sullivan, 202
They work together since 1995.
Joanne Tatham, born in West
Yorkshire, UK, in 1971.
Tom O'Sullivan, born in Norfolk,
UK, in 1967.
They live and work in Glasgow,
Scotland, UK.

Gert Tschögl, 189
Born in Vienna, Austria,
in 1959. Lives and works
in Vienna and Burgenland,
Austria.

Kuang-yu TSUI, 208
Born in Taipei, Taiwan,
in 1974. Lives and works
in Taipei, Taiwan.

Florin Tudor see
Mona Vatamanu & Florin Tudor

Roi Vaara, 198
Born in Moss, Norway,
in 1953. Lives and works
in Helsinki, Finland.

Jeanne van Heeswijk, 189
Born in Schijndel, The
Netherlands, nel 1965. Lives
and works in Rotterdam,
The Netherlands.

Erik van Lieshout, 189
Born in 1968 a Deurne, The
Netherlands. Lives and works
in Rotterdam, The Netherlands.

Mona Vatamanu & Florin
Tudor, 189
Mona Vatamanu, born
in Konstanz, Germany,
in 1968.
Florin Tudor, born in Geneva,
Switzerland, in 1974.
They live and work in Bucarest,
Romania.

Francesco Vezzoli, 160
Born in Brescia, Italy, in 1971.
Lives and works in Milan, Italy.

Urban Void, 189
Collective founded in Athens,
Greece, in 1998. Active
in Athens, Greece.

Cathy Wilkes, 202
Born in Belfast, Northern
Ireland, UK, in 1966. Lives
and works in Glasgow,
Scotland, UK.

Bedwyr Williams, 206
Born in St. Asaph, Wales, UK,
in 1974. Lives and works
in Rhostryfan, Caernarfon,
Wales, UK.

Alistair Wilson, 184
Born in the South Wales, UK,
in 1951. Lives and works
in Belfast, Northern Ireland,
UK.

Zafos Xagoraris, 189
Born in Athens, Greece,
in 1963. Lives and works
in Athens, Greece.

ZimmerFrei, 198
Group composed by:
Massimo Carozzi, born
in Massa, Italy, in 1967.
Anna de Manincor, born
in Trento, Italy, in 1972.
Anna Rispoli, born in Bassano
del Grappa, Italy, in 1974.
They live and work in Bologna,
Italy.